CHAUCER'S DRAMA OF STYLE

D0651881

C. DAVID BENSON

The University of North Carolina Press
Chapel Hill and London

CHAUCER'S DRAMA OF STYLE ❧ POETIC VARIETY AND CONTRAST IN THE CANTERBURY TALES ❧

TULSA JUNIOR COLLEGE
Learning Resources Center
Southeast Campus

For

Pam

and Mike, John, and Tom

© 1986 The University of North Carolina Press

All rights reserved

Manufactured in the United States of America

Library of Congress Cataloging-in-Publication-Data

Benson, C. David.

    Chaucer's drama of style. etc

    Includes index.

    1. Chaucer, Geoffrey, d. 1400. Canterbury tales.

2. Chaucer, Geoffrey, d. 1400—Techniques.

3. Chaucer, Geoffrey, d. 1400—Style. I. Title.

PR1874.B46   1986   821'.1   85-20849

ISBN-0-8078-1679-5

The publication of this work was made possible
in part through a grant from the National
Endowment for the Humanities, a federal agency
whose mission is to award grants to support
education, scholarship, media programming,
libraries, and museums, in order to bring
the results of cultural activities to a
broad, general public.

CONTENTS

Acknowledgments   vii

I.   Beyond the Dramatic Theory   3

The Dramatic Theory   3
The Pilgrims in the *General Prologue*   6
The Pilgrims in the Links   9
The Tellers and Their Tales   11
The Anachronism of the Dramatic Theory   16
The Many Poets of the *Canterbury Tales*   20
Medieval Precedents   22
Chaucer as Christian Poet   24

II. Chaucer the Pilgrim and His Contrasting Tales   26

Chaucer the Pilgrim   26
The Contrasting Tales of Chaucer the Pilgrim   31
The *Tale of Sir Thopas*   32
Telling Differences   34
The *Tale of Melibee*   37

III. Chaucer's Pardoner: The Man and His Two Tales as
a Defense of Christian Poetry   44

The Dramatic Interpretation of the Pardoner   44
The Pardoner as Corrupt Preacher   47
The Pardoner's Two Tales   51
The Pardoner's First Tale   52
The Pardoner's Second Tale   58

IV. The First Two Poets of the *Canterbury Tales*   64

The Dramatic Approach and the Link between
the First Two Tales   64
The First Two Poets of the *Canterbury Tales*   66
The Artistic Dialectic of the First Two Tales   72
The Thematic Dialectic of the First Two Tales   85

V.   Variety and Contrast in Chaucer's Fabliaux   89

The *Miller's Tale* and the *Reeve's Tale*   90
The *Shipman's Tale*   104
The *Merchant's Tale*   116

VI.   The Contrasting Religious Tales of the Prioress and
Second Nun   131

Contrasting Literary Prologues   133
Contrasting Narrators and Speech   135
Emotional versus Learned Art   138
Emotional versus Learned Faith   142

Epilogue   147

Notes   151

Index   179

ACKNOWLEDGMENTS

One advantage of a project that has lasted this long is all of the kind help I have received from both institutions and individuals. I wish to thank the University of Colorado for a Faculty Fellowship in 1979–80 which allowed me to begin this study and the National Humanities Center for a fellowship in 1983–84 which allowed me to finish it. I would particularly like to thank Kent Mullikin, Jean Williams, Karen Carroll, Maggie Blades, and Monica Frederick for helping to make my year at the Humanities Center so productive and Marc Plattner, John Reed, Timothy Breen, Vin Carretta, and Corbett Capps for making it so pleasant. I am more grateful than I can say for the unstinting generosity of my mother-in-law, Bernice Joseph, and for the long-suffering support of my parents. I am grateful to the *Chaucer Review* for permission to use material in chapter two that, in a different form, first appeared in its pages. I owe much to the Research Foundation of the University of Connecticut and its directors, Hugh Clark and Thomas Giolas.

Since I first took his graduate seminar, I have tried to learn from Charles Muscatine's unrivaled sensitivity to Chaucerian stylistics, and I am deeply grateful for his encouragement and advice throughout this project. Bruce Bassoff, Robert Hanning, and Emerson Brown read first drafts of this study and helped me greatly with their stimulating criticism. I learned much of what I know about Chaucer from the many wonderful students I have been associated with at Columbia, Colorado, and Connecticut. I want particularly to thank Jean Pfleiderer, David Rollman, Helen Hawkins, and Cathy Orr, who were there when the idea for this book began, and Professors Elizabeth Robertson and Charlotte Gross, who gave me the benefit of their considerable critical skills. At Connecticut, David Seaman, Jane Tolimieri, and Cindy Wagner saved me from many errors, and Jenny O'Neill also labored mightily with the index. Personal thanks to John Benson.

Many others have generously read all or parts of this book to my benefit. I am very grateful to Larry D. Benson and Thomas Cook for their suggestions about the fabliaux chapter and to John Seelye and Martin Meisel for their comments on the first chapter. John Fyler offered me solid advice and support at an important time in the project, and M. Teresa Tavormina, an invaluable colleague at the Humanities Center, vastly improved the final draft with her shrewd suggestions, formidable learning, and unflagging encouragement. Three colleagues at Connecticut, J. D. O'Hara, William Sheidley, and Raymond A. Anselment, made valuable comments on the entire manuscript. The enthusiasm, patience, and astonishing skill of Iris Hill of the University of North Carolina Press has been everything an author could imagine in an editor. Two readers for the press, who turned out to be Robert W. Frank and Derek Pearsall, delighted me with their support for the book and challenged me with their responses. I owe much to both.

I want to give special thanks to Donald C. Baker and Alain Renoir, two scholars and friends, whose learning and warm generosity have been a continual inspiration.

My greatest debt, acknowledged in the dedication, is to my family, and especially to my wife, Pam, always my first and best reader, who alone knows how much her scholarship and judgment have contributed to this book.

CHAUCER'S DRAMA OF STYLE

CHAPTER I ❧ BEYOND THE DRAMATIC THEORY

eaders have always recognized and responded to the exuberant variety of the *Canterbury Tales*. Within a generation after Chaucer, John Lydgate noted that the work includes both "desport" and "moralite," for some stories are about "knyghthode loue and gentillesse," others about "parfit holynesse," and still others about "Ribaudye." William Caxton echoed this view in introducing the first printed edition ("tales whyche ben of noblesse /wysedom / gentylesse / Myrthe / and also of veray holynesse and vertue"); and, at the beginning of the eighteenth century, John Dryden memorably declared that "here is God's Plenty."[1] Although his phrase well describes the diverse profusion of the tales themselves, Dryden is apparently here referring only to the portraits in the *General Prologue*, an emphasis on the pilgrims that dominated Victorian criticism and still continues today. Discussions of the variety of the *Canterbury Tales* in the twentieth century almost always attribute it to the different pilgrim-narrators, and this approach has come to be known as the "dramatic" theory. Chaucer usually intends there to be some appropriateness between his pilgrims and their stories, as he makes clear early in the work by warning that because the Miller and Reeve are churls they can be expected to tell "harlotrie" (I.3182–84). This natural, but quite general, correspondence between social class and kind of tale is very different, however, from the intense, even psychologically revealing, relationship between individual teller and tale assumed by so many.

The Dramatic Theory

Although such views had been developing for at least two centuries, the most influential proponent of the modern dramatic approach to the *Canterbury Tales* is undoubtedly George Lyman Kittredge. In his celebrated 1914 lectures at Johns Hopkins, subsequently published as *Chaucer and His Poetry*, Kittredge labeled the *Canterbury Tales* a "Human Comedy" (a conception still being echoed today). Decrying the habit of reading "each tale by itself, as if it were an isolated unit" and "as if Chaucer were telling it in his own person," he argued instead that it is "manifestly our paramount duty" to read the several tales "from the dramatic point of view."

Chaucer has as much interest in the pilgrims as in their stories, according to Kittredge, who flatly declared that "the Pilgrims do not exist for the sake of the stories, but *vice versa*. Structurally regarded, the stories are merely long speeches expressing, directly or indirectly, the characters of the several persons. They are more or less comparable, in this regard, to the soliloquies of Hamlet or Iago or Macbeth."[2]

Because of the powerful and still valuable readings produced by Kittredge, followers of many critical schools from his time to our own have enthusiastically elaborated on the supposed Roadside Drama of the *Canterbury Tales*. In a chapter entitled "The Human Comedy," John Livingston Lowes in his 1934 book on Chaucer declares that the "tales are not isolated entities," but rather the "whole is essentially dramatic"; and he insists that "Chaucer's ultimate glory is not his finished craftsmanship but the power by virtue of which he creates, through speech and action, living characters."[3] Twenty years later, John Speirs, influenced by the very different world of F. R. Leavis and *Scrutiny*, sounds much the same note. He also celebrates the *Canterbury Tales* as a Human Comedy and insists that the reader's interest is not simply in the tale, "but, at the same time, in the teller and in the tale as characteristic of the teller." He concludes that "each tale dramatically projects a distinct person."[4]

The excesses committed by the dramatic theory over the years ought to produce amusement rather than indignation. Even before Kittredge, the learned Robert K. Root could not resist a wonderfully preposterous biography of the Wife of Bath: "I conceive of the Wife of Bath as endowed originally with strong passions and vivid imagination, with what we are wont to call the poetic temperament. Had she been born in a palace, she might have become your typical heroine of romance, her inevitable lapses from virtue gilded over with the romantic adornments of moonlight serenades and secret trysts. But born heiress to a weaver's bench, there was no chance for her poetic imaginativeness to develop. Laughed at by others for her fine-spun fancies, she would certainly grow ashamed of them herself. I can believe that her excessive coarseness of speech was originally an affectation assumed to conceal the natural fineness of her nature, an affectation which easily became a second nature to her."[5] Root himself must have come to believe that such a re-creation of the Wife out of almost whole cloth could not be justified, for it is missing from the revised edition of his book.

The most exhaustive application of Kittredge's theory is surely Robert Lumiansky's *Of Sondry Folk: The Dramatic Principle in the Canterbury Tales*, whose thesis is reinforced by modern drawings of each pilgrim. Although less extreme in one way than Kittredge (he argues, not that the teller exists primarily for the tale, but that each illuminates the other), Lumiansky's claim is more extensive. Kittredge was content to describe the drama of only a few pilgrims, but Lumiansky applies the principle to all the tales. Because he regards each and every teller as an "actor-Pilgrim," Lumiansky believes that "in attempting to interpret a particular Pilgrim's performance in the *Canterbury Tales*, a critic must first establish, to his own satisfaction at least, the traits that Chaucer intended us to associate with that Pilgrim, and the dramatic forces that govern not Chaucer as author but the Pilgrim as teller of the tale."[6] As we can see, the dramatic principle is more comprehensive than its name might at first suggest; for its subject is not only the pilgrims' actions among themselves as they journey to Canterbury (the Roadside Drama proper), but also each of the tales as dramatic expressions of their individual tellers.

The dramatic approach has not been accepted by all. Such critics as Kemp Malone, Bertrand Bronson, Robert Jordan, and D. W. Robertson have vigorously attacked it, and, more recently, it has been dismissed as unhelpful by Martin Stevens, Judson Allen, Derek Pearsall, Helen Cooper, and others.[7] Despite these challenges, dramatic interpretations are still plentiful in contemporary Chaucer criticism, though usually practiced with more sophistication and flexibility than in the past. The pedagogical effectiveness of dramatic readings (a human personality will always seem more accessible to students than poetry) means that the approach is widely used in teaching Chaucer, and when the method appears either as support or at the center of an academic essay, its use is rarely justified. The continued popularity of the theory, whose specific applications we shall examine in more detail later in this chapter as well as in subsequent chapters, is indicated by its presence, to varying degrees, in four important, but otherwise dissimilar, books dealing with the *Canterbury Tales* that have been published within the last few years by Alfred David, Donald Howard, Charles Owen, and Robert Burlin.[8] Indeed, Burlin not only explicitly associates himself with the dramatic approach, while admitting it can be misused, but asserts that it is the underlying assumption of many of the best modern critics.[9]

Unquestionably, dramatic critics have made significant contributions to the study of the *Canterbury Tales* by providing, sometimes almost in spite of their theories, excellent readings of many individual stories and by alerting us to relationships between contiguous tales. The approach seems to work especially well with a few characters like the Wife of Bath, whose deafness mentioned in the *General Prologue* and explained at the end of her own prologue is one of the few examples of explicit correspondence between portrait and performance. But although the narrative frame is certainly an important and original element of the *Canterbury Tales*, it provides an uncertain foundation on which to base serious criticism. Dramatic critics apply anachronistic conceptions of realism and character consistency to Chaucer's work, and too often their responses to the pilgrims are disconcertingly subjective.

Having shed some of the most obvious naïvetés of the past, modern dramatic interpretations pose an even more insidious danger to sound literary analysis. Whatever their other faults, at least the older dramatic critics explained and defended their method at length, just as their application of the theory is usually clear and consistent. Today, however, the dramatic method is resorted to casually and unsystematically with few feeling the need to prove the worth of their approach or define its limits. Instead, it has become a convenient wild card that can be used at any time to reinforce almost any position. At the very least, the critical attention paid to the *General Prologue* and narrative links has been excessive, an imbalance I hope to redress in this study. For all its apparent appeal, the fascination with the human drama of the tellers obscures Chaucer's greatest achievement in the *Canterbury Tales*: the stylistic drama of the tales themselves.

The Pilgrims in the *General Prologue*

Despite the flexibility of the approach, especially among modern critics, dramatic readings of the *Canterbury Tales* are essentially based on two related assumptions: first, that the pilgrims, as we meet them in the *General Prologue* and the narrative links, are to some extent whole and consistent figures, perhaps even the "living characters" praised by Lowes and others; second, that the connection between teller and tale is usually close and revealing. Although each proposition has merit for some tales, both prompt so many questions and qualifications that their often unquestioned acceptance and free elaboration by dramatic critics have resulted in much confusion. The belief in the reality of fictional characters was an important strain of literary criticism in the nineteenth century, as witness the notorious *Girlhood of Shakespeare's Heroines*, and has lingered on in Chaucer studies despite its banishment elsewhere. Chaucer's portraits of the pilgrims are often vivid and memorable, but they do not describe believable individuals, and few have much to tell us about the tales that cannot better be found in the poetry itself.

A few critics have responded to Chaucer's extraordinary portraits as if they were accounts of actual people. The extreme example of this tendency is John M. Manly's *Some New Light on Chaucer*, which argues that the pilgrims were based on Chaucer's contemporaries and attempts to identify the real-life models.[10] Although Manly's learning provides useful information about English life in the late fourteenth century, his conclusions, at best, are suggestive rather than definitive. At this late date, it is hard to see how even a genuine name and a few biographical details could help us much with serious literary analysis because we would not be sure how to interpret these scraps of information, nor would they prove that the fictional character had been drawn with any accuracy.[11] Indeed, Chaucer's entire Canterbury pilgrimage probably appeared less realistic to its first readers than it does to us, for they would have had a surer sense of the unlikelihood of such a carefully diverse collection of pilgrims riding together and the impossibility of their being able to hear one another speak.

Even though only some modern critics have thought Chaucer's portraits were drawn from life, belief in the individuality of the pilgrims, even if mixed with typical traits, has been the norm.[12] In a valuable corrective to Manly, Jill Mann, in her *Chaucer and Medieval Estates Satire*, shows that, although Chaucer uses many techniques to give the impression of individuality, the portraits in the *General Prologue* are largely built on conventional details from the tradition of describing the various estates. Even when Chaucer invents new material, the result is often to emphasize the typical aspects of the portrait.[13] Mann's argument could be extended by noting that many of the pilgrims appear in the *General Prologue* as purely exemplary figures—either positive or negative ideals—who are simply too good (or bad) to be true. Neither Chaucer's Knight nor Parson, for example, represents a genuine individual (let alone an actual model), with the limitations and peculiarities that would imply, but instead each is described so as to celebrate all, rather than just some, of the virtues associated with his vocation.[14] Likewise, Chaucer's negative ideals, such as the Friar and the Monk, are not merely attacks on specific contemporary abuses or individuals, but are comprehensive descriptions that include the full range of vices traditionally associated with monkdom or friarhood.[15] Not all the portraits are as generic as these, but even Kittredge admitted that if "we had only the Prologue, we might, perhaps, regard the Pilgrims as types."[16] It is not necessary to agree with D. W. Robertson's claim that Chaucer's characters are nothing but moral allegories to accept his rejection of the pilgrims as convincing psychological portraits.[17]

The critic who relies on the portraits in the *General Prologue* to support a dramatic reading of the *Canterbury Tales* is faced with two contradictory problems. On the one hand, as we have just seen, the pilgrims are largely type figures rather than fully developed characters; on the other, the few unexpected details in the portraits that do suggest individuality are presented in a way that frustrates clear understanding. The famous observation about the Merchant ("This worthy man ful wel his wit bisette: / Ther wiste no wight that he was in dette" [I.279–80]) prompts many readers to conclude that the pilgrim is, in fact, in debt; but that is not necessarily what Chaucer has said. As Mann observes, "The exact meaning of these lines has been disputed. Do they mean that no-one could accuse the Merchant of being in debt because his prudence protected him from it? Or do they mean that although he *was* in debt, he was so circumspect that no-one knew of it?"[18] The reader may offer his own guess as to which is true, but Chaucer sees to it that we cannot surely know. Mann demonstrates that this is Chaucer's technique throughout the *General Prologue*. We cannot be certain that the Franklin's feasts are wastefully self-indulgent, as some have said, nor finally decide whether the Reeve escapes detection by his auditors because he is honest or because he is so skilled at hiding his thefts.[19] When Chaucer moves beyond the description of types in the Canterbury portraits, he does not create rounded characters so much as intriguing, incomplete puzzles. His method is to provide lots of smoke with no certainty that there is a real fire.

The pilgrims of the *General Prologue* are either too realistic or not realistic enough to support the dramatic theory. To the extent that the portraits are of types, they can tell us only the most obvious things about the tales; to the extent that they share the unknowable elusiveness of real people, we learn nothing so certainly that it can be applied with any confidence to the tales themselves. On the one hand, the nobility of the Knight or the rascality of the Miller, about which most (but not all) critics agree, prepares us only generally for the kind of story told by each, because rascals and nobles can have many voices. Even in those few cases when there is close similarity between portrait and tale, as with the Pardoner, the linkage is not as personal or revealing as some dramatic critics have claimed, as I shall attempt to show in my third chapter. On the other hand, with Chaucer's most subtle portraits, such as that of the Prioress (is she corrupting her holy calling or really an attractive, if sentimental, woman of style?), the reader risks misreading or even condemning an extraordinary tale if he relies too much on what can only be a subjective response to a brief and deliberately ambiguous portrait. Chaucer teases us with the unknowability of many of his pilgrims, without providing information that is either extensive or dependable enough to produce genuine characterization. The portraits in the *General Prologue* are among Chaucer's finest achievements, but their mixture of the enigmatic and the typical means that we cannot rely on them as a sound foundation on which to build convincing interpretations of the tales.

The Pilgrims in the Links

The dramatic links between the tales do not produce any more reliable characterizations of the pilgrims that might be helpful in interpreting their tales. Some links, such as the *Wife of Bath's Prologue*—if that long, virtuoso performance can really be considered only a link—genuinely extend our knowledge, but many others, such as the prologues to the *Miller's*, *Summoner's*, and *Friar's* tales, though exciting, add little to what we already know. Perhaps because the *Canterbury Tales* is unfinished, many tellers, such as the Squire, the Physician, the Second Nun, and the Shipman, make only token appearances, or none, outside the *General Prologue*. Critics have also noted apparent contradictions between what we learn about a pilgrim in the *General Prologue* and what we find subsequently in the frame: famous examples include the stiff, secretive Merchant, who later recklessly exposes his marital misery, and the self-indulgent Monk, who piously ignores the Host's suggestive repartee and tells his gloomy tragedies.[20] Of course, dramatic critics have offered explanations for such seeming tangles, often by recourse to irony (that most abused of Chaucerian qualities), but each depends on the frequently unexamined assumption that all the information about a specific pilgrim found throughout the *Tales* is designed by Chaucer to produce a unified character. If we do away with this novelistic view of the Canterbury pilgrims and accept that realistic character consistency, as we understand it, like "rational" perspective in painting, was not considered much of a virtue in the Middle Ages, we can then begin to appreciate the *Canterbury Tales* for what they are rather than trying to cobble them into something they are not.

Two pilgrims who are described only after the opening portraits, the Canon's Yeoman and the Nun's Priest, indicate that the links are no more helpful than the *General Prologue* in explaining the tales dramatically. In the links also, characterization tends to be either quite general or an elusive puzzle. The *Canon's Yeoman's Prologue* contains some fine action as the Canon and his Yeoman ride furiously to join the company ("But it was joye for to seen hym swete!" [VIII.579]), along with powerful dialogue in which the Yeoman soon admits to the Host that, despite his initial boasts about great alchemical powers, he and his master are frauds and failures. The Yeoman's sudden and complete confession defines no complex individual or convincing psychological crisis, however, but is the sort of conventional self-exposure familiar in medieval allegorical works like the *Roman de la Rose* and *Piers Plowman*. The Yeoman's abrupt decision to reveal all is prompted less by dramatic realism than Chaucer's need for a story. The prologue is certainly exciting, but it prepares us only generally for what is to come; the specific detail and interest are in the two-part *Canon's Yeoman's Tale* itself.

If the Yeoman in the frame is a kind of type figure, the Nun's Priest, who is seen before (and possibly after) his tale, is too vague to explain anything. Although Manly claims that the few words between Host and Priest before the tale allow us to know the latter "almost as well as if Chaucer had not neglected to paint his portrait," the lines in question actually tell us only that the cleric has an inferior horse, is quite polite, and intends to tell a merry tale (VII.2810–17).[21] The Nun's Priest's Tale is indeed among the merriest in Chaucer, but the lines of introduction reveal nothing significant about it. The brief epilogue to the tale, which Chaucer probably later decided to cancel, at first seems more promising. The Host declares that if the Nun's Priest were secular he would be a "trede-foul aright," for his physique suggests he would need more than seven times seventeen hens to satisfy his "corage" (VII.3447–60). Most critics have naturally read these lines to mean that the Priest is young and sexually able.[22] Lumiansky and some others take a startlingly different view, however: "I conceive of the Nun's Priest as a timid and frail person of indeterminate years, whom the Host is not afraid to address rudely."[23] The Host's apparent sexual praise is explained by Lumiansky as irony, in which "the intent of the passage is the opposite of its literal meaning."[24] At this point, the bewildered reader may well ask that if these lines are to be taken ironically, what dramatic episode could not be? Even if we could satisfy ourselves that one view of the epilogue was reasonably certain (and explain the apparent cancellation of the whole scene), how much does this tell us about the tale? Neither conception of the Nun's Priest begins to equal in complexity, let alone significantly interpret, what many have seen as one of the greatest of the Canterbury tales.[25] Rather than pursuing the shadowy Nun's Priest, a critic would do better to exercise his energy and wit on the tale.

I am not arguing that the links have no purpose in the Canterbury Tales, only that they, along with the portraits in the General Prologue, have frequently been given too much attention by dramatic critics. The links are interesting in themselves, but they are less important than the poems they enclose. As introductions, the links most often do little more than generally prepare us for what is to come; as endings, they are rarely the thematic or artistic culmination of a tale, though sometimes so regarded by dramatic criticism. Instead of apotheosis, the brief narrative moments that follow many tales commonly offer a new, more limited, and frequently humorous perspective. Examples include the gross foolery between the Pardoner and Host after the magnificent exemplum of the three revelers and the rollicking "Lenvoy de Chaucer" after the austerity of the Clerk's Tale. In addition to comic relief, not unlike that found in Shakespeare's tragedies, the links frequently return the reader to more ordinary experiences and values after the intensity of a tale, sometimes in the form of an obvious (and obviously inadequate) moral by Harry Bailly. We should enjoy and learn from the links, but, at the same time, be careful not to overestimate their importance.

The Tellers and Their Tales

Even when it is accepted that the pilgrims in the *General Prologue* and links are far from fully developed characters, we still cannot dismiss the dramatic theory. In addition to the opening portraits and frame narrative, dramatic critics also appeal to the undoubted individuality of the tales themselves to prove the psychological complexity of the pilgrims and thus justify their approach. Indeed, we will remember that Kittredge went so far as to assert that the tales exist primarily to define their tellers. Similar, if less extreme, readings of the tales as revelations of character appear throughout the four recently published books on Chaucer already cited. Burlin finds a foolish, overreaching Franklin and a willful, self-protective Merchant in their respective tales; David identifies a frustrated, *petit bourgeois* as the teller of the *Reeve's Tale*; Owen sees the Nun's Priest caught between literary sophistication and personal antifeminism; and Howard likens the extravagant Pardoner to Sartre's conception of the French thief and writer Jean Genet.[26]

As with attempts to see believably complex pilgrims in the *General Prologue* or links, the reasoning that finds the teller in his tale tends to be subjective and circular. Predisposed by their approach to discover a consistent personality regardless of the evidence, dramatic critics are condemned to pursue what is, at best, a less interesting and more unknowable question—the psychology of the pilgrim instead of the artistry of the tale. Chaucer's organization of the *Canterbury Tales* deliberately establishes some relationship between teller and tale, as we have seen, but usually this is no more than general and nominal (the low characters tell of "harlotrie" and their betters of "gentillesse," "moralitee and hoolynesse" [I.3179–84]). The intense, revealing association often assumed by followers of the dramatic theory is not very common and always difficult to prove. The tales of Canterbury cannot be read like Robert Browning's dramatic monologues, though this is commonly done, precisely because they are fictional narratives rather than personal reminiscences. Even the exceptional prologues of the Wife of Bath and Pardoner, for all their apparent self-exposure, are professional rather than personal confessions.

Dramatic criticism itself seems implicitly to acknowledge how sporadic the relations between teller and tale are in the *Tales*. Beginning with Kittredge, most of those who read the tales in terms of their pilgrims actually apply the method quite selectively: to only a few performances (most notably the Pardoner's) or to some selected aspect (the Man of Law's rhetoric or the Physician's misinterpretation of the Bible). Opponents of the dramatic approach have attacked what Lee Patterson calls "one of the most worn of interpretive strategies, the relation of teller to tale," by showing how often the tales fit their tellers only generally or not at all.[27] The polished art of the Miller's Tale, the moral delicacy of the Friar's Tale, the cleverness and learning of the Summoner's Tale, the dogged didacticism of the Monk's Tale—none of these qualities, but rather their reverse, is suggested by what we know of their pilgrims outside the tales. Similarly, only the most desperate arguments are able to make the speeches in the Wife of Bath's Tale in praise of gentility and poverty accord with the Wife's portrait in the General Prologue or with the very different values in her own raucous prologue.

Although most of the Canterbury tales have a general, if not especially deep, relationship with their nominal tellers, sometimes the two have nothing in common. A flagrant example is the obvious disjunction between the rough, murderous Shipman of the General Prologue and the cool, sophisticated art of the Shipman's Tale. One group of dramatic interpreters finds harmony between teller and tale on the grounds that a hostility to merchants (the occupation of the cuckold husband in the tale) can easily be attributed to the Shipman (see I.397), though others note that the merchant is not Chaucer's contribution to the story and, in any case, his role is only a small part of the tale.[28] Because the pronouns in lines VII.12–19 seem to suggest a female narrator, another set of dramatic critics has suggested that the tale was originally assigned to the Wife of Bath, on the grounds that she is the only female pilgrim who might possibly tell such a bawdy tale.[29] The argument by default (the Wife must be the teller because she is the only appropriate woman available) is inherently weak, even if we accept that the pronouns definitely point to a woman (still a debated issue), nor are the other general similarities that have been claimed between the tale and the Wife any more convincing.[30] The Wife would be an appropriate teller, but not especially so.

The limitations of the dramatic theory as an aid to serious literary criticism are made clear by a third group of dramatic critics, who assert that the Shipman's Tale might properly be told by either the Wife or Shipman: "not only is the tale, looking one way, an *exemplum* of the Wife of Bath's thesis, but, looking the other, it is also a satire by the Shipman on a merchant or merchants."[31] To say that both the Wife and the Shipman are fit tellers of the Shipman's Tale is finally to say that neither is. If these two disparate figures can reasonably be considered appropriate to the tale, who, except perhaps for the nuns or Knight, could not be? Indeed, one scholar has suggested that Chaucer at various times assigned the poem to no less than four pilgrims.[32] Such flexibility means the dramatic approach is of little use as a critical tool. The problem is not that it is sometimes difficult to link a particular tale to a plausible teller, but that, as with the *Shipman's Tale*, often it is much too easy. Without great ingenuity, several different pilgrims could be made to seem plausible narrators for any single tale.

As we have seen, caution is necessary even with the most fully characterized pilgrim in the *Canterbury Tales*, the Wife of Bath. Although readers have responded to her dramatically from the beginning, as seen by Justinus's citation in the *Merchant's Tale* and Chaucer's own mention in his "Lenvoy a Bukton," almost everything important we think we know about her comes from her own mouth, and one of her favorite themes is her skill at manipulating others with false speech. Because there is no way to evaluate the truth of what the Wife says (for example, we may suspect but cannot prove that her final relationship with her fifth husband was less perfect than she claims), the reader intent on defining the "real" woman behind the performance can do so only subjectively. As a result, she has been seen as illustrating everything from Chaucer's own love of life to the tragic consequences of a misspent life. In fact, the events of the Wife of Bath's life, if we believe her account, are the standard nightmares of medieval antifeminism; what makes her unique is not her "experience" but her manipulation of "auctorite." The voice we hear in her prologue is not that of a believable individual so much as that of an artist, a skilled user of words and sources. When we finally get to her tale, the pilgrim herself is even harder to locate. Certainly the story of the old hag who miraculously achieves both youth and a vigorous husband can be read as the Wife's wish fulfillment, but the voice of the teller has changed completely: the style of the tale is much more objective than that of the prologue (only an early dig at friars continues the earlier tone) and includes long speeches on gentility and poverty that come oddly from the Wife as we have known her. Even with this most obviously dramatic of Chaucer's pilgrims, the critic needs to tread carefully when interpreting the tale by means of its assigned teller.

Given such a loose connection between teller and tale, the frequent result of reading the *Canterbury Tales* dramatically is either banal generalizations (the *Knight's Tale* reveals the personality of the Knight because it is about war and chivalry) or highly speculative interpretations. Using the scraps of information actually provided, and their imaginations even more, some critics take it upon themselves to unearth the human complexity and individual psychology they assert Chaucer has hidden in the tales. The poet himself may seem to encourage such a response with his deliberate, teasing imprecision about the pilgrims, and the entire exercise can be enjoyable and relatively harmless as long as the practitioner realizes that he has left analysis for the headier delights of creativity. The most serious abuse comes when a critic begins to believe that his supplements to Chaucer are actually in the text. Thus we find critics who assert that the teller of the *Prioress's Tale* is everything from a naive country girl to a thwarted mother to a vicious anti-Semite.[33] These interpretations of Madame Eglentyne, achieved by a dangerous mixing of information from the tale and portrait, are questionable enough (as their sharp differences suggest), but when used as the foundation for criticism the circularity of the argument is apparent as well as its lack of objective proof. Rather than helping us understand the tale, the largely imaginary pilgrim thus generated becomes a definite hindrance.

There are more serious critical problems with this method than excessively subjective interpretations based on little textual evidence. Especially in the last generation, the dramatic approach has led many to argue that the perceived faults in a specific pilgrim signal us to understand his or her tale as either severely flawed or deliberately "bad." Such readings seem particularly popular with Chaucer's religious works, especially the tales of the Prioress, Second Nun, Man of Law, Physician, and Clerk, but they have also been offered for many other tales, especially those of the Squire, Franklin, Monk, and Manciple. It is possible that Chaucer intended all these poems to be ironic, but it is more probable that the dramatic principle is being used to support modern prejudices.

Dramatic criticism risks nothing less than trivializing some of Chaucer's greatest tales by associating them too closely with their assigned tellers. A flagrant example is the frequent attempt to read the pilgrim Merchant into the *Merchant's Tale*.[34] Although nondramatic critics who deny a close relation between pilgrim and poem usually take the tale too lightly and thus ignore its dark power, they have effectively exposed the weaknesses of the dramatic approach.[35] A few critics have even questioned whether the Merchant was the original teller of the tale; because of a passing reference to "thise fooles that been seculeer" (IV.1251) the Friar has been proposed instead, and the old view that the work was first assigned to the Monk has been revived.[36] Dramatic readings of the tale have also been undermined by the recognition that, once again, the different appearances of the teller do not seem to add up to a consistent or very profound character. Both the stiff, secretive Merchant so briefly encountered in the *General Prologue* (I.270–84) and the distraught husband of the *Merchant's Prologue* are little more than types, and the former, whose portrait contains no hint of marital discord or bitterness, is the last person, as Bronson notes, we would expect to reveal himself with the reckless indiscretion of the latter.[37]

Ignoring its apparent disharmony with the Merchant's portrait, many look principally to the *Merchant's Prologue* to justify a dramatic approach to the tale. The Merchant's sudden confession after the *Clerk's Tale* that his wife of two months is "the worste that may be"—a shrew who could overcome the Devil himself (IV.1213–39)—has prompted some critics to read the subsequent tale of marital unhappiness as an expression of the Merchant's own personal history, though there has been disagreement over the extent of the similarity.[38] In fact, as so often with the dramatic principle, the supposed correspondence has been created almost entirely by the critics themselves. The little we do know about the Merchant's own marriage explicitly contradicts the story of January and May: for example, whereas two months have been more than enough to convince the Merchant of his wife's shrewishness, January is still blissfully happy with May after at least a year of marriage.[39] Despite the lack of convincing parallels between January and the Merchant, dramatic critics resort to a form of circular reasoning by which the biography of the latter is derived almost wholly from the former, after which the two characters are, not unsurprisingly, found to be remarkably alike.[40] For example, the Merchant is often said to be old and a cuckold, though absolutely no evidence can be found for this in his portrait or prologue.[41] Similarly, one critic claims that the mock encomium on marriage at the beginning of the *Merchant's Tale* "expresses too closely for comfort the very sentiments in which the Merchant admittedly indulged before his fatal step," even though the Merchant says not a thing, here or elsewhere, about his views before he married.[42]

The relationship between the *Merchant's Prologue* and the tale that follows is general and prefatory rather than dramatic. Moreover, it works in one direction only: although the prologue effectively introduces the tale, the complex tale cannot be read back into the superficial comedy of the prologue. The Merchant's criticism of his wife is a conventional piece of medieval antifeminism rather than a revelation of individual personality, and, although it serves to prepare the reader for a tale of married woe, it does not determine the specific shape of what is to follow—the Merchant's problems with his wife are different and more familiar than January's. As with so many of the Canterbury tales, the connection between teller and tale, while appropriate, is not profound. There is not even a similarity of style. The clever intricacy of the *Merchant's Tale*, not to mention its complex mix of genres, differs completely from the compulsively frank, even naive outburst in the prologue.

Quite apart from the lack of correspondence, the most serious problem with reading the *Merchant's Tale* primarily in terms of the pilgrim Merchant is that it is reductive in the extreme to attribute all the corrosive skill and dark power of what many see as one of Chaucer's most challenging tales to the unspecified disappointments of a new husband. The Merchant is more vague and unknowable than most of the pilgrims, but the tale itself is one of the most distinctive in the Canterbury Tales. It is a self-contained work whose brilliance is not diminished if interpreted without the prologue, which is missing in over half of the surviving manuscripts. The Merchant's Tale clearly shows us, to adapt slightly D. H. Lawrence's warning about American literature, that we should trust the tale and not the teller.

The Anachronism of the Dramatic Theory

That the late Middle Ages had a genuine interest in dramatic narrative is undeniable, as collections such as Boccaccio's Decameron testify, but the close, psychologically revealing association between Canterbury teller and tale argued by so many Chaucerians depends largely on post-medieval values and assumptions about literature. I recognize that this assertion would seem to be refuted by the early and authoritative Elles-mere manuscript, whose magnificent illustrations of the pilgrims before each tale imitate Chaucer's descriptions in the General Prologue with amazing fidelity. But even though the Ellesmere portraits, which have un-doubtedly inspired many dramatic readings, are as vivid as Chaucer's originals, there is no reason to regard them as any more individual or complex; they, too, are essentially type figures as shown by the marks of office (the Physician's urinal, the Summoner's letter, the Clerk's book) unrealistically held aloft by several as they ride along.

Ian Doyle and Malcolm Parkes have convincingly argued that Chau-cer's literary remains were probably a collection of individual tales or groups of tales and that the special ordinatio of Ellesmere, which includes not only the famous illustrations but also running titles and additional headings, is not necessarily Chaucerian but rather a "sophisticated inter-pretation" of the Tales that "emphasizes the importance of the pilgrims" and "connects the tales with the General Prologue."[43] Other equally im-portant manuscripts, notably Hengwrt (apparently written by the same scribe as Ellesmere), lack such an elaborate apparatus, suggesting that the relatively limited "dramatic" organization of Ellesmere was only one of many medieval ways of responding to the Canterbury Tales. Indeed, the pilgrim portraits in another early illustrated manuscript, Cambridge Gg.4.27, although skillful, further call into question the dramatic ap-proach.[44] Although the surviving portraits in Gg are also found next to their appropriate tales, no effort has been taken to make them resemble Chaucer's descriptions in the General Prologue (the Cook is lavishly dressed, for example, whereas the Reeve and the Wife look quite young and the Pardoner normally virile), proving that this artist, at least, did not con-sider the pilgrims to be fixed personalities.[45]

Early printed editions of the *Canterbury Tales*, while emphasizing the connection between teller and tale with woodcuts, suggest that medieval and Renaissance readers considered the relationship to be quite general. Caxton's second edition (1484) contains woodcuts of each pilgrim in the *General Prologue* and of each teller before his tale, but individuality of character, let alone psychological realism, is not to be found. Instead, the portraits mark general social status, as indicated by the single figure who represents all five guildsmen. Even more significantly, the same woodcut is used for both the Doctor and the Parson, another for both the Shipman and the Canon's Yeoman, and a third for the Merchant, the Franklin, and, of all people, the Summoner (the Manciple's woodcut is also used before the Franklin's tale, though the latter has his own in the *General Prologue*). Subsequent illustrated editions take the same casual attitude in representing the pilgrims. In Thynne's 1532 edition of the *Works*, which uses many of Caxton's woodcuts but places them only with the tales, the Merchant-Franklin-Summoner portrait is also extended to the Manciple, the Prioress's woodcut is repeated before the Second Nun's Tale, the Plowman's woodcut is transferred to the Parson, and the Clerk's woodcut (showing him as in Caxton with bow and arrows!) is also used for the Canon's Yeoman. One of the issues of Stow's 1561 edition, which places the woodcuts back in the *General Prologue*, uses a very similar illustration for the Doctor and the Parson, as had Caxton, and another for two of the most disparate of the Canterbury pilgrims, the Prioress and the Wife of Bath. These confusions may testify primarily to the chaos of early printing methods, but they also reveal no great interest in the individuality of Chaucer's pilgrims.

Two fifteenth-century attempts to continue the uncompleted *Canterbury Tales* also suggest that the close connection between teller and tale argued by the dramatic theory is a modern way of reading the work. Both Lydgate's *Siege of Thebes* and the anonymous *Tale of Beryn* begin with lively and dramatic introductions that detail the adventures of the pilgrims in Canterbury, but nothing from these opening scenes or from the personalities of the supposed tellers (Lydgate himself and the Merchant) is allowed to enter into the tales themselves. Brief and perfunctory references to the pilgrimage occur before the first and second parts of the *Siege*, but the frame is completely forgotten before the third part and at the end of the poem.

Early readers of the *Canterbury Tales* appear to have held no strong belief in the pilgrims as fully developed characters. In his discussion of Richard Brathwait's *Comments on Chaucer's Tales of the Miller and the Wife of Bath* (first published in 1655 but written over thirty years earlier), the modern scholar R. H. Bowers laments "Brathwait's blindness to the rich drama arising from the social and personal antagonisms of the pilgrims," without considering that perhaps Brathwait's blindness is simply an older view of the *Tales*.[46] As is clearly revealed in the introduction to and selections from Derek Brewer's *Geoffrey Chaucer: The Critical Heritage*, Chaucer's first readers regarded him as a philosophical and rhetorical writer, a "Gothic poet" in Brewer's phrase. Only with the triumph in the late seventeenth century of neoclassic literary values, which regarded language as an inferior copy of reality, did Chaucer begin to be seen as a poet of Nature and Life.[47] In the eighteenth and nineteenth centuries this mimetic tradition, helped along by the dominance of the novel and the distorting deification of Shakespeare, finally resulted in the beginnings of the dramatic theory, as essentially amateur critics warmly responded to the vivacity and complexity of the *Canterbury Tales*.

Literary interest in the Canterbury pilgrims was stimulated by John Dryden's enthusiastic appreciation in his Preface to the *Fables* (1700): comparing Chaucer to Ovid he declares, "I see *Baucis* and *Philemon* as perfectly before me, as if some ancient Painter had drawn them; and all the Pilgrims in the *Canterbury Tales*, their Humours, their Features, and the very Dress, as distinctly as if I had supp'd with them at the *Tabard* in Southwark."[48] And yet Dryden, who like many since seems to be thinking primarily about the *General Prologue* while ignoring the tales, is not quite so modern as he may at first seem. Although he asserts that "Chaucer follow'd Nature every where," Dryden is not arguing for the individuality and psychological depth that later dramatic critics will claim; on the contrary, as a good neoclassicist, he means that the pilgrims conform to the universal laws of nature, or, in other words, that they are types: "their general Characters are still remaining in Mankind, and even in *England*, though they are call'd by other Names than those of *Moncks*, and *Fryars*, and *Chanons*, and *Lady Abbesses*, and *Nuns*: For Mankind is ever the same, and nothing lost out of Nature, though every thing is alter'd."[49] William Blake, whose engraved and written descriptions of the pilgrims are fully as vivid as Chaucer's and much less ambiguous (the Host and Monk, we are told flatly, are each "a leader of the age," the Wife of Bath "a scourge and a blight"), agrees with Dryden in seeing the pilgrims as types rather than individuals in the modern sense: "The characters of Chaucer's Pilgrims are the characters which compose all ages and nations. . . . some of the names or titles are altered by time, but the characters themselves for ever remain unaltered, and consequently they are the physiognomies or lineaments of universal human life, beyond which Nature never steps. Names alter, things never alter."[50]

The eighteenth century continued to develop Dryden's observations on the power of Chaucer's characters, stressing especially their fidelity to nature (in part to protect the poet from charges of obscenity), until the dramatic analogy began to become explicit. George Ogle claims in 1739 that Chaucer not only excelled at "the Distinguishing of Character from Character," but that in "Introducing them properly on the Stage" he is the equal of Plautus, Terence, or Aristophanes; and the dramatic metaphor is reinforced by the assertion in 1775 of Chaucer's first scholarly editor, Thomas Tyrwhitt, that the *Canterbury Tales* and the *Decameron* are "Comedies not intended for the stage."[51]

Two long essays in the *Retrospective Review* for 1823 and 1826 express fundamental opinions about the realism of Chaucer's characters and about the dramatic relationship of teller and tale that are still being echoed today. In his first essay, the anonymous author declares, with many of his time, that drama is the "most interesting, and perhaps the most instructive of all the forms of literary composition"; he then goes on to state that just as Homer is the father of ancient tragedy, Chaucer is the father of modern comedy, for both authors drew their materials not from books but from "observation of the living realities of human character."[52] The essay of 1826 again calls Chaucer the "Father of English Comedy" and asserts that his dramatic skill, especially "the delineation, grouping, and sustainment of diversified character," is equal to that of Shakespeare himself.[53] The author then argues for the close relationship of teller and tale, providing a full statement of the same dramatic principle that will be so brilliantly developed by Kittredge some eighty years later with the help of contemporary insights into individual psychology: "It is, indeed, worthy of particular note, how judiciously the poet has adapted throughout, not only the subjects of the respective narratives to the characters, conditions, and consequent associations of the respective narrators; but with what wonderful tact (or intuition rather) he has accommodated the style and language of each to the intellectual, educational, and moral habits, which should, in the course of things, pertain to them."[54]

For all its popularity, the dramatic theory is only one, limited, and increasingly outdated approach to the *Canterbury Tales*. Although its adherents continue to produce important criticism (my own considerable debt to their work will become clearer in the following chapters), the belief that Chaucer created coherent tellers through whom the tales are to be interpreted has also been responsible for much confusion and subjective imagining. A major problem with the theory has been a lack of consistency and rigor in its application. Because so many critics assume without question that there is usually a significant relationship between pilgrim and poem, they feel free to use the dramatic approach whenever it seems convenient without first establishing its validity for a particular tale. At the very least, dramatic critics need to become more self-conscious about their approach and deal frankly with the inconsistencies and anachronisms suggested above.

The Many Poets of the Canterbury Tales

Despite the limitations of the dramatic theory, its great contribution to the study of Chaucer has been to insist on the variety of the Canterbury Tales. Nondramatic critics sometimes discuss the tales as if all were written in a single, recognizable voice; though, as Kittredge recognized, nothing could be further from the truth in a work that includes, among other literary contrasts, both the complex, corrosive rhetoric of the Merchant's Tale and the elegant austerities of the Clerk's Tale. After opening with the startling contrast between the Knight's Tale and the Miller's Tale, Chaucer goes on to offer the reader an astonishing mixture of themes, genres, and narrative styles. The holy occurs next to the shameless and slapstick farce next to learned sermons.[55] Variety and conflict are everywhere, and no single "Chaucerian" style can be isolated. A false sense of the unity of the Canterbury Tales has sometimes been created by quietly excluding whole groups of tales that do not conform to current interests: the fabliaux were largely ignored at the beginning of this century, for example, and the religious tales more recently. Any full discussion of the Canterbury Tales must go beyond partial analysis and confront the total effect of such a complex and diverse work.

In my discussion of the Canterbury Tales, I intend to appropriate the most important insight of the dramatic approach (that each of the tales is fundamentally different from every other), yet I shall argue that this extraordinary variety ought not be attributed to the psyches of the pilgrims but to the different styles of the poems. It is my contention that each of the Canterbury tales is a unique work constructed on its own literary principles: principles that range from larger elements, such as the narrator and dialogue, down to the specifics of imagery, allusion, and vocabulary—all of which remain remarkably consistent throughout each work. General literary qualities may be signaled by a pilgrim or the narrative frame (the figure of the Knight prepares us for a chivalric romance, and the Miller, as Chaucer emphasizes, promises ribaldry), but the artistic individuality of the actual tale always goes much further than anything suggested by these dramatic hints. Chaucer has done nothing less than create a complete and original poetic for each tale. I know of no other literary work that is written in precisely this way, for the various parts are not mere parodies or only generally unlike; rather, each is a fully worked out expression of a special kind of poetry. The Canterbury Tales is not a dramatic clash of different pilgrims but a literary contest among different poets.

I am not, of course, arguing for the multiple authorship of the Canterbury Tales; I recognize that Chaucer and only Chaucer wrote all of the tales. Nevertheless, I think I am justified in using the metaphor of the "many poets" because it emphasizes just how far Chaucer goes to create a distinct and consistent artistry for each tale. Although a Henry James or Shakespeare has a considerable range in his works, it is usually not hard to recognize a novel by one or a tragedy by the other. To take an obvious example, Shakespeare uses different kinds and numbers of images from one tragedy to the next, but complex, vivid imagery itself is an essential element of each. The artistic variety I am claiming for the *Canterbury Tales* is more radical than this, like that between Shakespeare and James themselves; for in some tales, such as the *Miller's Tale* and the *Merchant's Tale*, Chaucer uses imagery extensively, whereas in others, even of the same genre, such as the *Shipman's Tale*, he uses virtually none at all. In what might be called the ultimate example of negative capability, Chaucer turns himself into a new poet for each tale. Awkward as it undoubtedly is, I sometimes choose to use the word "poet," rather than the more natural "voice" or "teller," in a deliberate attempt to depersonalize my analysis and prevent the reader from thinking of the pilgrim instead of the tale. As employed here, the term "poet" is comprehensive and not restricted just to the narrator, who is only one of his aspects. By "poet" I mean the literary sensibility of the entire work, as we would speak of the poet of the *Chanson de Roland* or the poet of *Sir Gawain and the Green Knight*.

By discussing poetics instead of pilgrims, the reader of the *Canterbury Tales* can avoid many of the limitations of the dramatic theory. The problem of how to interpret works that may have had more than one teller or that seem to fit their assigned pilgrims loosely or not at all can be largely dismissed because the tale itself (and the poet defined by that tale) is now our primary interest. It does not matter that the *Shipman's Tale* may once have been assigned to the Wife of Bath or even to someone else, because, whatever its title or nominal teller, the unique artistry of the work remains the same. The neglect of tales with undramatic tellers can also be remedied. Although Chaucer's pilgrims are often little more than types, each of his tales is strikingly individual. The Second Nun, for instance, is only a name in the *General Prologue* and link before her tale, but the *Second Nun's Tale* reveals a distinct and impressive poet who makes a significant contribution to the variety of the *Canterbury Tales*. Finally and perhaps most importantly, recognition of the poetic as opposed to the personal drama of the *Canterbury Tales* will allow us to make many more and more substantial comparisons among the various tales. In addition to familiar juxtapositions emphasized by the frame narrative (such as that between the tales of the Friar and Summoner), Chaucer has created even more interesting artistic and thematic contrasts between tales with absolutely no dramatic relationship, especially among works of the same genre. Although it has great potential for our understanding of the full complexity of the *Canterbury Tales*, such wide-ranging comparative criticism has been largely blocked by the more limited concerns of dramatic criticism.

Previous Chaucerians have occasionally suggested the principle of poetic variety and contrast that I wish to explore at length. When Dryden declares that "even the Ribaldry of the Low Characters is different: the *Reeve*, the *Miller*, and the *Cook*, are several Men," he is talking only about the pilgrims, but his observation is perhaps even truer when applied to the different kinds of low poetry in each tale, as we shall see in chapter V.[56] More recently, Derek Brewer, while asserting that the pilgrims have a life of their own, has observed that "the essential quality of *The Canterbury Tales* as a whole lies in the interplay of stories, rather than in the interaction of the characters who tell the stories," and Lee Patterson, near the end of a long and impressive essay on the *Parson's Tale*, calls the *Canterbury Tales* "a series of poetic experiments in various styles," though he, too, links these styles with the personalities of their tellers.[57]

Medieval Precedents

Although Chaucer's creation of a radically different poetic for each of his tales is unparalleled in medieval or later literature, others who had exploited the possibilities of different kinds of variety might well have influenced the construction of the *Canterbury Tales*. Beginning in the thirteenth century, as A. J. Minnis has recently shown, commentators no longer saw the Bible as the unmediated inspiration of the Holy Spirit, but began to explore the implications of its different authors and kinds of discourse.[58] Chaucer himself in the link between *Thopas* and *Melibee* refers to the single *sentence* but various styles of the four evangelists ("Al be ther in hir tellyng difference" [VII.948]), in a passage that I shall discuss further in chapter II, and earlier in the *Canterbury Tales* the poet defends his inclusion of different kinds of stories, even low ones, by recalling that "Crist spak hymself ful brode in hooly writ" (I.739). The *Metamorphoses* of Ovid, who is the classical poet Chaucer seems to have known best, contains much variety among its stories; and a similar diversity of matter and genre is characteristic of many medieval story collections, the most famous example being Boccaccio's *Decameron*, though scholars do not agree whether Chaucer himself actually knew this work.[59]

General precedent for the stylistic experiments of the *Canterbury Tales* is provided by Chaucer's favorite philosophical work, Boethius's *Consolation of Philosophy*. Its alternation of prose exposition and soaring poetry (later imitated, though hardly matched, in such works as Alan de Lille's *De Planctu Naturae*) may have suggested something of what different kinds of artistries within the same work could accomplish. Boethius himself seems clearly to have understood that each literary mode has its own special ability to apprehend and express truth.[60] The influential Roman de la Rose may also have taught Chaucer the possibilities of different styles. Literary variety and conflict are obvious to the most casual reader of the Roman because its two, very different authors—Guillaume de Lorris and Jean de Meun—are writing what is ostensibly the same story and using many of the same characters. In addition, the Roman contains many contrasting voices, especially in Jean de Meun's section, each expressing plausible but limited views of the world whose ultimate value the reader must judge for himself.[61] The poetic variety of the Canterbury Tales may also be seen as a further development of the well-known thematic complexity in Chaucer's fellow Ricardian poets: the many conflicting, incomplete perspectives of Piers Plowman, for example, or the three judgments on Gawain's quest at the end of Sir Gawain and the Green Knight, or even the sometimes uncertain relationship between the stories and their lessons in Gower's Confessio Amantis. Chaucer's special achievement in the Canterbury Tales is to extend the method of constructing a work out of many contrasting parts to the style as well as the matter of his poetry.

Chaucer's own earlier work foreshadows the stylistic variety and contrast so fully exploited in the Canterbury Tales.[62] The House of Fame, which is centrally concerned with questions of artistry, deliberately experiments with various kinds of poetry. Each of the three books of the poem differs absolutely in both substance and style: the scientific, comic form of the second could not be predicted from the dreamy, bookish first, nor the richly allegorical third from the second. An even more revealing example of poetic contrast occurs in the first book where Chaucer complicates our response to the story of Aeneas by telling parts of it in the manner of Virgil, who is sympathetic to the hero, and another part in the manner of Ovid, who is not. In a small way, the two versions of the Aeneas story anticipate the artistic differences in the Canterbury Tales among works of the same genre. In the Parliament of Foules also, diversity of style and material is common. The several parliamentary speakers, in particular, each of whom talks in his own distinctive style, have frequently been seen by dramatic critics as forerunners of the variety of the Canterbury Tales, though there is no danger that readers of the Parliament will assume its characters are psychologically believable individuals because, in addition to being birds, they are clearly identified as types representing different avian classes. Troilus and Criseyde also contains its share of experiments in literary variety, as seen most clearly in the contrast between the noble, idealizing language used by Troilus and the practical, manipulative language of Pandarus, each of which is echoed in turn by Criseyde, depending on whether she is speaking with her lover or uncle. Stylistic variety in the Troilus is also found in the several layers of material Chaucer has added to

Boccaccio's romance, including philosophical speculation, mythological allusions, and Trojan history.

Chaucer as Christian Poet

Despite general precedents in medieval literature and Chaucer's own poetry, the stylistic drama of the *Canterbury Tales* is something entirely new and daring. Other medieval works do not go so far in creating contrasting poetic voices, and few can equal its balance of *sentence* and *solaas*. With an ambition reminiscent of Dante, Chaucer is attempting to be both Christian teacher and true poet. Both offices are important to him, and he will not slight one for the other, though critics often do. In response to the freshness of Chaucer's stories and his ironic, sophisticated wit, some modern readers, echoing Arnold, deny the seriousness at the core of the *Canterbury Tales*. All Chaucerians therefore owe a debt to Professor D. W. Robertson, Jr., and his followers, despite their well-known excesses, for insisting that any study of the poet must begin with a recognition of his Christianity. For their part, exegetical critics often ignore Chaucer's achievement as a poet—a poet, in contrast to so many others in the Middle Ages, even in the exalted post-Renaissance ideal of the vocation. In their eagerness to explain Chaucer's message, the Robertsonians do not pay enough attention to the artistry that transmits and creates that message.[63] Poetry for Chaucer is not simply an attractive but disposable shell covering the harsh doctrinal kernel within; rather, it is the most effective method of apprehending certain truths and making them understood by others. Poetry is a way of knowing.

Although I am calling attention to the virtuosity of the poetic experiments in the *Canterbury Tales*, I do not mean to suggest, as is fashionable in literary analysis these days, that its only subject is poetry itself. Whatever his lack of high seriousness, Chaucer is not frivolous. Although he wears his morality lightly, he is a Christian poet who uses stylistic variety to instruct as well as delight. Poetry and preaching were often linked in the Middle Ages, as the purpose of both is to explore and revivify truth. For Chaucer such a crucial task is best accomplished through the full resources of his art, which has the power to involve a reader in serious themes. Harry Bailly, who is always quick to draw a moral from literature (even if it is usually the wrong one), expresses what every good teacher understands: even the best lesson is useless unless it reaches those for whom it is intended. He tells the Monk, who has almost put the company to sleep with his dull tragedies, that his tale has been told in vain because "Whereas a man may have noon audience, / Noght helpeth it to tellen his sentence" (VII.2800–01). As we shall see in more detail in the next chapter, Chaucer knew that even the most valuable *sentence* can better succeed with the *solaas* of poetry.

Although deeply Christian, the *sentence* of the *Canterbury Tales* is no simple lesson, but as complex as its *solaas* is various. By creating a new poet for each tale, Chaucer allows his reader to experience many different kinds of art and so appreciate the achievement (and limitation) of each. Furthermore, the poet's artistic complexity inevitably leads to moral complexity. Each of the tales is a poetic experiment that offers a unique view of the world, and therefore none is authoritative or final. The best reader of the *Canterbury Tales* will be the one who can fully respond to this rich mixture of contrasting visions, each of which, even the comic *harlotries* that gave poetry such a bad name in the Middle Ages, has something to contribute. As a sophisticated Christian poet, Chaucer does not mechanically indoctrinate his readers; rather he trains them in judgment, for it is they who finally decide the relationship and value of the different tales. The artistic variety and conflicts of the *Canterbury Tales* are as demanding as they are exhilarating.

CHAPTER II ✤ CHAUCER THE PILGRIM AND HIS CONTRASTING TALES

n our attempt to understand Chaucer's special accomplishment in the *Canterbury Tales*, there is no better place to begin than with the role the poet assigns himself. The "Chaucer" who narrates the *General Prologue* and then reappears to tell both *Sir Thopas* and the *Tale of Melibee* exposes the limitations of the dramatic theory while, at the same time, demonstrating the principle of literary variety. For all his vivacity, the first-person narrator never develops into a fully realized character but remains vague and elusive. The poet uses this flexible but disembodied voice in the *General Prologue* to produce a convenient series of narrative perspectives too diverse ever to coalesce into a single, definite personality. When the pilgrim is later called on to perform as storyteller, we are meant to see through him to the more important individuality of his tales.

Chaucer the Pilgrim

In suggesting that the narrator of the *General Prologue* is deliberately contradictory, I realize that I am opposing the widely accepted view of E. Talbot Donaldson. In his elegant and influential essay "Chaucer the Pilgrim," Donaldson correctly took issue with those critics who had identified Chaucer the pilgrim with the actual poet, and he argued instead that the figure is a carefully constructed and consistent fictional character. Easily impressed by important people and good companions (whatever their morals), the pilgrim Chaucer is "a bourgeois exposed to the splendours of high society, whose values, such as they are, he eagerly accepts." He can spot some kinds of rascality, but only if present among the lower classes and "provided it was, in any case, somewhat wider than a barn door." This naive and quite ridiculous figure, so unlike our sense of the real Chaucer, is not finally a bad man, "merely an average man."[1] Despite some dissent, Donaldson's portrait of the pilgrim as a wide-eyed, rather simple observer has been adopted with enthusiasm by all varieties of critical opinion and has become central to modern ironic readings of the *Canterbury Tales*. The result has been a new manifestation of the dramatic principle: the historical Chaucer is banished from the pilgrimage only to be replaced by a dramatic persona.

The foolish bourgeois defined by Donaldson is certainly one of the voices in the *General Prologue*, but his is hardly the only one. Diversity, not uniformity, is the most obvious quality of the *Prologue*. Chaucer's art of stylistic contrast, which is the essence of the *Canterbury Tales*, is practiced from the very beginning of the work. After opening in the best medieval high style with a formal description of the spring season (I.1–18), the *General Prologue* quickly switches to a chatty, highly individualized voice (I.19–42). The portraits that follow are similarly different in form and content and thus prepare us for the variety of the tales themselves. Some portraits describe the pilgrims physically (Squire), others morally (Parson). Some suggest only a casual knowledge (Yeoman), others reveal personal secrets (Wife of Bath and Friar), while still others are both intimate and distant (the narrator refers to the Merchant's possible indebtedness but does not know his name). Some of the portraits are long (Friar) and others quite short (Cook). Their tone varies from biting satire (Pardoner), through gentle mockery (Prioress), to admiration (Clerk). Some portraits judge the pilgrims by spiritual values (all of the religious and the Plowman), others by social values (the guildsmen). Some incorporate the characters' points of view and actual words (Monk), though others remain far outside (Squire). Some pilgrims are arranged in groups (Knight, Squire, and Yeoman; Summoner and Pardoner), others appear as individuals.

No single "Chaucer" will explain such variety. A foolishly credulous pilgrim accounts for only some of the more ironic portraits, like those of the Monk, Prioress, and Friar (to which, significantly, Donaldson devotes most of his essay), and parts of a few others, such as the Shipman's and Miller's. Even in these limited examples, the narrative voice identified by Donaldson is less a convincing dramatic character than an expression of innocence pushed so far that it eagerly endorses both nonsense and sin.[2] Chaucer did not intend the narrator to become a uniform character of novelistic verisimilitude; rather, the various portraits of the pilgrims are held loosely together by a nonspecific and flexible "I" who is capable of adopting many perspectives, even contradictory ones.[3] Other medieval first-person narrators mentioned by Donaldson, such as Dante in the *Commedia* or the dreamer in *Pearl*, are far more believable and consistent characters: each is a central figure who appears throughout the work and whose education is a primary focus of the action. Chaucer the pilgrim is none of these things; instead, he is a shadowy figure who disappears immediately after the *General Prologue* and then reappears before *Thopas* only to confirm his elusiveness. He seems never to learn anything.

More than once, the grace and wit of Donaldson's writing cannot overcome the logical difficulties of insisting on a totally consistent narrator. For example, he asserts that the stab at the Man of Law ("And yet he semed bisier than he was" [I.322]) does not violate the characterization of Chaucer the pilgrim because he is now describing one of his fellow bourgeois and can allow himself to be patronizing.[4] Yet it is hard to believe that the narrator who, according to Donaldson, worships all success and outward show would be less impressed by the magnificent Man of Law than by the Prioress or Friar. Harder still to account for is the quality of the praise for the truly good characters. Donaldson's explanation ("It is the nature of the pilgrim to admire all kinds of superlatives") is disingenuous and inadequate.[5] The narrator's praise of the good pilgrims is not that of an easily impressed naïf; on the contrary, especially with the Parson, but also with such as the Clerk and Plowman, he sets out clearly and intelligently the grounds for his admiration. In a brief discussion of the portrait of the Clerk, Donaldson pays most attention to the joke about the scholar's lack of money (I.298–99): "is not this still typical of the half-patronizing, half-admiring ununderstanding that practical men of business display towards academics?"[6] Even if we agree that Donaldson's statement represents a general truth about business and scholarship, it is a red herring in regard to the portrait. In order to maintain the consistency of Chaucer the pilgrim, Donaldson seriously misrepresents the narrator's obvious respect for the Clerk and for the value of knowledge for its own sake.

Donaldson's Chaucer the pilgrim is perhaps hardest to imagine as the speaker behind the portrait of the Parson. The following passage is an excerpt from the description of that good priest, every line of which expresses the values not of a naive or even average man, but of the Middle Ages at its most serious:

> And though he hooly were and vertuous,
> He was to synful men nat despitous,
> Ne of his speche daungerous ne digne,
> But in his techyng discreet and benygne.
> To drawen folk to hevene by fairnesse,
> By good ensample, this was his bisynesse.
> But it were any persone obstinat,
> What so he were, of heigh or lough estat,
> Hym wolde he snybben sharply for the nonys.
> A bettre preest I trowe that nowher noon ys.
> He waited after no pompe and reverence,
> Ne maked him a spiced conscience,
> But Cristes loore and his apostles twelve
> He taughte, but first he folwed it hymselve.
>   (I.515–28)

Portraits like these are created by one, in contrast to Donaldson's pilgrim, who is capable of a learned understanding of goodness.

The dramatic unity claimed for Chaucer the pilgrim is not apparent when we meet him again during his brief appearances before and between the tales of *Sir Thopas* and *Melibee*. Previous readers have commented on the inconsistency between the character's aloofness here and his own account of his sociable conduct in the *General Prologue* (I.30–34). The little we learn about the pilgrim Chaucer when the Host calls him forth to tell a tale in the *Prologue to Sir Thopas* suggests that he is a difficult character to grasp—literally because the size of his waist makes him a handful for any woman to embrace (VII.700–702) and figuratively because he always remains somewhat apart from the rest of his fellows. He may be plump, but he is not a rounded character. In fact, he is presented as more than a little unreal. As with no one else of the company, the Host seems completely ignorant about him; he does not know his profession or what to call him (the name "Geoffrey" or "Chaucer" is never used). "What man artow?" (VII.695) Harry first demands, after noticing him, apparently by accident, while attempting to lighten the sober mood after the *Prioress's Tale*. The pilgrim-narrator speaks in the first person throughout the scene, but he makes no attempt to define himself or reveal his feelings;[7] instead, he allows the Host to present him as an awkward outsider, one who stares at the ground and has to be ordered to join the group and take part in the fun: "Approche neer, and looke up murily" (VII.698). The pilgrim appears even less normal and quite mysterious when the Host calls him "elvyssh" and notes that "unto no wight dooth he daliaunce" (VII.703–4). The reader is left with the overwhelming impression of a distant, hidden figure, who not only illustrates Chaucer's gift for self-mockery, but frustrates those who read the *Canterbury Tales* dramatically. With the possible exceptions of the Second Nun and the Nun's Priest, there is less description of "Chaucer" than of any of the other pilgrim-tellers.

The reader gets no clearer sense of a consistent Chaucer the pilgrim during his appearance in the link between *Thopas* and *Melibee*. When the outraged Host stops his tale of foolish knightly deeds, the pilgrim Chaucer is deeply offended and demands to know why he has been treated so unfairly:

> "Why so?" quod I, "why wiltow lette me
> Moore of my tale than another man,
> Syn that it is the beste rym I kan?"
>   (VII.926–28)

This comically indignant pilgrim, who is not obviously identical with the shy, mysterious figure of the prologue to the tale, then gives way a few

lines later to what might be considered a third character, one who presents a detailed, if not necessarily profound, argument about the relation
of style to substance in literature (VII.943–66). We need not go so far as
Bernard Huppé and think that the third voice is actually that of the real
Chaucer to admit that, far from contributing to consistent characterization, this sudden outbreak of literary criticism seems to undercut any
claim to dramatic unity because it is so much more intellectual than
anything we have heard from the pilgrim before.[8] Of course, it would be
possible to construct a character who combines all these different qualities (conviviality with shyness and poetic naïveté with a taste for critical
theory), but the poet gives us no reason to do so. A Henry James might
well have been fascinated by such a complex personality, but Chaucer
has other interests, and so he allows apparent discrepancies to occur
without attempting to reconcile them or explain them away. Chaucer the
pilgrim demonstrates that inconsistency need not mean believable
complexity.

Despite the little they have to work with, and its apparent inner contradictions, many critics have attempted to see the teller of *Thopas* and
Melibee as a fully developed character. As is so often true of the dramatic
approach, the results have been idiosyncratic rather than persuasive, depending more on imaginative reconstruction than on the text itself. To
take only two brief examples, one critic understands Chaucer's apparent
shyness before his tale to result from the powerful emotional impact of
the *Prioress's Tale*, whereas another suggests that the pilgrim "is staring at
the ground in an effort to prevent the Host's seeing the merry twinkle
which has come into his eyes at the prospect of the joke he plans."[9] Such
contrary dramatic explications of brief narrative moments, though intriguing, cannot really be either proved or disproved because the necessary evidence simply is not available. The problem here is not with different literary interpretations, but with the creation of something unsanc-
tioned by the text. Nothing in the *Prologue to Sir Thopas* indicates what
Chaucer the pilgrim thought of the *Prioress's Tale* or the condition of his
eyes. Such subjective readings finally depend more on the critic's ingenuity than on Chaucer's poetry, and so the Host's opening question concerning the pilgrim Chaucer still remains: "What man artow?"

In questioning the dramatic realism of Chaucer the pilgrim, I do not
mean to suggest that his appearance before and between *Thopas* and
Melibee is either irrelevant or uninteresting. The exchanges with the Host
contain some of the poet's most delightful comedy at his own expense.
For our purposes, however, the significance of the pilgrim has less to do
with who he is than with what he does. Chaucer appears in the *Canterbury
Tales* not as a consistently developed personality, but as a teller of tales. In
fact, he tells twice as many as any other pilgrim and by so doing teaches

us through his own performance how we should understand each of the pilgrims. They are not so much characters in a drama as signals of artistic individuality. The main function of the tellers is to point the reader to the tales. Therefore, I suggest we dismiss the futile pursuit of Chaucer the pilgrim, who never becomes a convincing personality in the few lines devoted to him, and concentrate instead on his literary production.

The Contrasting Tales of Chaucer the Pilgrim

The significant drama of the *Thopas-Melibee* section is not in the confrontation of Host and pilgrim, but in the artistic opposition of the two tales themselves. Paul Ruggiers has referred to the "rich contrast" of the two works, and Alan Gaylord has argued that they are part of a fragment whose subject is tale-telling and that they themselves represent the two goals of the story competition announced by the Host in the *General Prologue: Thopas* is all *solaas* and *Melibee* all instructive *sentence*.[10] Valuable as such insights are, more detailed discussion about the pairing of these tales is needed. First and most importantly, we must come to see that the tales are not simply different, they are radically so. Elsewhere in the *Canterbury Tales*, *solaas* alternates with *sentence* less absolutely, as when the *Knight's Tale* is followed by the Miller's, for instance, or in the other examples from Fragment VII noted by Gaylord—the tales of the *Shipman* and *Prioress*, or those of the *Monk* and *Nun's Priest*. Although each pair sets up a conflict, no single tale has a complete monopoly on entertainment or instruction; but the opposition between the mirth of clever parody in *Thopas* and the morality of earnest exposition in *Melibee* is absolute. No coherent personality is defined by such schizophrenic tales; instead, by assigning two totally different works to himself, Chaucer unmistakably proclaims the art of literary variety that distinguishes the *Canterbury Tales*.

Just as significant as the thematic clash between *solaas* and *sentence* in *Thopas* and *Melibee*, though less commented upon, is their literary contrast. It is the style, not the substance, of *Thopas*, after all, that the Host criticizes and demands changed, with the result that the second tale is told in a completely different way from the first. The fundamental stylistic opposition is between poetry and prose, but the conflict goes far deeper. *Thopas* is art at its nimblest, *Melibee* art at its most dogged. So great is their contrast that little would suggest they come from the same imagination. By telling them one after the other and putting them both under his own name, Chaucer seems to have foreclosed any notion of a single "Chaucerian" style.

Thopas and *Melibee*, like every one of the Canterbury tales, are unique literary works, almost as if each had been written by a different author.

No other Canterbury tale is very much like the *Melibee*. In its use of prose
rather than verse and its overt didacticism, the *Parson's Tale* is undoubtedly
the closest, but it is finally quite different in form (*Melibee* is a story, however attenuated), narrative style, and material. *Thopas* is even more obviously one of a kind—it contains many nonce words, employs a metrical
scheme unparalleled in Chaucer's other works, and is the only example
of sustained parody in the *Tales*. This sharp opposition of literary styles
does not mean that one tale is all good and the other bad or even that
one work must necessarily be preferred to the other. Instead, because of
their artistic dialectic, each helps the reader understand the strengths and
weaknesses of the other. In addition, the stylistic contrast between the
two tales defines some of the practical problems of the Christian artist
that we shall see Chaucer struggle with throughout the *Canterbury Tales*.
The subject of the *Thopas-Melibee* unit is not so much the difference between art and meaning (*solaas* versus *sentence*) as it is the need to combine
the two.

The Tale of Sir Thopas

The achievement of *Sir Thopas* is its bright, nimble wit, as readers since at
least Skelton have always appreciated.[11] The tale offers pure fun without
the slightest hint of edification or moral improvement. As he does often,
the Host requests "a tale of myrthe" (VII.706), and for once he gets exactly what he asked for. The poet promises to tell "Of myrthe and of
solas" (VII.714), and he delivers nothing else. Even the element of satire
against the excesses of tail-rhyme romance is without malice and far from
wounding. The mock romance has no desire to reform, but finds only
pleasure in the conventions it uses so nimbly. *Sir Thopas* is all lightness,
literary decoration, and entertainment. In contrast to the foully martyred
boy of the preceding *Prioress's Tale*, "child Thopas" (VII.830) inhabits a
more fanciful children's world of elf queens, giants with three heads, and
abundant sweets and stories—a place in which despite the promise of
hunting and war, despite many strange beasts and much sudden movement, there is no real danger, pain, or loss. The story exists in the imagination with the real world far away, more like the adventures of Peter Pan
than even the most extravagant marvels of Arthur. Thopas himself seems
unable to manage any real involvement with another human being. He
scorns the flesh-and-blood women who long for his love ("many a
mayde, bright in bour" [VII.742]); instead, after falling in love in response
to a bird song (VII.772–73), he pursues a Fairy Queen whom he sees in a
dream (VII.787–88). With his small sides and fair bearing, the knight often seems too delicate for practical action. He tires easily from "prikyng

on the softe gras" (VII.779), and, despite the speed with which he travels from town to the country of Fairy, a few stones are sufficient to drive him away. The poem casually suspends the normal laws of cause and effect, of time and space, and even of knightly conduct (the only resemblance Thopas has to genuine knights like Percival, as the last stanza tells us, is that both "drank water of the well" [VII.915]). This gingerbread knight never actually lays eyes on the Elf Queen and never fights the giant. Instead his world is all cakes and mead, all "game and glee" (VII.840).

The style of the poem is also agreeably self-indulgent. Just as Thopas pampers himself with sweet things to eat and delightful tales to hear when he is supposed to be preparing for mortal battle (VII.845–56), so Chaucer ignores plot and theme to heap up wonderfully irrelevant lists of sports (VII.736–41), herbs (VII.760–65), birds (VII.766–71), and especially armor (VII.857–87). Delightful as these passages are, they do not advance the plot nor do they have any of the thematic importance of lists in the more serious Knight's Tale. Similarly, the poet uses a long physical description of his hero principally to set up a crude and delicious anticlimactic joke that is sprung in the concluding tail-rhyme: "And I yow telle in good certayn, / He hadde a semely nose" (VII.728–29). The poem is almost all show and filigree, like Thopas's gold shield (VII.869), whose beauty is matched by the uselessness of such metal against real weapons.

Thopas certainly delivers the "myrthe" demanded by Harry Bailly (if only he had the wit to know it), but perhaps its most remarkable achievement is that the comedy is so innocent, with no other aim than pleasure. Although, as John Burrow has shown, the tale has moments that remind us of Chaucer's poetry at its most serious, Thopas is a stylistic send-up that uses the tail-rhyme romance as little more than a pretext for its comedy.[12] Chaucer celebrates his own skill for its own sake. As an exercise in ars gratia artis, the tale is a literary tour de force whose very lack of moral or practical purpose is delightful to the aesthete, but incomprehensible, even offensive, to a literalist like Harry Bailly. Helen Corsa notes that "although the jog-trot never lets up, nothing in the poem seems to move," and Burrow observes that the tale "seems to narrow away, section by section, towards nothingness."[13] Surely, this is precisely the point. Without meaningful characters or a message of any kind, Sir Thopas proves that, in literature at least, something can be made out of nothing. It stands at the head of a long and peculiarly English tradition of sophisticated nonsense whose more recent practitioners include Gilbert and Sullivan, Max Beerbohm, and P. G. Wodehouse. Like Thopas, the works of these writers are never dull because they are never tempted by solemnity. Style is all and inspired silliness enough.

Despite the delight that many have long properly found in the wit and technical brilliance of Sir Thopas, we must consider that a medieval reader (including Chaucer himself) would surely have regarded the poem more ambivalently.[14] Neither pleasant nothingness nor the interest in poetic self-reflexiveness that dominates criticism today would have been considered a great virtue in the Middle Ages. G. K. Chesterton refers to *A Midsummer Night's Dream* to suggest that, like Shakespeare, Chaucer in *Sir Thopas* is marking the limitations of his craft as well as celebrating it: "Chaucer is mocking not merely bad poets but good poets; the best poet he knows; 'the best in this kind are but shadows.' "[15] Similarly, Donald Howard notes that *Thopas* is "escapist" and "mindless," especially when compared to the *Melibee*.[16] To the Middle Ages, the tale might have suggested the aimless and self-indulgent trivialities to which fiction at its worst could descend, confirming the harsh criticisms that Boccaccio tries to answer with his defense of poetry in the *Genealogy of the Gods* and illustrating Langland's constant warning about the abuses of minstrels.[17] There is an empty and mechanical center to *Sir Thopas* for all its cleverness, and no reader could endure much more of it because it lacks *gravitas* of any kind. Like cotton candy its airy lightness would not make a steady diet; and, though his grounds may be the wrong ones, the Host is in one sense perfectly correct to cut off the pilgrim's performance.

My suggestion that *Thopas* is a severely limited work may seem ludicrous to the modern reader and simply serve to associate me with the Philistine views of Harry Bailly. Nevertheless, as Anne Middleton notes in another context, although the Host often comes to what we, or Chaucer, would consider the "wrong" artistic answer, "he always knows where the questions are."[18] The Host is certainly wrong to consider *Thopas* incompetent, but his objections are useful in raising more profound questions than he is capable of considering about the aims and functions of poetry. Despite its brilliance and its deserved popularity among readers of Chaucer, *Sir Thopas* is far from the ideal of Christian poetry because it finally has almost nothing to say, although it says it so very well.

Telling Differences

The link between *Thopas* and *Melibee* ("Heere the Hoost stynteth Chaucer of his Tale of Thopas"), in addition to offering comedy between Host and pilgrim, explicitly discusses the main concerns of my study of the *Canterbury Tales*: stylistic variety and its effect on the reader. As we have seen, the link makes little contribution to a coherent conception of Chaucer the pilgrim; instead, it emphasizes the extreme literary contrast of *Thopas* and *Melibee* and explores the relationship between the way a tale is told and its ultimate meaning. At the beginning of the link, the Host makes clear that his reasons for stopping *Thopas* all have to do with style. He criticizes the form of the poem and not its content. With his ears aching from Chaucer's "drasty speche" (VII.923), the Host insists that the pilgrim's poetry is "rym dogerel" (VII.925) and denies it any skill whatsoever: "for pleynly, at a word, / Thy drasty rymyng is nat worth a toord!" (VII.929–30). For all his bluster, Harry is on the wrong side of the right fence. He is correct to focus on the style of *Thopas* as its most distinctive feature, but he then mistakes an extremely sophisticated spoof for ignorant incompetence. This is something like criticizing Sheridan for not making the vocabulary of Mrs. Malaprop more correct and is a joke that has been used before in the *Canterbury Tales*. Chaucer the poet is discussed in similar terms by the Man of Law, who praises him for the number and decency of his stories, even as his skills as a poet are slighted: "thogh he kan but lewedly / On metres and on rymyng craftily" (II.47–48). Both Harry Bailly and the Man of Law come to a conclusion that is exactly the opposite of the truth: the creator of the dazzling set of stylistic experiments known as the *Canterbury Tales* is labeled an incompetent rhymester. Of course we laugh at Chaucer's self-mockery, but, at the same time, we have been invited to think about the literary style of *Thopas*.

The Host does more than reject the form of *Thopas*; he occasions the artistic contrast of Chaucer's two tales by suggesting the pilgrim try something completely different. If he is incapable of poetry, let him "telle in prose somwhat, at the leeste" (VII.934). Substituting prose for poetry is a large change, but it only hints at the radical stylistic differences between the two tales. In abandoning *Thopas* for *Melibee*, the pilgrim has moved about as far as possible from one end of the literary spectrum to the other.

The topic of style is continued in a speech by the pilgrim that occupies the rest of the link, although now the subject is not different forms of literature, but the effect of slight variation in works that are basically similar. In a more serious tone than we have yet heard from him, and after noting that the "moral tale vertuous" he proposes to offer has been told "in sondry wyse / Of sondry folk" (VII.940–42), the pilgrim discusses the four evangelists and the changes in his version of the story of Melibee:[19]

> ye woot that every Evaungelist,
> That telleth us the peyne of Jhesu Crist,
> Ne seith nat alle thyng as his felawe dooth;
> But nathelees hir sentence is al sooth,
> And alle acorden as in hire sentence,
> Al be ther in hir tellyng difference.
> For somme of hem seyn moore, and somme seyn lesse,
> Whan they his pitous passioun expresse—
> I meene of Mark, Mathew, Luc, and John—

But doutelees hir sentence is al oon.
Therfore, lordynges alle, I yow biseche,
If that yow thynke I varie as in my speche,
As thus, though that I telle somwhat moore
Of proverbes than ye han herd bifoore
Comprehended in this litel tretys heere,
To enforce with th'effect of my mateere,
And though I nat the same wordes seye
As ye han herd, yet to yow alle I preye
Blameth me nat; for, as in my sentence,
Shul ye nowher fynden difference
Fro the sentence of this tretys lyte
After the which this murye tale I write.
                    (VII.943–64)

A central purpose of this passage is undoubtedly to prepare us for the moral seriousness of what is to come by comparing *Melibee* to the Gospels, but the stylistic discussion is of interest for itself. Of course, we need not take these somewhat disingenuous lines as a sincere expression of Chaucer's own views; the structure of the *Canterbury Tales* makes it hard to accept any statement as fully authorial, and this passage resembles other ironic "defenses" of the *Tales* in which the narrator seeks to avoid blame (I.725–46 and 3171–86). Nevertheless, although the method is characteristically indirect and comic, the lines ask us to consider the relationship between stylistic variation and the persuasive power of literature, a major concern of the *Canterbury Tales*.

At first, the argument in this passage may seem to undercut my emphasis on artistic contrast and variety because it apparently dismisses the importance of "tellyng difference." A closer look will show otherwise. Although Chaucer the pilgrim is here discussing religious prose and not the more obvious verbal complexities of poetry (and though we need never accept his conclusions as the whole truth), he does not deny that there are obvious differences of presentation even in the Gospels, because some of the four evangelists "seyn moore, and somme seyn lesse" (VII.949). His point is only that, however variously told, the *sentence* of the four accounts of Christ's passion is identical, as is that of the different versions of the *Melibee*. *Sentence* is an important word in the *Canterbury Tales* and expresses many overlapping meanings, from the narrow "maxim" or "saying" to the broader sense it apparently has here of "drift, purport" or "doctrine."[20] But the *sentence* of a literary work, while central, is not everything. The assertion that several works have the same *sentence* means only that they share the same general theme or purpose; it says nothing about their particular literary qualities or what the result of variation in these may be.

On this very question, the pilgrim goes on to suggest that an identical *sentence*, if presented differently, may not have the same effect on the reader. The difference in telling can have a telling difference. He says that he has varied the telling of his own version of the *Melibee* through the addition of proverbs in order "To enforce with th'effect of my mateere" (VII.958). Although brief, the statement is crucial, for the pilgrim is now saying the opposite of what he initially seemed to mean. In respect even to the *Melibee*, which is in expository prose and thus presumably less concerned with literary ornamentation than is poetry (and which all scholars agree is little changed from its sources), the pilgrim admits that a change in style (even the rather simple one of adding proverbs), while not altering the *sentence*, is designed to have a significant impact on the reader: "To enforce with th'effect of my mateere." Even for such artistically unsophisticated literature, the manner of presentation is crucial to result, and the relative effectiveness of works with the same *sentence* will depend on their individual artistries. In the *Thopas-Melibee* section we are asked to consider not only the obvious opposition of moral *sentence* to pleasant *solaas*, but also more subtle contrasts between different telling of similar material.

The pilgrim concludes the link by requesting that his audience "herkneth what that I shal seye" (VII.965). But what the previous discussion of style and meaning strongly suggests, and what the *Canterbury Tales* as a whole demonstrates, is that the specific way a work is told determines whether and how the reader hearkens to it. Chaucer's experiments with different styles in the *Canterbury Tales*, even within the same genre, are a direct result of his belief in the crucial importance of the particular artistry by which a story is presented. Of equal significance with what you say is how you say it. As one signal of this concern, Chaucer assigns himself two tales that taken together seem to define two poles of literary variety.

The Tale of Melibee

Although it still appears to be little read in the classroom, Chaucer the pilgrim's second tale, *Melibee*, a long prose work with allegorical touches in which Prudence finally succeeds in persuading her husband of the folly of revenge and the need to forgive his enemies, seems more and more to be accepted as a sound if somewhat dull work of moral instruction. A few recent interpreters like John Gardner and Trevor Whittock go beyond even the dismissive criticism of W. P. Ker ("perhaps the worst example that could be found of all the intellectual and literary vices of the Middle Ages") and consider the *Melibee* a joke, though it certainly damns Chaucer more to regard the tale as his idea of humor than to take it seriously.[21] In contrast to these negative views, most modern critics who discuss the work seem to agree that it is a sincere tale, if not one much suited to the taste of our time. Donaldson, who asserts that the *Melibee* is no hoax, perhaps best expresses the tale's relationship to Chaucer and his age: "the story (or sermon) was nevertheless a very popular one in the Middle Ages when readers did not entirely distinguish between pleasure in literature and pleasure in being edified. Chaucer himself probably did distinguish between these pleasures—but he also probably felt more pleasure in being edified than we are apt to."[22]

One of the principal reasons the *Melibee* has never inspired much enthusiasm, even among its admirers, is also my main interest: its unexciting style. Although not totally without narrative skill, *Melibee*, in Glending Olson's phrase, is, with the exception of the *Parson's Tale*, the "least fictive" of the *Canterbury Tales*.[23] Despite the thoroughly admirable message of peace and reconciliation, the artistry of the tale is embryonic. The narrative is diffuse, inert, and repetitive to the point of weariness, so that *Melibee* is easier to admire than to enjoy. Religious prose can be exciting in Middle English, as the *Ancrene Wisse* and even the lurid *Hali Meidenhad* testify, but *Melibee* is written in a style that is both plain and overly explicit. The slow, nondramatic presentation of the story seems all the more disappointing in the midst of Fragment VII, which contains some of the most brilliant poetry of the *Canterbury Tales* and is particularly concerned with questions of tale-telling. Chaucer's other prose works have not drawn the criticism of the *Melibee* in part because of their location; the *Boethius* and *Astrolabe* are independent works judged on their own terms, and the *Parson's Tale*, if not the most popular tale, has often been seen as an appropriate conclusion to the Canterbury collection. None of these other works has to come immediately after the lively *Thopas* and shortly before the incomparable *Nun's Priest's Tale*. But the placement of *Melibee* is not a miscalculation; rather, it is the essential literary point. By juxtaposing *Melibee* so starkly to *Thopas*, and including both in such a complex and artistically self-conscious fragment, Chaucer makes the tales under his own name a microcosm of the whole: they are extreme examples of the stylistic experiments and contrasts that run throughout the *Canterbury Tales*.

Unlike *Thopas*'s clever manipulation of romance motifs into the striking originality of parody, *Melibee* is thoroughly conventional in form and content. As Chaucer announces in the link, *Melibee* is a close translation of its source, and it depends heavily on popular proverbs and familiar quotations. It has no desire to say anything new, but instead heaps up a profusion of traditional knowledge. One authority is never enough when two or three more can be found, even if they say exactly the same thing.

For instance, in the course of asserting that it is a sin for a private person to take vengeance, Prudence notes that it is equally a sin for a judge to neglect to punish the guilty. Although the latter point is merely incidental to the main argument against private vengeance, it is fully supported with appropriate citations:

> "For Senec seith thus: 'That maister,' he seith, 'is good that proveth shrewes.' / And as Cassidore seith, 'A man dredeth to do outrages whan he woot and knoweth that it displeseth to the juges and the sovereyns.' / And another seith, 'The juge that dredeth to do right, maketh men shrewes.' / And Seint Paul the Apostle seith in his Epistle, whan he writeth unto the Romayns, that 'the juges beren nat the spere withouten cause, / but they beren it to punysse the shrewes and mysdoers, and for to defende the goode men.' / If ye wol thanne take vengeance of youre enemys, ye shul retourne or have youre recours to the juge that hath the jurisdiccion upon hem, / and he shal punysse hem as the lawe axeth and requireth."
> (VII.1437–43)

Such piling up of authorities, which occurs throughout Melibee, does nothing to advance the argument; it merely reinforces it. At times the tale reads like a demonstration of the different kinds of amplification so often recommended by medieval rhetorical manuals.

Melibee is a clear, dull, lengthy, and somewhat suffocating work without the irony or stylistic virtuosity that so baffled the Host in Chaucer's first tale. Melibee never aims for the sparkle or wit of Thopas; its undramatic, flatly allegorical approach is established in the opening line: "A yong man called Melibeus, myghty and riche, bigat upon his wyf, that called was Prudence, a doghter which that called was Sophie" (VII.967). Chaucer's one change from his source, the addition of the name Sophie, only makes the passage more didactic. Having scant regard for mere aesthetics, the work throughout avoids obvious opportunities for lively dramatic scenes in favor of straightforward exposition. For example, fairly early in the work, Melibee declares that he will not follow Prudence's advice because she is a woman, a stand he lays out dutifully with reference to standard authorities (VII.1055–63). Should the reader think that Melibee's perfunctory expression of such an exciting topic as antifeminism lacks passion or individuality, he need only look at the answer given by Prudence, which is an even longer and more conscientious piece of inert didacticism (VII.1064–1111). She identifies each point raised by Melibee (there are five) and answers it thoroughly with her own extensive set of authorities before concluding with a positive view of women. Prudence's whole speech is much too long to give here, but its flavor may be judged from the beginning of her answer to her husband's second point: "And as to the seconde resoun, where as ye seyn that alle wommen been wikke; save youre grace, certes ye despisen alle wommen in this wyse, and 'he that al despiseth, al displeseth,' as seith the book. / And Senec seith . . ." (VII.1070–71). Such a style produces a comprehensive statement that is clear and easy to follow, but at the expense of all narrative excitement. The passage is simply incapable of capturing any of the dynamics of a real dispute, especially one between husband and wife. The reader can only imagine how differently, and more entertainingly, the Wife of Bath or Proserpina in the *Merchant's Tale* would have exploited a similar opportunity. The debate in *Melibee* is a good, if somewhat superficial, summary of traditional views for and against women, but it is not very convincing or much fun.

As opposed to the profusion of details and narrative speed in *Thopas*, the material of *Melibee* is developed slowly and with great care. Once raised, a subject is explored fully, even if, as in the long discussion of riches (VII.1551–1671), it is only loosely related to the main argument. In the best medieval manner, topics are formally divided and even subdivided into separate units, which are then considered in order (see, in addition to Prudence's defense of women already mentioned, the discussion of *ire*, *coveitise*, and *hastifnesse* at VII.1120–37). In contrast to the plot of *Thopas*, which moves quickly, sometimes even bewilderingly, from incident to incident, transitions in the *Melibee* are always extremely deliberate: "Now, sire, sith I have shewed yow of which folk ye shul take youre conseil, and of which folk ye shul folwe the conseil, / now wol I teche yow how ye shal examyne youre conseil . . ." (VII.1200–1201).

The loose, paratactic style of *Melibee*, which finds no virtue in conciseness, means that minor points are explored with the same numbing thoroughness as major points, dissipating much of the force of the argument. Even painfully obvious statements are proved with earnest thoroughness. Prudence begins her exposition of whose counsel Melibee should avoid by advising him not to listen to fools or flatterers. Hard as it is to imagine any disagreement here, the first recommendation is supported with quotations from Solomon and Ecclesiasticus, the second with two quotations each from Cicero and Solomon and one from Cato (VII.1172–81). Not that the advice of Prudence is wrong, but the manner of presentation keeps it general and conventional. Rather than being offered a genuine exploration of some difficult topic, the reader is reassuringly reminded of universally accepted truths.

The conflict between *Thopas* and *Melibee* goes far beyond that between *solaas* and *sentence*. Innumerable medieval religious works, including

Chaucer's own *Second Nun's Tale*, demonstrate that *sentence* equal in seriousness to that of *Melibee* can be presented with literary skill and real excitement, just as *solaas* in literature need not be as frivolous and poetically self-conscious as *Thopas*. The styles of the two tales precisely reflect the different themes of each. The plain, careful, conventional artistry of *Melibee* echoes the virtues of self-control and moderation that Prudence unceasingly recommends to her husband. While *Thopas* celebrates knightly action and the easy gratification of appetite (corresponding to its flashy, excited style), *Melibee*, in form and precept, urges prudence, patience, and humility. Indulgence in selfish passion is criticized in the treatise, which instead values self-restraint through consideration of others and the social control of law. Despite its emotional constraint and lack of drama, moreover, *Melibee* contains a title character with family and friends who feels pain, loss, and love, unlike the frivolous, solitary *Thopas*. In contrast to the make-believe world of Chaucer's first tale, his second tale, though conventional, is heavy with thoughtfulness and genuine human problems. *Thopas* is a childish fantasy of selfish delights, whereas *Melibee* sets forth the principles of an ideal Christian society.

But for all its undeniable seriousness, *Melibee* is not a perfect tale or the end to which Chaucer has been working in the *Canterbury Tales*, as some critics seem almost to suggest. Because its art is unsophisticated, the effectiveness of the message of this "moral tale vertuous" remains potential rather than fully realized. The simple Host is excited by the tale, but not in the most edifying way: he thinks its lesson should apply only to his wife Goodelief. The most disturbing question about *Melibee*, however, is whether it can, or ever could, deeply involve a sophisticated reader. While approving the good intentions of the work, one may still feel unconvinced by a plodding narrative with allegorical characters whose motivations are so didactically obvious. Near the end of the work, *Melibee* suddenly submits to Prudence's argument and gives up his desire for vengeance: "I shal nat konne answere to so manye faire resouns as ye putten to me and shewen. / Seyeth shortly youre wyl and youre conseil, and I am al redy to fulfille and parfourne it" (VII.1711–12). The reader applauds Melibee's conversion, while looking to the text in vain for some plausible reason (besides exhaustion) to believe it. Even those modern readers who admire the tale have little praise for its art.

Melibee itself shows an awareness that style is as necessary as substance if an audience is to be genuinely reached and moved. At the first council called by Melibee, a wise old man gets up to oppose the young hotheads who want war. He states his position, but is never allowed to make it convincing. In the words of the link before the tale, he is not allowed "to enforce with th'effect of my mateere" (VII.958): "And whan this olde man wende to enforcen his tale by resons, wel ny alle atones bigonne they to rise for to breken his tale, and beden hym ful ofte his wordes for to abregge. / For soothly, he that precheth to hem that listen nat heeren his wordes, his sermon hem anoieth" (VII.1043–44). Although the reader might be inclined to sympathize with the young men's impatience if the speaker intended to prove his position with the mere repetition of authorities so common in *Melibee*, the passage does make a serious point. Truth alone is not enough; to be properly effective it must be presented skillfully.

Prudence herself is aware that the art with which one says something is as important as what one says. Like Boethius's Lady Philosophy, she knows that she must not only show her pupil the error of his ways, but also find a way to get him to listen to and accept her words. She is a strategist as well as a preacher. At the opening of the work, for instance, she waits for her husband to calm down and stop weeping before beginning her instruction—with words from Ovid no less (VII.974–80). Prudence knows that the manner of approach is important: "Thanne dame Prudence, whan that she saugh how that hir housbonde shoop hym for to wreken hym on his foes, and to bigynne werre, she *in ful humble wise, whan she saugh hir tyme*" (VII.1051—my emphasis; see also VII.1726–28). Throughout, she consistently looks for the right time to speak and the right words to use. Even Melibee acknowledges her skill: "Whan Melibee hadde herd the wordes of his wyf Prudence, he seyde thus: / 'I se wel that the word of Salomon is sooth. He seith that "wordes that been spoken discreetly by ordinaunce been honycombes, for they yeven swetnesse to the soule and hoolsomnesse to the body"'" (VII.1112–13). Although *Melibee* contains little artistic ingenuity of its own, it nevertheless asserts that differences in style and presentation can be crucial.

The *Melibee's* lack of complex art does not mean that it is a failure, but it does suggest the limitations of the work. Dolores Palomo correctly notes that it "contains only minimal indications of setting, characterization, and plot," and Donaldson, who takes the tale seriously, points out its "lack of literary qualities and of any real imagination."[24] *Melibee* is not the ideal of Christian art. Because it is so abstract, dull, and repetitious, the reader is less likely to absorb or act on its thoroughly admirable message.

Although I disagree with Trevor Whittock and John Gardner, who dismiss the tale as a joke, their comparison of *Melibee* with the Host's flamboyant reaction after the tale is instructive. In the prologue to the *Monk's Tale*, Harry Bailly regrets that his impatient wife had not heard the *Tale of Melibee* that has just concluded:

> By Goddes bones! whan I bete my knaves,
> She bryngeth me forth the grete clobbed staves,

And crieth, "Slee the dogges everichoon,
And brek hem, bothe bak and every boon!"
(VII.1897–1900)

The Host's lament (of which this is only a part) is a delightful scene, one of the many comic links that join the Canterbury tales, and Gardner is right when he says that it is a comment on what is missing in Prudence's sermon: "The *Melibee* ignores the force of human passion—the force Melibee talks about with such remarkable detachment, for an angry man, and which the Host's wife Goodelief embodies."[25] Whittock's observation is even more relevant for our purposes because it stresses the contrast in style between *Melibee* and the Host's speech: "How clogged and clumsy the language of *Melibeus* is seen to be beside this passage whose life, of course, is achieved by a craftsmanship so skilful that it almost conceals itself. Here language prickles with bodily sensation."[26]

In the contrast between *Melibee* and the Host's speech, as in the larger contrast between *Melibee* and *Thopas*, Chaucer is not comparing bad to good, but illustrating different ways of using language. The vivacity and drama of the Host's words represent a positive value, but Chaucer's view of art is broader than that understood by Gardner and Whittock; he also recognizes the value of *Melibee*'s moral instruction. The Host's coda does not invalidate the tale of *Melibee*, but it does suggest the limitation of its bloodless, flat presentation of virtue. *Melibee* contains much of the truth of Christianity, as Chaucer saw it, but there is a real question of how effectively, then or now, it is able to convince an audience of that truth. Similarly, *Thopas*, for all its wit and skill, lacks the substance to sustain its clever art. Given such a stark contrast, it is not clear that Chaucer would prefer one tale over the other. Each has its own virtues and weaknesses, which are most clearly revealed by comparison with the other. Although we can be sure that neither represents the poet's own ideal of literature, together they define the outer boundaries within which the Christian artist must work.

The elaborate dramatic frame that Chaucer creates around *Thopas* and *Melibee* teaches us very little about the pilgrim-narrator, but it does force his two tales into sharp juxtaposition and thereby announces the method of the entire work. This kind of unparalleled stylistic variation, and not the Roadside Drama, is the great achievement of the *Canterbury Tales*. Our natural interest in Chaucer the pilgrim is proper, provided that it is not at the expense of a more substantial figure we meet in this section: Chaucer the poet, who struggles with the many demands and techniques of his craft to produce an art of contrast that challenges, while it entertains, any reader who seeks to follow its complexity.

CHAPTER III ❧ CHAUCER'S PARDONER ❧ THE MAN AND HIS TWO TALES AS A DEFENSE OF CHRISTIAN POETRY

he outrageous Pardoner of Rouncivale, the last of a group of shady characters described at the end of the *General Prologue*, has long played a central role in dramatic interpretations of the *Canterbury Tales*. Chaucerians of all varieties from Kittredge's time to the present have been almost unanimous in seeing him as one of the most realistic of the pilgrims and have provided detailed, if contradictory, analyses of his character, desires, and innermost motivations. Paul Ruggiers speaks for many when he calls the Pardoner "the ultimate example of Chaucer's subtle handling of human psychology."[1] Despite the apparent appeal of this approach, I wish to join the small but diverse company that has questioned the psychological depth of the Pardoner and suggest instead that he provides a clear example of the limitations of the dramatic theory.[2] The image of the Pardoner as a complex, dark soul tortured especially by his aberrant sexuality, which has been so enthusiastically developed by scholars in this century, often rests on extremely weak evidence and has diverted attention from Chaucer's more important accomplishments in this extraordinary tale. The Pardoner is not so much a personality as a verbal performer—a skilled but corrupt artist of language. Our attention should not be on the man, but on his words, for Chaucer's real interest in the Pardoner is as a tool to explore the dangers and potential of literature in the service of morality. The *Pardoner's Tale*, as we shall see, is nothing less than Chaucer's defense of Christian poetry.

The Dramatic Interpretation of the Pardoner

It is easy enough to understand why the figure of the Pardoner has fascinated so many readers. His portrait is among the longest and most vivid in the *General Prologue* (I.669–714), emphasizing his grotesque physical appearance and ability to win money with his tongue. He then interrupts the Wife of Bath to praise her preaching and to ask for advice on marriage (III.163–87). When his turn comes to tell a tale, he apparently baits the Host and certainly stirs up the fears of the "gentils" (VI.320–28) before offering an unparalleled confessional prologue during which, in contrast to the Wife of Bath's defense of her activities, he reveals all his wicked tricks and freely admits to being a vicious hypocrite concerned only with personal gain. The tale he finally tells continues the focus on himself, for, instead of being a story, it is an actual demonstration of his preaching techniques. This is followed by a highly dramatic conclusion in which, after trying to peddle his pardons to the pilgrims (most likely as a joke), the Pardoner is so roughly insulted by the Host that he can no longer speak, though a reconciliation of sorts is arranged by the Knight. Without doubt, the Pardoner is an extraordinary literary character and the relationship between him and his tale is one of the most interesting in the *Canterbury Tales*; but, instead of reading the Pardoner's performance for information about the man, I suggest the teller is most significant as he points to the tale. Chaucer is not primarily interested in the Pardoner himself, still less in having us go behind the characterization to discover coherent motives and real feelings; instead, the poet uses this lively performer to illustrate the relationship of art to morality that is the central concern of the *Pardoner's Prologue and Tale*.

Dramatic interpretations of the Pardoner as a fully developed character depend on very little evidence but much critical ingenuity. Few solid facts about the pilgrim's life emerge, and some of these, like his claim to have a wench in every town (VI.453), are regularly disbelieved. Most of what we do learn is untrustworthy because it comes from the mouth of the Pardoner himself, a self-admitted verbal trickster. John Halverson properly cautions that the "figure of the Pardoner with which we have to deal is almost entirely an image that the Pardoner himself projects. (Of the 'real' Pardoner we know next to nothing)."[3] This has not stopped critics from trying to discover the inner man, however, and the conclusion to the tale has been a special target for their speculations.[4]

Kittredge's reading of the scene is still among the best, but it is also one of the most inventive because he makes all depend on the Pardoner's brief recommendation of Christ's pardon at the end of his sermon:

> And Jhesu Crist, that is oure soules leche,
> So graunte yow his pardoun to receyve,
> For that is best; I wol yow nat deceyve.
> (VI.916–18)

Although these lines are perfectly conventional, Kittredge finds in them an extraordinary emotional crisis in which the pilgrim, remembering that he has not always been such a spiritual renegade, "suffers a very paroxysm of agonized sincerity." But the feeling cannot last: "The crisis passes, and the reaction follows. He takes refuge from himself in a wild orgy of reckless jesting."[5] Of course, the real author of this powerful scene of self-recognition is not Chaucer but Kittredge, and, while admiration for the reading has been general, few have ever believed it true. Instead, it remains an extreme example of just how much can be made by a persuasive critic from almost nothing.

In their valuable summaries of interpretations past, both G. G. Sedgewick and John Halverson spend much of their time burying similar dramatic imaginings that have died for lack of convincing evidence: for example, the theory that the Pardoner's performance is explained by drink or that his sermon is delivered inside a tavern, thus allowing him simultaneously to denounce and to enjoy the sins of the table.[6] Variety is essential to literary criticism; but looking at the range of contradictory recreations of the Pardoner, we may suspect that we are dealing more with idiosyncratic response than with genuine literary analysis. Although all dramatic critics cast the Pardoner as the star of a play, each proposes a different genre—from high tragedy through theater of the absurd to slapstick farce.

To a degree that is not true with even the most problematic characters of literature like Shakespeare's Hamlet, critics cannot agree on basic questions about the Pardoner: is he thoroughly evil ("the one lost soul" among the pilgrims), merely an entertaining pitchman explaining his tricks, or actually quite innocent, even Christ-like?[7] Nor is there any agreement about what the Pardoner really wants from the other pilgrims—is it money, revenge, admiration, approval, compassion, or even love?[8] These different interpretations are argued skillfully by their proponents, but they are also almost entirely subjective, as their sharp differences suggest. The reader can neither refute nor support them very convincingly because they depend on so little, and such selective, textual evidence. If most are interesting in themselves, none of these hypothetical re-creations of the Pardoner is reliable enough to support a literary interpretation of the tale.

Although many previous dramatic theories have had to be abandoned over the years, recently a new one has gained general popularity and is currently the basis for most psychological explanations of the Pardoner: the sexual interpretation, an approach that may have more to do with the obsessions of contemporary society than with anything in Chaucer's poetry. This interpretation derives largely, though not entirely, from a single line in the *General Prologue*: "I trowe he were a geldyng or a mare" (I.691). The line is not as clear as it may first seem because it is subjective ("I trowe"), metaphorical (a gelding is not necessarily a human eunuch, nor a mare a male homosexual), and contradictory (gelding or mare). Although many write with certainty about the Pardoner's sexuality, there is once again, as with other dramatic interpretations, no general agreement. Some consider him a eunuch (either *ex nativitate* or spiritual), whereas others assume he is homosexual.[9] Several critics appear to regard these two states as identical or complementary, but occasionally the Pardoner is diagnosed with breathtaking precision: he is, according to one, "a manic depressive with traces of anal eroticism, and a pervert with a tendency toward alcoholism," and, according to another, "characteristic of the testicular pseudo-hermaphrodite of the feminine type."[10]

Elsewhere I have argued against the sexual interpretation at length, attempting to show that the supposed "scientific" proof from medieval physiognomy manuals for the Pardoner's eunuchry is much weaker than is usually thought and that the evidence for his homosexuality is even less convincing.[11] The poet undoubtedly hints at sexual disorder of some sort as one part of the Pardoner's basic corruption, but he defines no specific condition. Perhaps it is best to see the Pardoner as generally effeminate (which in the Middle Ages could mean too much interest in women), like Absolon in the Miller's Tale, another lustful cleric who is not so much incapable of heterosexual lovemaking as he is incompetent at it. This is exactly the way the Pardoner appears in the introduction to the fifteenth-century pseudo-Chaucerian Tale of Beryn. Like other dramatic theories, the sexual interpretation of the Pardoner is based on scant textual evidence and distracts us from the real issues of the Pardoner's Tale.

The Pardoner as Corrupt Preacher

Belief in the psychological reality of the Pardoner may come in part from a confusion between literature and life. That a literary figure is made exciting and vivid to the reader does not necessarily mean that the author has imagined human depths for him or realistic motives for his actions. All fictional characters are two-dimensional in fact, but late medieval and early Renaissance writers and their audiences had a sense of literary personality far different from one shaped by the realistic novel and modern film. Langland's Gluttony and Shakespeare's Falstaff have the same powerful effect on the reader as Chaucer's Pardoner, but both derive from the medieval allegorical tradition and are not individuals in the modern sense at all. We accept drunkenness as central to both Gluttony and Falstaff without thinking to ask, as we would with more realistic characters, what it was that made them drink in the first place. Although Chaucer's art makes the Pardoner seem more naturalistic than his allegorical model, Faus Semblant in the Roman de la Rose, he still remains very much a type of falseness, though a brilliant realization of the type.[12]

The Pardoner is exactly what he so repeatedly says he is: a pure example of the corrupt preacher. He has no more private life than any other allegorical character; rather, the essence of his being is his misuse of the art of preaching for profit. For all the seeming revelations, his own great verbal skill is finally all that we really know about him (it is what he talks about in his apparently "personal" prologue and then demonstrates in his tale). The man escapes us, but we have his clever, fraudulent words.

That the Pardoner is essentially a deceitful linguistic performer is emphasized when we first see him in the *General Prologue*. After the description of his odd physical appearance, the main purpose of which is to prepare us for the deeper professional corruption to come, the focus of the Pardoner's portrait is on his skill with words at the expense of an audience. The narrator notes that the Pardoner "seyde" his bogus relics were genuine (I.695 and 696) and that by means of "feyned flaterye and japes" he makes "the peple his apes" (I.705–6). Although the Pardoner reads the lesson well and eagerly sings the offertory, his real brilliance is in the pulpit, for then he is able to "wel affile his tonge / To wynne silver" (I.709–13). When the Pardoner interrupts the Wife of Bath, it is to declare, presumably as an expert, that she is "a noble prechour in this cas" (III.165).

The Pardoner as preacher is carefully established by Chaucer because his is a useful profession through which to examine the dangers and potential of Christian poetry. Not only were poetry and preaching considered similar disciplines in the Middle Ages (the *ars praedicandi* closely resembled the *ars poeticae* in form and precept), but of all literary genres at the time preaching was both the most prestigious and the most popular. Christ himself was a preacher, and the sermons of many of the leading figures of Christianity from Augustine to Bernard were closely studied and imitated in Chaucer's day; moreover, preaching was the only form of medieval literature that would have been known to virtually every Christian, however humble. In a sense, then, the preacher is the most important literary figure of the Middle Ages. Of all who use words, he has the greatest ability to do good and to do evil. He can be Satan or Christ—the father of lies or the *verbum Dei*.

The prologue to the *Pardoner's Tale* illustrates and deepens the portrait of the Pardoner as a clever performer with words—a corrupt preacher whose great abilities are perverted to serve base and selfish ends. The Pardoner boasts that his professional skills are used solely for evil purposes: "For myn entente is nat but for to wynne, / And nothyng for correccioun of synne" (VI.403–4). He repeatedly insists that he is a hypocrite concerned only with personal gain and completely indifferent to the spiritual fate of his *lewed* audience: "I rekke nevere, whan that they been beryed, / Though that hir soules goon a-blakeberyed!" (VI.405–6). In a voice bursting with self-assertion, he concludes by claiming a willingness to commit the most heartless crimes:

> I wol noon of the apostles countrefete;
> I wol have moneie, wolle, chese, and whete,
> Al were it yeven of the povereste page,
> Or of the povereste wydwe in a village,
> Al sholde hir children sterve for famyne.
> (VI.447–51)

Such lines are not very convincing as realistic self-revelation (who would seriously describe himself as so unredeemably wicked?), and it is not surprising that dramatic critics have felt the need to account for such extreme statements. Drink was long ago seized upon. A Pardoner whose tongue has been loosened by the "moyste and corny" ale he requests before he will speak (VI.315) is not just an idea of older critics, but has been proposed by several contemporary ones as well.[13] Recently another explanation has been offered by those who accept a realistic Pardoner but find his claims of absolute wickedness too melodramatically exaggerated to take seriously. James Calderwood sees the confession as a deliberate parody of how the Pardoner imagines the respectable pilgrims see him, and Halverson calls it a "put on."[14]

Dramatic explanations of the *Pardoner's Prologue* turn our attention away from Chaucer's text to the supposed psychology of the pilgrim. Even more seriously, they discount the importance of what we learn by labeling it as no more than a spoof or the result of drink. Instead of trying to explain away the Pardoner's horrible self-portrait in the prologue, we would do better to accept it as a serious description of a corrupt preacher. As such it prepares us for the artistic and moral conflicts of the *Pardoner's Tale* itself by addressing the question of verbal skill divorced from truth. Although the prologue tells us less about the human pilgrim than is usually thought, it tells us everything we need to know about him as a preacher, and it is to the preacher rather than to the person that I am referring when I use the name "Pardoner" from now on.

In the description of his preaching skills in the prologue, the Pardoner celebrates only the effective manipulation of words, never their truth. Talbot Donaldson comments that nowadays the Pardoner "would probably represent himself as an image-maker, an advertising man,"[15] and he indeed has that profession's concern with style and practical result at the expense of content. For all his deceitful superficiality, it cannot be denied that the Pardoner puts on a good show of the sort still found all over the United States in revival tents and on evangelical broadcasts. His is a multimedia happening with "bulles" from Rome, a "patente" from the bishop, and various relics (VI.336–37 and 347ff.), though it is not clear that any of them is genuine. Of course the Pardoner's principal medium is language, and he knows all the tricks of that trade. He rings out his speech like a bell (VI.331), complete with slightly smutty jokes about a wife sleeping with priests "two or thre" (VI.371) to balance his showy Latin (VI.344–45). Again and again, the Pardoner ignores morality to concentrate on the practical question of what works with an audience. Justly proud of his skill, he declares that lewed people love his old stories (VI.435–38), and he calls attention to the show he puts on in the pulpit with his "hundred false japes" and active neck, hands, and tongue: "it is joye to se my bisynesse" (VI.391–99).

The Pardoner is all technique and nothing but technique, and his explanation of his methods makes it easy to understand the distrust of art and fiction that runs throughout medieval Christian thought (and is found even in Chaucer's own Retraction). The Pardoner's performance for the lewed folk is no amusing exercise in style like Sir Thopas, for its intent is truly satanic—the employment of knowledge, skill, wit, and energy for evil. And yet, as he repeatedly boasts, the Pardoner is always able to reach and sway those who listen to him, an achievement whose importance is repeatedly stressed in medieval preaching manuals. In contrast to the plodding Melibee, whose worthy sentiments lack all inspiration and fire, the Pardoner's performance demonstrates the potential power art has to affect an audience, an essential quality even Christian literature must have to succeed, though here used for all the wrong reasons.

At the end of his prologue, the Pardoner asserts that even though he is a "ful vicious man" he can still tell a "moral tale" (VI.459–60). But a more interesting question is what happens when moral tales are told by men who are not only vicious but also possess great literary skill. This is much harder to deal with than the problem posed by the opposition of Thopas and Melibee. Each of them is a good, if limited, work; their contrast makes us consider only the right mix of art and morality, not the utter perversion of both at the hands of a talented but unscrupulous artist. Melibee may be dull, but it is earnest and pure, and although Thopas can be seen as no more than a clever trifle, it is successful within its own terms and never pretends to any kind of moral weight. In contrast, the prologue to the Pardoner's Tale deals with matters that are altogether more serious: evil able to masquerade as good because of its author's command of words. In the tale that follows, Chaucer first reveals the dangers that can result when Christian themes are handled by a skilled, corrupt artist, but he then goes on to show how effective the right mix of great art and true doctrine can be.

The Pardoner's Two Tales

The themes of language, truth, and audience response, which Chaucer raises in the *Pardoner's Prologue*, are further explored in the tale itself through the sharp contrast between two kinds of religious poetry. Instead of possessing a single, unified style, the *Pardoner's Tale* is in radical opposition to itself. Critics have often found powerful contradictions in the psyche of the pilgrim (the former servant of Christ who now preaches only for gain, the skilled public speaker who is privately miserable, the grotesque sexual defective who believes he rides in the latest fashion, and so forth), but the most significant drama in the *Pardoner's Tale* is artistic rather than personal; not within the Pardoner himself but within his tale. As we have seen in the juxtaposition of *Thopas* and *Melibee*, artistic contrast between tales is a central principle of the *Canterbury Tales*, but here the contrast is internal, almost as if the *Pardoner's Tale* were really two different poems.

The first of the Pardoner's two tales is the energetic but superficial denunciation of the tavern sins (VI.463–660) along with the final address to the pilgrims (VI.895–918); the second is the magnificent exemplum of the three revelers contained within this frame (VI.661–894). Although the exemplum is a section of the larger homily, I shall use the term "sermon" to mean only the denunciation of the sins. The verbal skill of each part is equally accomplished (Charles Muscatine sees here the only narrator "given literary powers comparable to those of Chaucer himself"),[16] but the results differ completely as the Pardoner abuses his craft in the first tale before revealing its full moral power in the second. Chaucerians have not sufficiently appreciated how completely different artistically, and therefore morally, the two parts of the *Pardoner's Tale* are. Even when some contrast between the sermon and the exemplum has been noted, comment has been brief and only in passing, without the detailed literary comparison necessary to understand the significance of such a conflict.[17]

St. Thomas Aquinas makes a distinction between two kinds of literary art in preaching that is relevant here: "The use of secular eloquence in Sacred Scripture is in one way commendable and in another reprehensible. It is reprehensible when a man uses it for display or when he aims mainly at eloquence. He who strives principally after eloquence does not intend that men should admire what he says, but he strives rather to gain their admiration for himself. Eloquence, however, is commendable when the speaker has no desire to display himself but wishes only to benefit his listeners, . . . and out of reverence for Holy Scripture."[18] The two parts of the *Pardoner's Tale*, the sermon and the exemplum, are almost exact demonstrations of these opposite ways of using literary skill in Christian art.

The Pardoner's First Tale

In the Pardoner's Tale two varieties of religious poetry are contrasted under
the form of a sample homily. The exemplum is medieval moral poetry at
its most subtle, but the opening denunciation of the tavern sins is a more
flamboyant, crowd-pleasing performance of the sort Chaucer must have
frequently heard (and presumably despised). The respect often given to
this first of the Pardoner's tales needs careful qualification. While techni-
cally accomplished and ostensibly devout, the denunciation illustrates
the misuse of language condemned by Aquinas and discussed in the
prologue. It is therefore misleading to call the sermon, as one critic does,
"a piece of grand rhetoric in the best medieval manner."[19] An undeniable
facility with words, which will be properly employed in the exemplum,
is here used to produce a spectacular but ultimately empty example of
trite moralizing. The sermon is a flamboyant performance with a dazzling array of different levels of language that is never dull, but, despite its
accomplishments, the reader may well agree with the critic who finds
the rhetoric "extravagant" and "self-indulgent" and with another who
likens the effect to that of "slight sickness, almost of vertigo."[20]

Our unease comes from the preacher's efforts to impress an audience
at any cost. There is no denying the power of this flexible, fluent voice,
seen especially in the mastery of certain set pieces, such as the virtuosic
description of how the whole world labors to feed the glutton:

> Allas! the shorte throte, the tendre mouth,
> Maketh that est and west and north and south,
> In erthe, in eir, in water, men to swynke
> To gete a glotoun deyntee mete and drynke!
>   (VI.517–20)

Nevertheless, for all its skill, the effect of the sermon is manipulative,
demagogic, and often vulgar. The tone is deliberately extravagant, careen-
ing from a pompous high style ("superfluytee abhomynable" [VI.471])
to the homeliest expressions ("Thou fallest as it were a styked swyn"
[VI.556]). Sometimes the two are violently fused: "That of his throte he
maketh his pryvee, / Thurgh thilke cursed superfluitee" (VI.527–28).

Superfluity, in fact, accurately describes the style of this first part: it is
packed with lists, laments, threats, and famous names in compulsive profusion as if to prevent any attempt by the audience to reflect, even for a
moment, on what they have heard. The quality of the sermon may be
questioned, but the sheer quantity of its examples and the energy of its
rhetorical devices are undeniable. Thomas Waleys, the fourteenth-century English Dominican writer of a treatise on preaching, specifically
warns against "superfluity ad nauseam" in homilies because it will lead a

listener to reject food for the soul just as the stomach rejects too rich a diet.[21] Because of its showy style, the attack on gluttony in the *Pardoner's Tale* is itself guilty, Waleys would say, of the verbal equivalent of that same sin.

The beginning of the sermon in particular does not inspire or educate; it harangues. A preacher is supposed to appeal to the emotions of his audience, but the Pardoner too easily indulges in melodramatic flights of exaggerated rhetoric of the sort Chaucer parodies in the *Nun's Priest's Tale*:

> O glotonye, ful of cursednesse!
> O cause first of oure confusioun!
> (VI.498–99)

> O glotonye, on thee wel oghte us pleyne!
> (VI.512)

> O wombe! O bely! O stynkyng cod,
> Fulfilled of dong and of corrupcioun!
> (VI.534–35)

These sudden bursts of mechanical emotionalism contain little moral seriousness or artistic taste, but they might well arrest the attention of an unsophisticated audience.

As we would expect from the *Pardoner's Prologue*, the sermon is a skilled performance that misses no opportunity to display its dramatic prowess, as in this fervent address to a drunk man:

> O dronke man, disfigured is thy face,
> Sour is thy breeth, foul artow to embrace,
> And thurgh thy dronke nose semeth the soun
> As though thou seydest ay "Sampsoun, Sampsoun!"
> (VI.551–54)

The lively last effect ("Sampsoun, Sampsoun!") is then resorted to again only twenty lines later.

Striking as much of the first part of the *Pardoner's Tale* is, the result is closer to that of a used-car salesman than a serious Christian artist. We are impressed by the urgent tone of voice and sweeping claims rather than by any depth of thought. The command of language that is capable of producing genuinely moving moral art, as the exemplum will demonstrate, is here perverted into mere hucksterism, in which the virtuosity of the performer rather than the importance of his message dominates. Although it is undoubtedly clever and was probably widespread, this style of preaching was constantly attacked during the Middle Ages. We have already quoted St. Thomas's disapproval of self-regarding eloquence; in addition, Alain de Lille and others insist that preaching ought to be direct and nontheatrical, and Humbert of Romans cites Augustine as support for his statement that "a sermon should be simple, and devoid of all the empty ornaments of rhetoric."[22]

More damning than its sensational style, the denunciation of the tavern sins, for all its overt didacticism, lacks real moral force. Although it mimics many of the devices and topics of the medieval sermon, it contains surprisingly little spiritual content.[23] Chaucer seems well aware of the dangers that could result when a form so important to Christian life as preaching was used dishonestly, and he may even be specifically mocking the failures of actual sermons he had heard. In the approved manner, the sermon sets out a specific theme (*Radix malorum est Cupiditas*), and then subdivides it into three parts, also a common practice.[24] Although its form is proper and its theme potentially important, for cupidity (or avarice as the Pardoner calls it at VI.428) was often seen in the late Middle Ages as the source of all evil,[25] the sermon itself is severely reductive. The specific sins the Pardoner discusses (gluttony, gambling, and swearing) are relatively minor ones and, in his treatment, as much social errors as spiritual faults. Not that these sins are ignored in real medieval sermons, but they are usually seen as only a part of larger and more serious patterns of evil. Donaldson is surely right to conclude that the three were chosen because "they are the sins that can be made to sound most exciting."[26] They would undoubtedly jazz up the performance for the peasants, but they do not really engage the most difficult questions of Christian sin. In his influential treatise on preaching, Robert of Basevorn also provides a sample homily for laymen; but the three sins he examines (and this is echoed by an actual Middle English sermon from MS Royal 18.B.xxiii) are central: pride, avarice, and luxury, the so-called Three Temptations traditionally believed to have caused Adam to fall and which Christ resisted in the desert.[27]

In order to excite the audience and encourage them to buy indulgences, the Pardoner's sermon sensationalizes its three sins. Although one sin is actually from the Three Temptations—gluttony, which is often substituted for luxury—the treatment is superficial. To say that "corrupt was al this world for glotonye" (VI.504) is to follow a long medieval tradition that connects the sin with the Fall, but, rather than explore the subject seriously, the Pardoner exploits it in overwrought rhetorical excess:

> O glotonye, ful of cursednesse!
> O cause first of oure confusioun!
> O original of oure dampnacioun,
> Til Crist hadde boght us with his blood agayn!
> (VI.498–501)

It is a further exaggeration to then go on to suggest that gluttony alone lost Paradise:

> Adam oure fader, and his wyf also,
> Fro Paradys to labour and to wo
> Were dryven for that vice, it is no drede.
> For whil that Adam fasted, as I rede,
> He was in Paradys; and whan that he
> Eet of the fruyt deffended on the tree,
> Anon he was out cast to wo and peyne.
> (VI.505–11)

The source for this last passage is St. Jerome's *Adversus Jovinianum*, 2:15, as the Latin gloss to Ellesmere and other manuscripts indicate, but Jerome's thought has been distorted by taking the words out of context. In *Jovinianum*, the passage is part of a larger discussion of the difference between physical and spiritual values, in which fasting is linked with prayer, and whose ultimate point, which goes far beyond anything in the Pardoner's sermon, is that the things of this earth keep us from achieving the divine. For the Pardoner gluttony itself is the Original Sin; for Jerome it is an example of a fundamental separation between man and God.[28] The prominence given to gluttony in the Pardoner's sermon undoubtedly makes for a more dramatic presentation, but such oversimplification, which is perhaps most dangerous because it contains a core of truth, does little for the moral education or spiritual growth of the audience.[29]

At the end of the sermon, the Pardoner makes extraordinary claims for the importance of his third sin, swearing. He says that it is worse than murder—because its prohibition occurs earlier in the Ten Commandments (VI.643–47)—and declares that God will take vengeance on those who practice it (VI.648–50). Yet for all the danger the Pardoner professes to see in this sin, his discussion is relatively brief and unhelpful. It begins by asserting that both false and idle oaths are terrible things, reinforces this with a reference to Matthew and a quotation from Jeremiah, and concludes with a lengthy list of forbidden expressions. Compare this superficial treatment with a late-medieval English sermon on swearing from the Royal manuscript previously mentioned.[30] This sermon also condemns both kinds of swearing (though each is discussed in more detail) and warns of God's vengeance, but the preacher then goes on to urge careful self-examination by the individual to discover if he is guilty of the sin and whether it has led to others like pride, covetousness, or gluttony. The sermon then concludes by asserting that, although God surely punishes the guilty, he is very good to man and fully rewards those who repent. Rather than a sensationalized denunciation designed to frighten its listeners into buying more pardons, the sermon from the

Royal manuscript is a thoughtful, complex mixture of emotion and reason that appeals for personal repentance while attempting to promote real moral insight.

Even though the Pardoner's sermon on the tavern sins echoes phrases, imagery, and themes from authoritative medieval works, we should not therefore conclude that Chaucer meant us to read it as a serious exposition of Christian thought. Many passages in the sermon have general parallels, and perhaps even their source, in Innocent's De Contemptu Mundi, and are echoed in the Parson's Tale;[31] and yet, as with the quotation about Adam and Eve from Jerome, similar words in another context may produce a very different result. The Pardoner's sermon contains tags from its betters, while ignoring their deeper purpose. Traditional religious discourse is looted for shiny nuggets of wisdom to decorate the performance, but the denunciation has no interest in serious instruction or moral reform. Even when his writing is most rhetorically charged, Innocent, along with the more sober Parson, avoids the flashy, insubstantial effects of the Pardoner's sermon; instead, each of these genuinely moral writers creates a solid, carefully argued work that systematically considers the whole range of human evil (not just a few entertaining sins) and then, most important of all, suggests specific remedies to combat them. In contrast, the Pardoner offers only his fraudulent indulgences.

A sermon, especially one for laymen, will usually be briefer and more dramatically appealing than full-scale moral treatises like those of Innocent or the Parson, but even superficially similar English sermons are significantly more serious and less worldly than the Pardoner's performance. G. R. Owst has shown how popular the topic of the "Sins of the Tavern" was with medieval English preachers, perhaps because such sins were a frequent problem and their castigation would make for useful as well as exciting homilies. Nevertheless, although contemporary English attacks on the tavern sins contain many lively scenes and, like the Pardoner, stress the practical disadvantages of these vices, they do not forget the wider social and spiritual costs.[32] We are told by one preacher that gambling, with its allied vices, not only wastes time and deserves misfortune, but it also "greeveth God" and men's "owne soules."[33] As for gluttony, and especially drink, preachers note that, in addition to its physical ravages and effect on family life, it often keeps a man from church and the sacraments: "glotenie maketh a man or a womman nat onliche blynd bodiliche but also gostliche."[34] The most powerful example of such ghostly blindness in medieval English literature is Langland's Gluttony, who stops in at the tavern on the way to confession and becomes not only disgustingly sick, but more deeply in need of repentance.[35]

The sermon in the Pardoner's Tale, however, stresses almost exclusively the practical effects of sin without much attention to the spiritual. In recording the evils of drink, the Pardoner, along with giving two biblical quotations that threaten death (VI.521–23 and 529–33), declares that it produces "manye maladyes" (VI.513–16), foul sounds at either end of the body (VI.536), physical unattractiveness (VI.551–54), and loss of intellectual control (VI.556–61). These are serious disadvantages to be sure, but there is nothing specifically Christian about them. With gambling as well, it is not so much the spiritual toll that is reckoned as the social: other sins are mentioned, but the Pardoner's emphasis is on the loss of time, goods, and honor caused by the vice (VI.593–96) and its disadvantage to the reputation of kings (VI.603–28).[36]

For all the literary prowess of the denunciation, it has nothing new or even serious to say about these sins. In his discussion of preaching, the twelfth-century monk Guibert de Nogent warns against telling an audience only what they already know: "it follows that in expounding the lessons of the holy Gospel we must do something more than mouth traditional platitudes; we bring in the moral application, bringing in new stones, as it were, for the reconstruction of an old wall."[37] This the Pardoner's sermon conspicuously fails to do. It never gives us more than sensationalized clichés about gluttony, swearing, and gambling, and never convincingly shows how these relatively minor sins may lead to major ones. Instead of real analysis, the denunciation depends on the intensity of its abuse and the sheer number of examples crammed into the performance. And yet, although the sermon is packed with illustrative exempla, each remains undeveloped and thus of limited value. In the section on gluttony, for example, there are references to Lot, Herod, John the Baptist, Seneca, Adam, Paul, Sampson, Attila, and Lamuel (who is not Samuel); but these names flash by with little effect. None is allowed to become a real story, and so none has the literary power to move or teach the listener. This array of "olde stories longe tyme agoon" (VI.436) is clearly designed to dazzle the Pardoner's lewed audience, but one wonders how relevant to their humble lives is the knowledge that the Bible proves sobriety necessary for a leader to succeed in battle (VI.573–87) or that it hurts the reputation of a great lord to be known as a gambler (VI.597–628). Comparable stories in real sermons to illustrate the dangers of sin are often about ordinary people in common situations—the harm a drunkard might do to his family or a gambling priest to his calling.[38] They are less showy than the Pardoner's exempla, but probably more useful.

Finally, for all its overt moralizing, the Pardoner's sermon offers little real help against sin. The good preacher is supposed to provide encouragement as well as criticism, but the Pardoner can only rant at the vices. He has nothing positive to offer and commends no virtues. In contrast to Innocent, to the Parson, and to many contemporary English preachers, the sermon in the *Pardoner's Tale* contains no spiritual remedies for the sins it discusses; self-examination, prayer, and repentance go unmentioned, all the better to promote the only recourse left open: the profitable pardons whose sale is the only purpose of the whole performance.

An even more serious flaw is that the effect of the sermon, as A. C. Spearing notes, is not at all prohibitive: "the sins are not diminished but magnified."[39] At times, the audience seems actually encouraged to participate, at least vicariously, in what is supposedly being condemned, as in the detailed discussion of different wines and their powerful effects (VI.562–72) or the list of prohibitive oaths whose number and detail produce a virtual primer of swearing for the gambler:

> "By Goddes precious herte," and "By his nayles,"
> And "By the blood of Crist that is in Hayles,
> Sevene is my chaunce, and thyn is cynk and treye!"
> "By Goddes armes, if thou falsly pleye,
> This daggere shal thurghout thyn herte go!"
>   (VI.651–55)

While acknowledging that the first part of the *Pardoner's Tale* is rhetorically spectacular and addresses themes treated seriously by other medieval writers and preachers, we must still conclude that the sermon does exactly what Malcolm Pittock says the Pardoner's pardons do: "offer an easy and corrupt substitute for repentance."[40] Because the energy and skill of the sermon seem to promise so much, its actual failure is all the more disappointing.

The Pardoner's Second Tale

The exemplum of the three revelers is in direct contrast, both morally and aesthetically, to the denunciation of the tavern sins. Although both parts of the *Pardoner's Tale* display great verbal skill, only the second deals seriously with the announced theme of the work: *Radix malorum est Cupiditas*. From the moment the story of the three revelers at last gets under way, the style and even vocabulary of the poetry change completely, becoming more direct and profound:

> Thise riotoures thre of whiche I telle,
> Longe erst er prime rong of any belle,
> Were set hem in a taverne for to drynke,
> And as they sat, they herde a belle clynke
> Biforn a cors, was caried to his grave.
> That oon of hem gan callen to his knave:

"Go bet," quod he, "and axe redily
What cors is this that passeth heer forby;
And looke that thou reporte his name weel."
(VI.661–69)

Even in these opening lines, the story proceeds quickly but effectively, with telling detail and colloquial dialogue in the service of an important theme—death.

Despite the controversies surrounding other aspects of the Pardoner and his performance, all varieties of critics have united in asserting that the exemplum is one of the great achievements of Chaucer's art. As opposed to the verbal tricks and empty ranting of the first tale, the second is an understated and ultimately mysterious poem of great moral force. Robert K. Root long ago described its power: "full of tragic terror; dramatic in its structure, transacted as it is almost wholly in dialogue; never hurried, but marching forward with sure strides, unimpeded with a single superfluous detail, irresistible and inevitable as death and night."[41] The verbal facility first described in the prologue, and practiced fraudulently in the denunciation, is now under full artistic control and used for genuinely spiritual ends. The exemplum fulfills the Horatian demands made before the performance: it is an entertaining story, and thus the "myrie tale" the Host had wanted (VI.316), while also being instructive and thus the "moral thyng" requested by the *gentils* (VI.325).

Impossible as it undoubtedly is to explain the full power of the exemplum, previous Chaucerians have identified many of the elements of its success. The story, in which dialogue and action are paramount, has a spare and elegant plot whose swift narrative and stunning climax are presented as effectively as in Chaucer's best fabliaux.[42] Instead of the "ensamples many oon" (VI.435) that pass by so quickly in the sermon, this single exemplum is fully developed and thus effective in engaging (and instructing) the reader. Its energy comes not from a dominating narrative voice, but from the action of the story itself. Perhaps most revealing is what is *not* in the second tale: no empty rhetoric, mechanically emotive apostrophes, or ostentatious display of famous names. There is no clutter. Unlike the sermon, the exemplum is told in the simple, modest style recommended to medieval preachers. Every detail in the story advances the narrative and contributes to its final meaning without the constant repetition that exposes the superficiality of the sermon. Although the tale is thoughtful and challenging to the intellect, its explicit learning consists of just one direct quotation from the Bible (VI.742–44) and a closing reference to Avicenna that leads us back to the style of the first tale (VI.889). In contrast to the excesses of the denunciation, the exemplum avoids the temptation of melodrama implicit in its subject and achieves the economical yet evocative effect of archetypal myth.[43] A significant paradox of the tale is that the Pardoner best impresses as a rhetorician when he is least ostentatious and most direct. For although it lacks all the flashy verbal fireworks of the sermon, the exemplum succeeds at every level: its art is simple enough to be understood by the *lewed* audience but profound enough to satisfy the most sophisticated.

In place of the shrill and false language of the sermon, the exemplum has a subtle irony that works through powerful understatement, as previous critics have shown. Early examples of this are the proposal by one of the revelers that each "bicomen otheres brother, / And we wol sleen this false traytour Deeth" (VI.698–99)—exactly the opposite of what actually happens—and the trio's vow to "lyve and dyen ech of hem for oother" (VI.703). Perhaps the most chilling line occurs when the three first see the treasure that will destroy them all: "No lenger thanne after Deeth they soughte" (VI.772). We know, as they do not, that they need no longer seek Death because he has found them. Other examples in which this poem exploits the full power of language without calling attention to itself include the "croked wey" (VI.761) down which the Old Man directs the revelers to the tree of death, the use of the Christian term "grace" (VI.783) and the Boethian "heigh felicitee" (VI.787) by the worst of the three to describe the fatal treasure, and the "vermyn" (VI.858) that the youngest says he wants poison to kill.

Beyond even these stylistic accomplishments is the symbolic significance the exemplum gives to a group of physical objects, especially the "breed and wyn" (VI.797) the three rioters are to share and the tree under which they find both the treasure and their deaths. While essential to the literal working out of the narrative plot, these objects also link the story with the central episodes of Christian salvation history: the Fall of Man at the Tree of Knowledge and the eventual redemption of the world through the passion of Christ, as reenacted in the bread and wine of the Mass.[44] In keeping with its deliberately humble style, the exemplum in no way calls attention to these symbols, but they add much to its artistic and moral weight.

The mysterious Old Man in search of death because he can find no one with whom to exchange his age for youth is an appropriate microcosm of the artistry of the exemplum as a whole. Although he has been identified with such diverse figures as Death, penitent avarice, the Wandering Jew, Old Adam, and a devil, and seen as both positive and negative, the full significance of this character has never been convincingly defined.[45] Yet all critics have testified to his importance in the story and his eerie effectiveness. As A. C. Spearing and others suggest, the key to the Old Man may be that he is deliberately ambiguous and therefore all points of view have something to contribute to his explication.[46] As such, he provides a revealing contrast to the crude, repetitive, and often trite moralizing of the Pardoner's first tale.

Just as the restrained but powerful artistry of the exemplum is far superior to the empty rhetoric of the sermon, so, too, the moral depth and sophistication of the second tale answer the superficiality of the first. In addition to being a genuinely exciting narrative, the exemplum succeeds in being what the first tale can only parody: a complex and highly effective work of Christian instruction. The exemplum is both a good story and a true sermon, combining the moral *sentence* of *Melibee* with the literary *solaas* of *Sir Thopas*. Like the first part of the tale, the exemplum begins with the "Sins of the Tavern," but then it goes beyond such relatively minor failings to show how they lead to more deadly temptations, as with the youngest rioter:

> And atte laste the feend, oure enemy,
> Putte in his thought that he sholde poyson beye,
> With which he myghte sleen his felawes tweye;
> For-why the feend foond hym in swich lyvynge
> That he hadde leve him to sorwe brynge.
> (VI.844–48)

The announced theme of the entire homily (*cupiditas* or love of worldly things) is not ignored or reduced in the second tale, but deeply explored. Gluttony, gambling, swearing, and the love of money all appear in the exemplum without being its major concerns. Even the triple murders at the end, horrible as they are, are not the root evil of this story, but only the consequences of the two fundamental sins of cupidity: the revelers' separation from God and from each other (the opposite of Jesus's twin commands to love God and one's neighbor), whose biblical prototypes (the Fall and Cain and Abel) are replayed at the end of the exemplum. In contrast to the more worldly sermon, the exemplum shows that, for all the material harm that sin may bring, the real damage is done to one's soul: the revelers' physical death is only a confirmation of their earlier and more important spiritual death.

Like the sermon, the exemplum has the ability to reach and affect its audience; but while the first tale merely aims to make them its dupes, the second allows the audience to get imaginatively close to evil without identifying with it. Instead of merely haranguing, it genuinely teaches. The difficult idea of humans deliberately choosing damnation, for example, is presented clearly and with convincing inevitability. The art of the exemplum continually forces us to go beyond the surface narrative to find a hidden and more complex spiritual meaning. As readers so instructed, we are far different from the revelers who judge by appearance and find reality only in the physical.[47] Living in a purely carnal world, they do not understand that the Death they seek to destroy with force can only be conquered by Christ, the one whom they help to kill with their oaths. Likewise, they ignore the spiritual meaning of the bread and wine, but in a parody of transubstantiation physically change it from its potential as a life-giving sacrament to an instrument of horrible death.[48]

The Pardoner's first tale, the denunciation of the tavern sins, shares many of the rioters' limitations: like them, it ignores the spiritual to concentrate on the physical consequences of evil, though it is able to confront that evil only with a furious, and ultimately superficial, attack of the sort the revelers direct at Death. The Pardoner's second tale is a far superior kind of Christian art because it succeeds as both imaginative fiction and a moral lesson. Many critics have noticed that the story contains a careful mixture of the physical and spiritual in its movement from tavern realism to religious allegory.[49] In this respect, the exemplum is like the divine liturgy of the Church—among the most authoritative uses of language in the Middle Ages—in that its words and actions are simultaneously specific and universal, literal and symbolic.

When the story of the three revelers comes to its awful conclusion, its serious, thoughtful mood is immediately shattered, as others have noted.[50] With many "O's" and "allas's," we are thrown back into the false and overwrought style of the first part of the tale:

> O cursed synne of alle cursednesse!
> O traytours homycide, O wikkednesse!
> O glotonye, luxurie, and hasardrye!
> (VI.895–97)

This cheap rhetoric seems all the more inadequate after the subtle power of the exemplum and explicitly confronts us once again with the artistic contrast of the Pardoner's two tales and their different kinds of Christian art.

The *Pardoner's Tale* concludes with an animated dramatic scene in which the Pardoner offers his indulgences to the pilgrims, and especially to the Host because "he is moost envoluped in synne" (VI.942). If the invitation is meant as a joke, as seems likely, Harry fails to appreciate it; instead, he coarsely insults the Pardoner, though the Knight eventually effects a reconciliation of sorts. This brief dramatic episode has been at the center of many interpretations of the *Pardoner's Tale* from Kittredge to Howard, but the tomfoolery is probably better seen as a comic modulation down from the serious issues of the tale itself—a function the frame often performs in the *Canterbury Tales*. Although some have believed that one or another of the Pardoner's "secrets" are finally revealed here, the lines instead support the notion that the Pardoner is essentially a creature of words. Humiliated by the Host and laughed at by the company, the Pardoner's performance ends when he loses that which is his only being, command of language:

> This Pardoner answerde nat a word;
> So wrooth he was, no word ne wolde he seye.
> (VI.956–57)

The relationship between art and morality is a common theme in the *Canterbury Tales*. Another preacher with whom the Pardoner has often been compared, the Parson, explicitly states that fiction poses dangers to Christian values. When asked for a tale, the Parson declares, "Thou getest fable noon ytoold for me" (X.31), echoing a common distrust of purely imaginative stories among medieval churchmen. The Parson says that his subject is "moralitee and vertuous mateere" (X.38) and that he will not speak in alliterative verse or in rhyme, but straightforwardly in prose (X.42–47). The Parson explicitly opposes morality to art, and one critic, comparing him to the Pardoner, insists that the priest provides "the true sermon of which the Pardoner's is the false copy."[51] But nothing is ever that simple in Chaucer. The Parson's sermon is certainly superior, morally and even artistically, to the Pardoner's first tale: his complex but lucid analysis of the way to Christian repentance, which not only identifies sin but also suggests remedies for it, is in every way more valuable than the Pardoner's superficial and self-promoting denunciation of the tavern sins. Nevertheless, the Pardoner's second tale has a power and appeal that the *Parson's Tale* does not begin to match.

The exemplum of the three revelers is Chaucer's defense of poetry because it proves the power of skillful art to communicate Christian themes. Any modern reader will find the story of the rioters in search of Death superior in both art and moral instruction to the *Parson's Tale*, but even the original audience of the exemplum must have realized it possessed a moral depth and literary effectiveness denied to mere expository prose. The *Pardoner's Tale* is one of Chaucer's most audacious creations. It contains all the best and all the worst the poet had to say for imaginative literature. While illustrating the dangers when clever language and the powers of fiction are misused, the Pardoner's prologue and two tales also succeed in justifying the ways of Christian poetry to medieval (and modern) man.

he first, and perhaps the most striking, literary contrast in the *Canterbury Tales* is that between the *Knight's Tale* and the *Miller's Tale*. Every reader feels their difference, and Derek Brewer well expresses one of the givens of Chaucer scholarship when he declares: "The contrast between *The Miller's Tale* and *The Knight's Tale* is very refreshing, and very typical of Chaucer. We turn from 'sentence' to 'solas,' from art in the service of serious conviction to art in the service of fun."[1] The change that Brewer and others have noted is true enough, but more needs to be said: the literary opposition between the first two tales is far more profound, consistent, and deliberate than generally recognized. To begin the *Canterbury Tales*, Chaucer created a dynamic conflict between two completely different kinds of secular poetry. This opening contrast is unlike the mixture of corrupt and sublime poetry in the *Pardoner's Tale* or the juxtaposition of witty trifle and inert didacticism in *Sir Thopas* and *Melibee*. Neither the *Knight's Tale* nor the *Miller's Tale* is corrupt art, but rather each, through its own brand of magnificent poetry, reveals a particular truth about the world, and thus each contains both *sentence* and *solaas*. Yet good as they are alone, their triumph is in dialectic. When the tales are read together, they produce a complex literary experience much greater than the sum of their individual parts.

The Dramatic Approach and the Link between the First Two Tales

Dramatic critics have naturally paid special attention to the drunken Miller's boisterous interruption to demand that he be allowed to "quite" the *Knight's Tale* (I.3127), and they deserve much of the credit for insisting on the opposition between the first two tales. Nevertheless, because the dramatic approach understands the contrast as personal and social rather than artistic, it can identify only the most obvious differences and actually hinders the detailed literary comparisons I shall attempt here. When Paul Ruggiers states that "in tone and attitude, vocabulary and word choice, figure of speech and word play, in genre and philosophy, the two pilgrims stand utterly opposed," he expresses the essence of my argument; but because Ruggiers sees the opposition occurring between pilgrims and not poems, he does not develop further his valuable literary insights.[2] As long as the first two tales are regarded as essentially "a dramatic collision of generalized social differences," as one recent critic puts it, discussion of their opposition must remain superficial.[3] Not much can be said about the personal conflict between Knight and Miller because, as with most of the pilgrims, we finally know so little about either. In their eagerness to identify differences of class and temperament, critics often slight the more important poetic quarrel between the opening tales.

As often in the *Canterbury Tales*, the relationship between the first two tales and their tellers, though generally appropriate, is not so close that a different narrator is impossible to imagine. Nothing in the *Knight's Tale* absolutely conflicts with the pilgrim Knight of the *General Prologue*, but neither are the similarities especially striking.[4] An epic of ancient chivalry is fitting for the Knight, although we might have expected something more specifically Christian from one who is described less as a courtly hero than as the model of a crusader.[5] There also seems to be some conflict between the story told by the Knight and the views the pilgrim expresses after interrupting the Monk's Tale (VII.2767–79). The *Knight's Tale* is a serious philosophical work that does not deny the pain or difficulties of life, whereas the Knight's later words seem to approve only a simple, optimistic kind of literature.[6] Such apparent differences between teller and tale are relatively minor and can be explained away, but at the very least they support the view that a general and nominal relationship between the Knight and his tale is as justified by the text as a detailed and dramatic one.

The *Miller's Tale* has an even looser relationship to its pilgrim.[7] Although a bawdy tale of deceit and low deeds is appropriate to a thief who speaks mostly of "synne and harlotries" (I.560–63), as Chaucer himself suggests just before the tale (I.3167–84), the subtle brilliance of the actual poetry comes oddly from the mouth of such a "thikke knarre" (I.549). The Miller's skill at breaking down doors by running at them with his head is the very opposite of the poem's highly polished art. Although they describe two interesting character types, the portraits of the pilgrim Knight and Miller only hint at the complex artistries of their contrasting tales.

The link between the *Knight's Tale* and the *Miller's Tale*—usually called the *Miller's Prologue*—is much discussed by dramatic critics because it seems to unleash so many personal and class tensions, but the passage is even more valuable for its introduction of literary conflict. The drama of style that is the essence of the *Canterbury Tales* first begins only after the drunken Miller shatters beyond repair the Host's proposed order of telling with the aggression for which he is so well known. The Host intends that the Monk should give the second performance, and a little reflection will make clear how different things would have been if the *Monk's Tale* actually had followed the *Knight's Tale*. A certain thematic tension would exist (we have already noted the Knight's objections to the Monk's endless list of tragedies), but the effect on the reader of beginning the collection with two such long and serious works would be oppressive, though not unmedieval. After proposing and deliberately rejecting such a dull beginning, Chaucer turns to the crude Miller to initiate the structure of complex literary contrasts that gives excitement and meaning to the *Canterbury Tales*. Despite the Reeve's fear that he will hear nothing better than "lewed dronken harlotrye" (I.3145) from such a ruffian, the skilled art of the *Miller's Tale* is the equal, if also the opposite, of the *Knight's Tale*. Now that the "male" is finally "unbokeled" (I.3115), what had threatened to become a dreary "game" is truly "wel bigonne" (I.3117).

The dramatic dispute in the first link signals a deeper artistic conflict between two kinds of poetry. The Knight and the Miller never actually quarrel (or even address a single word to one another), for Robin's challenge is more literary than personal. He declares that his tale, too, will be "noble" and insists that it will not merely follow, but actually "quite" the *Knight's Tale* (I.3127). Although the drunken Miller, who can barely sit on his horse, is portrayed as a burlesque of the Knight,[8] the tale he tells is much more than a mocking parody of a superior work. The fabliau uses many of the same literary materials as the romance for different, but equally valuable, purposes. There may be many a "bettre man" (I.3130) than the churlish Miller, but few poems in or out of the Canterbury collection are superior to the *Miller's Tale*. It requites the *Knight's Tale*, as promised, not by discrediting the former work, but by providing a completely different literary experience.

The First Two Poets of the *Canterbury Tales*

As the link between them suggests, the key to understanding the first two Canterbury tales is our recognition of their dynamic literary contrast. Chaucer's initial juxtaposition of an idealistic chivalric romance and a witty tale of sex and deceit, which defines two extremes of secular literature, is more surprising, and deliberately so, than the variety found in other collections of stories such as Ovid's *Metamorphoses* or Boccaccio's *Decameron*. The artistic individuality of the first two tales goes far deeper than their obvious difference in genre: the *Knight's Tale* has a plain earnestness and philosophical ambition lacking in most continental romances (including its source in Boccaccio's *Teseida*), whereas the *Miller's Tale* is one of the most ornate fabliaux ever written.[9] The contrast becomes still more interesting when we realize how many elements of the two stories are complementary. Critics have long noticed that the Miller's Tale parallels the Knight's Tale in such things as character, situation, and structure: for instance, a courtly love triangle in the romance is followed by an earthier threesome in the fabliau and lordly Theseus as patriarch is replaced by silly John the carpenter.[10] The tales demand comparison because of their different handling of shared elements, a comparison that reveals the individual poetic sensibility and world view at work in each. In length, characterization, word choice, imagery, speech—whichever element we care to look at—the first two Canterbury tales, though equally impressive, are radically and consistently opposed. At the very beginning of the Canterbury Tales Chaucer introduces an extreme example of the literary contrast that will distinguish the entire work.

The contrasting artistries of the Knight's Tale and the Miller's Tale announce themselves from the first. The direct yet magnificent art of the romance appears within its opening five lines:

Whilom, as olde stories tellen us,
Ther was a duc that highte Theseus;
Of Atthenes he was lord and governour.
And in his tyme swich a conquerour,
That gretter was ther noon under the sonne.
(I.859–63)

Although its style and vocabulary are relatively simple, the passage moves with a leisurely stateliness that is appropriate to the tale's exalted themes. In the first line we learn that the subject is not only ancient, but also popular enough so that several stories (note the plural) have already been told about it. Theseus is introduced by name, a name (along with that of the famous city of Athens) that is both familiar and impressive to the reader. Theseus is then assigned a series of titles ("lord," "governour," and "conquerour"); although the terms themselves are not uncommon, they suggest power and control and are suitably grand without being grandiose. The phrase "lord and governour" in the third line is typical of the many doublets found throughout the poem. While redundant and thus not strictly necessary for sense, such phrases, like the equally superfluous "and in his tyme" in the next line, give dignity to the narration while contributing to its slow, careful development. The image with which the quotation ends, "That gretter was ther noon under the sonne," is, like the passage as a whole, both simple and magnificent. "Under the sonne" is another redundancy, but it hints at the scope of the poem, which deals with both heaven and earth, and it is thus an appropriately lordly image with which to describe Theseus.[11]

When we turn to the beginning of the Miller's Tale, its contrasting poetic is immediately apparent:

> Whilom ther was dwellynge at Oxenford
> A riche gnof, that gestes heeld to bord,
> And of his craft he was a carpenter.
> With hym ther was dwellynge a poure scoler,
> Hadde lerned art, but al his fantasye
> Was turned for to lerne astrologye.
>   (I.3187–92)

Although the fabliau opens with the same word as the romance and also immediately describes the oldest male character in the story, its style is very different. Unlike the steadily developed grandeur of the Knight's Tale, the first lines of the Miller's contain a series of anticlimaxes and frustrated expectations. The story takes place in Oxford, but the first character is not an academic. The churl is rich, but he takes in boarders; and though he has a craft, it is the fairly low one of carpenter. The scholar, for his part, has been educated in the liberal arts, but his real interest is in astrology. The opening account of Theseus in the Knight's Tale magnified his importance until he seemed little less than the sun, but description of character here is deliberately reductive. For instance, the term "gnof" is in striking contrast to the noble titles given the romance hero: used nowhere else by Chaucer, and, according to the Middle English Dictionary, nowhere else in Middle English, it is clearly a comic, even insulting label, so that the phrase "riche gnof" is probably meant to be somewhat oxymoronic.[12]

In contrast to the dignified and smooth opening of the Knight's Tale, the narration here shifts quickly from the unnamed carpenter, who is nominally head of household, to the unnamed scholar, making us wonder, as we do not in the romance, who is to be the central character and who will dominate. Theseus is clearly established as a figure of accomplishment and control from the beginning of the tale, but the effect of the first lines of the fabliau is conflict and tension. Whereas the simple dignity at the beginning of the Knight's Tale suggests the coherence of its world, the Miller's Tale opens with a series of sharp oppositions (rich versus poor, landlord versus tenant, town versus gown, study versus play, and, implicitly, old versus young) whose instability will be exploited during the rest of the tale for comic effect. The sharp contrast of these initial passages first announces the individual sensibilities and values of the two poems.

The different kinds of art that Chaucer has given to each of the first two tales determine what we see and how we see it, even when the events described are superficially similar. A good example is the marriage mentioned early in each tale. The account of Theseus's conquest of the

Amazons and subsequent marriage to their queen, Hippolyta (I.866–85), contains the same direct, dignified poetry found in the opening lines of the tale. Although the passage uses many exalted words, such as "glorie," "solempnytee," "victorie," "noble," and "chivalrye," and deals with extraordinary events, the style is relatively simple and unadorned: for example, "He conquered al the regne of Femenye, / That whilom was ycleped Scithia, / And weddede the queene Ypolita" (I.866–68). If the passage reads like the voice of sober historical truth, this is in part because the verse is devoid of concrete imagery, similes, or literary allusion. The most noticeable literary device in the passage is *occupatio*, which introduces an authoritative but friendly narrative voice ("And certes, if it nere to long to heere" [I.875]), which both asserts the scope of the story (so extensive that it must be cut short) and demonstrates an ability to manage such rich material. The solid artistry of the *Knight's Tale* allows it to deal with large and even symbolic subjects (a great war between Athens and the Amazons and, implicitly, the right relationship between men and women), while maintaining a clear, coherent narrative. Order is celebrated in the *Knight's Tale* and illustrated by the poet's sure control, although the many difficulties of this world, from war to the hostile weather during the couple's return, are not ignored.

The first mention of the much less successful marriage between John and Alisoun in the *Miller's Tale* just as surely defines its special poetry (I.3221–32). The courtship and wedding are dismissed in a single line, and the focus is instead on the couple's life together afterward—an almost certain guarantee of comedy rather than romance. The marriage is less noble in the *Miller's Tale* than in the *Knight's Tale*, and the verse employs a greater variety of literary devices in fewer lines. Unlike the romance account, the fabliau passage contains vigorous imagery and even a literary allusion to Cato. Alisoun is likened to an animal held "narwe in cage" who yet remains "wylde," suggesting that, in contrast to the ultimately harmonious union in the romance, the natural impulses of the wife in this tale are unwillingly constrained: an unstable and thus potentially comic situation. The marriage of Theseus and Hippolyta can be seen as an emblem of personal and political order; but precisely because we are invited to read the couple symbolically, they remain rather vague as human beings. In contrast, the wedded pair in the *Miller's Tale* is more rooted in physical and psychological reality. We are told Alisoun's exact age and John's fear of cuckoldry. A final difference is that the narrative voice in the second passage is less pleasant; it remains distant, giving no sign that it is in any way shaping the story, and draws a lesson that offers not comfort but only a cool determinism: "He moste endure, as oother folk, his care" (I.3232). No reader of Chaucer will be surprised to learn that marriage in the *Miller's Tale* is described differently from marriage in the Knight's Tale, but detailed comparison reveals that the obvious clash of two genres extends farther than we would expect, to the smallest particulars of style.

Other parallel scenes in the first two tales also contribute to defining their contrasting poets. For example, each tale contains an unexpected physical catastrophe near the end of its story: the fatal fall of Arcite from his horse (I.2671–2966) and the ridiculous fall of old John from the rafters when he thinks Noah's flood has come (I.3816–49). In its elaborate account of the consequences of Arcite's fall, the romance combines narrative action, moving speeches by several characters, and detailed reports of exotic funeral ceremonies to produce a powerful pageant of heroic death that contrasts sharply to the fabliau's clever mix of rapid action and dialogue to depict silly John's hurt and humiliation. Recognition of these artistic differences enables us to see the poetry of each tale more clearly, and this leads to larger thematic differences: the Knight's Tale takes Arcite's death very seriously and tries to find meaning in it, whereas the Miller's Tale, with its funny and cruel narrative climax, turns all John's "harm unto a jape" (I.3842).

The first two Canterbury tales are conspicuous examples of poetry that calls special attention to the way in which it is told. In both tales a close connection exists between artistry and meaning, so that art itself becomes an important theme in each. Critics of the Miller's Tale have long been aware of the flamboyant skill of its imagery, elaborate character portraits, parodies, and puns. The deliberate art of the Knight's Tale, so obvious in its opening lines, has also been recognized by many. In his influential essay on the first tale, Charles Muscatine stresses the importance of its artificial style and balanced structure, which does not aim to represent real life, but instead produces a "poetic pageant" concerned with ceremony, ritual, and the creation of order.[13] Robert Jordan suggests a direct link between the style of this romance and its philosophical ideas and, in an approach recently echoed by others, shows that "the idea of form itself becomes a major theme" of the tale, thus forcing the reader to examine closely the poet's own art.[14]

The artistic self-consciousness of the first two tales is seen most clearly in an element both share: a major character who functions as an artist-figure within the story. Theseus, who works to establish harmony and order, plays this role in the Knight's Tale, while Nicholas, an instigator of deceit and confusion, does so in the Miller's. Once he has conquered the Amazons and Creon, Theseus often seems as much a humanist, or at least a patron, as a warrior; in addition to his vast building projects, he is a rhetorician of love and philosophy and the generous impresario of noble ceremonies that include the chivalric tournament and Arcite's funeral. Nicholas is a very different but equally accomplished artist, whose talents extend far beyond his musical skills and general handiness; he arranges the dumb show in his room that alarms the carpenter and is a gifted storyteller, as his account of the coming flood proves.[15] In their separate ways of converting the stuff of life into art, Theseus and Nicholas epitomize the poetic method of each tale.

Each of the two artist-figures creates a construction that is central to the plot of his poem and also defines its special artistry. In the Knight's Tale the revealing artifact is Theseus's "noble theatre" (I.1885)—which in Boccaccio's Teseida is not built for the occasion but already exists—a perfectly round structure of simple but harmonious beauty, which takes on great symbolic significance.[16] The stadium expresses the theme of the tale as well as its art: like the romance as a whole, it does not deny that the universe contains malevolent forces (seen primarily in the baleful influence of the pagan gods), but attempts to contain and rationalize them. Both the stadium and the Knight's Tale are attempts to produce harmony and even love out of human conflict, though the success of each is limited. Almost at the beginning of its description, we are told that the stadium is "ful of degrees" (I.1890). Although this phrase really means little more than that the theater had many rows of seats, it perfectly describes the romance as a whole, which deals with degree in the widest sense— the right ordering of both human society and the universe, especially as expressed in Theseus's speech on the divine Chain of Love.[17] The stadium is said to be built so that "whan a man was set on o degree, / He letted nat his felawe for to see" (I.1891–92), a good analogy to the clear and direct art of the Knight's Tale itself. Yet within this symbolically round structure are also the many intricate carvings and paintings that decorate the temples of the gods (I.1914–17), a reminder of the complex literary skill beneath the deliberate simplicity of the tale, just as the often terrible events described in the temples reflect the work's serious, even tragic themes.

The corresponding artistic construct in the Miller's Tale is the tubs that Nicholas persuades John to hang in anticipation of a new flood. These homely and somewhat ridiculous objects may seem insignificant in comparison with a grand amphitheater, but they accurately represent the different, but not inferior, art of the fabliau. Although presented more briefly than Theseus's noble theater, the tubs are given a physical solidity and precision lacking in the romance account of the building of the lists: we see John collecting and hanging the three different kinds ("knedyng trogh," "tubbe," and "kymelyn"), making a ladder to reach them, climbing up "by the ronges and the stalkes," and stocking them with bread, cheese, and "good ale in a jubbe" (I.3620–29). The art of the Knight's Tale is more idealistic and philosophical, but the Miller's Tale conveys a better sense of the tangible objects and actual processes of this world. The tubs also accurately reflect the cleverness, deceit, and fun of the fabliau. Nicholas devises a cruel trap—so elaborate that it suggests love of inventiveness for its own sake—that he gets the victim himself to set. Hanging high in the rafters and containing a profoundly ignorant man, the tubs create a delicious tension in the reader, who, even if momentarily diverted by other events, knows that what has gone up must inevitably come crashing down to John's sorrow and our delight.

The Artistic Dialectic of the First Two Tales

The individual, contrasting artistries of the first two tales—symbolized by the differences between Theseus and Nicholas and their two constructs—is found at all levels and throughout each work. The frequent resort in the *Knight's Tale* to doublets that slow down the verse while giving it greater dignity, already mentioned and another manifestation of the balance and symmetry that is the essence of the poem, is very much the opposite of the puns, double entendres, and clever rhymes in the *Miller's Tale*.[18] In contrast to the well-known physical solidity and precise descriptions of the *Miller's Tale*, which need no further illustration here,[19] the abstract *Knight's Tale* often ignores the everyday world and instead presents a significant number of ceremonies (funerals, weddings, tournaments, feasts) and symbolic events. Even when the *Knight's Tale* is most vivid, as in its accounts of the sculpture and paintings of the three pagan temples, the poetry often remains in the service of allegorical abstraction, as in this famous example: "The pykepurs, and eek the pale Drede; / The smylere with the knyf under the cloke" (I.1998–99).

Valuable as it is to recognize these general differences, only a detailed comparison between specific literary elements, like the one tentatively offered in the following pages, can begin to reveal the full depth and consistency of the artistic contrast in the first two tales. The special poetic achievements (and limitations) of each are seen most clearly when the two tales are read together, one in the light of the other, as their juxtaposition invites. Such a dialectic demonstrates the individual poetic of both the *Knight's Tale* and the *Miller's Tale* (though any specific conclusion may be rejected or modified by others), confirming the proverbial wisdom of Pandarus in *Troilus and Criseyde*: "By his contrarie is every thyng declared" (I.637).

Narrative Voice

Our brief comparison of a marriage in each of the first two tales revealed a contrast between the involved narrator of the *Knight's Tale* and the cool, somewhat contemptuous narrator of the *Miller's Tale*—a difference that is consistently developed throughout each poem. I should at once make clear that in the following discussion I am restricting the term "narrator." When using the word, I am not referring to the general exposition of the tale (that is the product of what I call the "poet"), but only to those specific passages in which the narrative voice intrudes to speak directly to the audience.

The authoritative, conscientious, and at times even warm voice of the narrator of the *Knight's Tale* is frequently heard throughout the romance. Ruling the tale as firmly as Theseus does Athens, it shapes, controls, and attempts to bring order out of confusion. The narrator's self-conscious manipulation of his material is evident from the very beginning of the story. Within the first twenty lines, in the only passage that refers specifically to the larger tale-telling contest, he says that if it were not "to long to heere" (I.875), he would tell us of the battle and wedding between Theseus and Hippolyta, but "I have, God woot, a large feeld to ere, / And wayke been the oxen in my plough" (I.886–87). This *occupatio* is the first of many in the tale: a major shaping device of the narrative voice that allows it, as Muscatine shows, "to shorten the story without lessening its weight and impressiveness."[20]

The narrator's control of his material is also revealed by the care with which he makes transitions. Because of its vast scope, the romance must often move between different locales or characters, and when it does the narrator goes out of his way to inform the reader of what is happening. One example that will have to stand for several others (my own *occupatio*) is an early transition from one of the lovers to the other:

> Now wol I stynte of Palamon a lite,
> And lete hym in his prisoun stille dwelle,
> And of Arcita forth I wol yow telle.
> (I.1334–36)[21]

Assertions of narrative authority such as *occupatio* and careful transitions not only define the special narrative voice of the *Knight's Tale* but also reflect the themes of order and responsibility in the tale as a whole.

If the narrator of the *Knight's Tale* takes conspicuous command of his tale, he is no fierce and distant ruler. Although many of the events in the romance are strange and glorious, as befits such an ancient, heroic tale, the narrator's voice is remarkably personal. He often uses the pronoun "I" and is engaged with both his characters and readers to a degree unprecedented in Boccaccio's *Teseida*. When Arcite is freed from prison on the condition that he never return to Troy, the narrator comments, "Lat hym be war! his nekke lith to wedde" (I.1218); when the same knight lies fatally wounded, the narrator bursts out, "Fare wel phisik! go ber the man to chirche!" (I.2760).[22] The narrator easily admits his limitations as a versi-fier (I.1459–61) and theologian (I.2809–14), and, like Theseus, though often formal, he can also be rustically proverbial: "Now in the crope, now doun in the breres, / Now up, now doun, as boket in a welle" (I.1532–33).

The audience (or at least the lovers in it) is directly addressed at the end of the first section (I.1347–54) and is throughout spoken to in con-versational, even friendly tones: for example, "Ther as the knyghtes weren in prisoun / Of which I tolde yow and tellen shal" (I.1058–59). The longest formal set piece in the poem, the account of the three pagan temples, is made more intimate and vivid by narrative involvement. The voice first ingenuously claims to have forgotten to describe the oratories (I.1914–17), and then says that he would like to tell everything about the portraits ("Why sholde I noght as wel eek telle yow al / The portreiture that was upon the wal" [I.1967–68]), even though that is impossible ("I may nat rekene hem alle though I wolde" [I.2040]). He dramatizes the sights in the temples by constantly repeating "ther saugh I" or a similar phrase (for example, I.1995, 2005, 2011, 2017, 2028, 2056, 2062, 2067, and 2073).

The careful but kindly narrator of the *Knight's Tale*, whom the reader both likes and trusts, is strikingly different from the impersonal, often contemptuous narrator of the *Miller's Tale*, who delights in the foolishness of his character as much as the reader does. A direct narrative voice is rarely heard in the *Miller's Tale*, whose action is generally allowed to un-fold quickly without the exterior comment that would get in the way of its comedy. In contrast to the romance, narrative transitions in the fabliau are either brief ("Now, sire, and eft, sire, so bifel the cas" [I.3271]) or so smooth that they are hardly noticed, as when we go from the initial description of Absolon in church to an account of his wooing that eve-ning: "The moone, whan it was nyght, ful brighte shoon" (I.3352). The brisk style of narration forces the reader directly into the action of the story, so that often the only indication of transition from one scene to another is an insistent demonstrative—"this parissh clerk, this amorous Absolon" (I.3657) or "this Nicholas" (I.3798). Such is the form of one of the most dazzling transitions in all literature, when, after the searing of Nicholas and his anguished cry, we suddenly return to the all-but-forgot-ten John in his tub:

> This carpenter out of his slomber sterte,
> And herde oon crien "water" as he were wood,
> And thoughte, "Allas, now comth Nowelis flood!"
>   (I.3816–18)

The few first-person statements in the Miller's Tale are perfunctory and not at all personal: for example, "I dar wel seyn" (I.3346) or "as I gesse" (I.3644). In contrast to the friendly, informative *occupatio* in the Knight's Tale, expressions of abbreviation in the Miller's Tale are simply curt ("I may nat rekene hem alle" [I.3198] or "as I have told biforn" [I.3302]) and never indicate the slightest affection for the characters or audience. When the narrator notices the former at all, his response is either noncommittal ("Now ber thee wel, thou hende Nicholas" [I.3397]) or infinitely superior, as when John is alarmed for his wife's safety: "Lo, which a greet thyng is affeccioun!" (I.3611). The last words of the narrator in the Knight's Tale warmly address both the happiness of Palamon and Emelye and the audience ("And God save al this faire compaignye" [I.3097–3108]), but when the fabliau narrator reappears at the end of his tale, it is to offer a smug, heartless, and wonderfully funny summing up:

> Thus swyved was this carpenteris wyf,
> For al his kepyng and his jalousye;
> And Absolon hath kist hir nether ye;
> And Nicholas is scalded in the towte.
> This tale is doon, and God save al the rowte!
> (I.3850–54)

The contrasting narrators of the first two tales are a function of the different kinds of poetry Chaucer has created for each work and should not be closely associated with the nominal tellers. Although the serious, kindly narrator of the Knight's Tale seems generally (but not much more than generally) similar to the pilgrim Knight, the cool, superior narrator of the Miller's Tale is nothing like the drunken Miller. Nor are the different narrators simply a result of genre. Medieval romances of the ancient past often have a less personally involved, more formal narrative voice than we find in the Knight's Tale, the most relevant example being its immediate source—Boccaccio's *Teseida*. The narrator in Chaucer's other long classical romance, *Troilus and Criseyde*, though even more prominent, has a very different voice (more nervous and bookish, for example) than the one heard here. Correspondingly, the narrative voice often plays a much greater role in other fabliaux than it does in the Miller's Tale, as we shall soon see in Chaucer's own Reeve's Tale and Merchant's Tale. As is best realized through the dialectic of comparison, Chaucer has given each of the narrators in his first two tales a unique and highly effective voice.

Character Portraits

The extreme change in genre from romance to fabliau in the first two tales inevitably results in two sets of characters unlike one another in class, manners, values, and interests. More revealing than these inevitable, objective differences, however, is the significant contrast between the way each poet chooses to present his characters in formal description. The method of characterization, as distinct from the characters themselves, is unique to each tale and another indication of the deep and consistent artistic conflict at the beginning of the *Canterbury Tales*.

The principal women of the two tales, Emelye and Alisoun, provide the most obvious illustration of each poet's approach. The characterization of Emelye in the *Knight's Tale* is simple and idealized, as the opening lines of her description reveal:

> Till it fil ones, in a morwe of May,
> That Emelye, that fairer was to sene
> Than is the lylie upon his stalke grene,
> And fressher than the May with floures newe—
> For with the rose colour stroof hire hewe,
> I noot which was the fyner of hem two.
> (I.1034–39)

The images of May, rose, and lily are common and associate the heroine with a traditional type of romance heroine.[23] They are not meant to individualize or vivify her. The leisurely passage, which goes on for sixteen more lines to describe Emelye's yellow hair and angel's voice, is clear and straightforward, but, in contrast to her portrait in the *Teseida*, allows us to see Emelye, even when she walks before us, only as a distant ideal.

The characterization of Alisoun in the *Miller's Tale* proceeds from a deliberately different, though equally skillful, literary sensibility. Alisoun is described in a long and elaborate portrait (I.3233–70) so famous that I shall quote only a few lines from the end:

> A brooch she baar upon hir lowe coler,
> As brood as is the boos of a bokeler.
> Hir shoes were laced on hir legges hye.
> She was a prymerole, a piggesnye,
> For any lord to leggen in his bedde,
> Or yet for any good yeman to wedde.
> (I.3265–70)

In contrast to the romance portrait, what we are told about Alisoun is specific and physical. Although generally objective, the poet is capable of sudden, revealing thrusts: "And sikerly she hadde a likerous ye" (I.3244). The most original quality of this portrait, however, is the concentration of vivid imagery whose effect is comically reductive rather than idealizing. Alisoun is associated with a series of rustic images (such as milk, sheep's wool, apples) and likened not to a lily or rose but to a "pigges-nye," which, as Donaldson has shown, if a flower, also "remains, unmistakably, a pig's eye."[24] Although we never see Alisoun perform any real action, the method of characterization—which links her with several frisky animals (including a weasel, swallow, calf, kid, and colt), while emphasizing her active look, shining hue, and playful skipping—produces a lively, tangible woman, to whom we do not respond as we did to Emelye. The poet involves the reader with Alisoun as a physical and sexually attractive creature by reminding us of the body beneath her clothes and even turning her around for our inspection.[25]

The different method of characterization in each of the first two tales is not dictated by their separate genres. Although largely absent from the Knight's Tale, detailed, physical description of major characters, especially women, is a common feature of medieval romance, the most obvious examples of which are found throughout Troilus and Criseyde. Correspondingly, the average fabliau, far from containing elaborate portraits like that of Alisoun, relies on quite perfunctory character description of the kind found in Chaucer's own Shipman's Tale. Critics have long recognized that Chaucer greatly altered the characterization he found in the sources for his first two tales. The principal figures in the Knight's Tale, with the exception of Theseus, are less vivid and individualized than their models in Boccaccio's Teseida, whereas the complex portraits of Nicholas, Alisoun, and Absolon are almost certainly Chaucer's contribution to the Miller's Tale.[26] What has not been stressed is the extreme contrast. Chaucer's changes in the first two tales, though not demanded by genre, are in exactly opposite directions—from significantly less detailed characterization in the Knight's Tale to significantly more detailed characterization in the Miller's Tale. The unique poetry of each tale is once again seen most clearly when the two works are read closely together.

Although neither of the first two Canterbury tales describes all its characters in exactly the same way, each has its own special approach, which remains consistent throughout the work. Characterization in the Knight's Tale is symbolic, distant, and ideal, whereas that in the Miller's Tale is ironically reductive, local, and helpful to the plot. The difference is perhaps best seen in the contrast between secondary rather than major characters: Absolon in the fabliau and the two champions, Lygurge and Emetreus, in the romance.

On the surface at least, the long portraits of Lygurge and Emetreus (I.2128–89), constructed with great care from accounts of many different warriors in Boccaccio, seem unlike the description of Emelye and closer to the detailed characterization of the Miller's Tale. Looked at more closely, however, especially in direct comparison with the fabliau, it is clear that the form of the portraits, like that of characterization elsewhere in the

Knight's Tale, is essentially emblematic.[27] By this I mean that, although the champions add to the splendor of the poetic pageant and reflect its concern with balance and symmetry, neither is essential to the plot, and the considerable information provided in their portraits is never referred to again. As with Emelye, the champions are not seen as individuals, but rather as traditional types. Both heroes are described in an objective, rather stiff style, without irony or insinuation, that is closer to the conventional medieval catalogue portrait than character description elsewhere in Chaucer, including the *General Prologue*. The portrait of Emetreus, for example, begins with a general view and then moves from his hair to his nose, to his eyes, to his lips, to his complexion, to his beard, to his voice, to his head as a whole, to his hand, and, finally, to what is around him.

The long portrait of Absolon in the *Miller's Tale* has its own ornateness, but one in the service of an entirely different poetic. Its function is not emblematic but practical. Absolon's vanity (I.3314–16), personal fastidiousness (I.3319–24), involvement in nonreligious activities (I.3325–30), music making (I.3331–33), flirtations among the lower classes (I.3334–36), and dislike of farting (I.3337–38) will all be used in the plot of the *Miller's Tale*. Even the surprising detail that his eyes are as "greye as goos" exactly defines the clerk's difference from the genuine courtly lover (I.3317): the usual phrase in the romances is "gray as glass," but Absolon is, indeed, a silly goose and the change accurately predicts his amatory incompetence.[28] In contrast to the exotic descriptions of the pagan heroes in the *Knight's Tale*, which contribute to the noble tone of the romance, the portrait of Absolon is made familiar by the use of ordinary and parochial details, any one of which is impossible to imagine in the *Knight's Tale*: the windows of St. Paul's, a *kirtel*, shoelaces, a surplice, a land charter, a *rubible*, a *giterne*, and a tavern (I.3318–34). The difference from characterization in the *Knight's Tale* goes beyond genre; other fabliaux, even those by Chaucer, contain nothing like this profusion of specific detail.

The different kinds of characterization in the first two tales require opposite responses from the reader. We have every reason to trust the heroic portraits of Lygurge and Emetreus in the *Knight's Tale*, but the description of the "myrie child" in the *Miller's Tale* contains so much satire and ironic comment that we cannot accept it at face value. The reader must alertly interpret the portrait, discovering for himself (because the narrative stance is so disingenuously admiring) the implications of such things as Absolon's biblical name, his hair and dress, and his many secular pursuits. Not that the *Miller's Tale* demands more from the reader than the *Knight's Tale* (responding to the ancient and ideal is also difficult), but its demands are radically different. The characterizations of the pagan champions and of Absolon are each excellent and appropriate to their individual works.

Speech

Because it is uttered by the characters themselves, direct speech cannot easily be attributed to the pilgrim tellers and is thus rarely discussed in dramatic interpretations of the *Canterbury Tales*. Nevertheless, the different use of speech in the first two tales is an essential part of their opposing artistries and can tell us much about the two poets. The formal, often quite serious and emotional monologues that are characteristic of the *Knight's Tale* are nothing like the rapid, witty dialogue found throughout the *Miller's Tale*. The significant difference between speech in these tales once again goes beyond genre. Chaucer's other romance set in ancient times, *Troilus and Criseyde*, has much more variety of speech than the *Knight's Tale*, just as his other fabliaux, especially the *Shipman's Tale* and the *Merchant's Tale*, contain more formal and extended speech than anything in the *Miller's Tale*.

The different kinds of speech in the first two tales are clear from the first spoken words in each. Although the opening speech in the romance, which is given by Theseus, is an angry demand to know why the ladies in black have disturbed his homecoming, his words remain elevated and carefully balanced:

> "What folk been ye, that at myn homcomynge
> Perturben so my feste with criynge?"
> Quod Theseus. "Have ye so greet envye
> Of myn honour, that thus compleyne and crye?
> Or who hath yow mysboden or offended?
> And telleth me if it may been amended,
> And why that ye been clothed thus in blak."
> (I.905–11)

In response, the eldest of the grieving widows delivers a long speech whose rhetorical intricacy does not exclude either literary brilliance or deep feeling (I.915–47).[29]

Compare this formal but emotional exchange in the romance with the opening spoken words in the *Miller's Tale*: the vivacious, tricky, and quite insincere dialogue between Nicholas and Alisoun, which cleverly uses courtly parody to produce a magnificent juxtaposition of act and utterance:

[Nicholas] seyde, "Ywis, but if ich have my wille,
For deerne love of thee, lemman, I spille."
And heeld hire harde by the haunchebones,
And seyde, "Lemman, love me al atones,
Or I wol dyen, also God me save!"
And she sproong as a colt dooth in the trave,
And with hir heed she wryed faste awey,
And seyde, "I wol nat kisse thee, by my fey!
Why, lat be," quod she, "lat be, Nicholas,
Or I wol crie 'out, harrow' and 'allas'!
Do wey youre handes, for youre curteisye!"
                                              (I.3277–87)

These contrasting kinds of speech remain consistent throughout the two tales. When Palamon first catches sight of Emelye, he initially utters only a single syllable—"A" (I.1078)—but he and Arcite soon deliver three relatively long, formal speeches on love and fortune, whose earnestness may provoke a smile from the reader (I.1081–1111 and 1118–22). Then, after one of the few examples of dialogue in the poem (I.1125–27), the knights deliver an additional pair of even longer speeches on the subject of who should love Emelye (I.1129–86). The poet has no desire to make the words of the rivals sound realistic, nor does he distinguish between them; as with speeches in Thucydides or classical drama, these lines are to be read as heightened presentations of the characters' thoughts and general position rather than as actual expressions.

The speeches of Theseus, the central character in the Knight's Tale, are similarly abstract and thematically important. When Theseus comes upon Palamon and Arcite fighting in the wood, the poet reveals his hero's changing will through a series of deliberately stylized utterances. Theseus first angrily pronounces a death sentence against the two knights (I.1743–47), which prompts Hippolyta and Emelye to offer a courtly plea for mercy (I.1757). After considering the request seriously (for speech in the Knight's Tale can persuade the noble to good action as the widows of the Theban warriors have already learned), Theseus utters an address on the need for mercy in a lord, which is no less formal for being addressed to himself (I.1773–81). The noble duke then gives a long discourse on the comedy of love (I.1785–1825)—perhaps the most amusing and rhetorically skilled speech on love ever delivered by a political ruler on horseback—which is followed, once the two knights pray for mercy, with an ex tempore, yet comprehensive and well-organized, statement describing the tournament he will arrange to decide who shall marry Emelye (I.1829–69). Of course, none of these utterances sounds much like real speech, for that is not their purpose; instead, they carefully, if perhaps a bit too schematically, define an ideal of the just and sensitive ruler.

Speech in the Knight's Tale, while frequently passionate and never obscure, is always elevated and thoughtful, as befits a poem so deeply concerned with crucial matters like order, justice, and man's relation to the cosmos. Even when the young knights are most smitten by their love for Emelye, they nevertheless talk philosophically of fate and fortune, just as Theseus's witty meditation on the folly of love makes an important point about the limitations of this world, and Arcite's last, deeply emotional words remain rhetorically sophisticated and in control despite his imminent death (I.2765–97). The final long speech in the poem is Theseus's magnificent First Mover speech, which puts all that has happened in a divine context of harmony and love, while also bringing about the marriage of Palamon and Emelye to strengthen the political union between Thebes and Athens (I.2987–3093).

In contrast to the formal, persuasive, and often philosophical discourses of the Knight's Tale, speech in the Miller's Tale is tricky, manipulative, and intended primarily to deceive. Like the poem as a whole, the characters create elaborate, witty fictions full of tricks and surprises. In addition to its frequent cruelty and clever deceit, talk in the Miller's Tale is impressively colloquial and individualistic. As opposed to the romance in which everyone sounds alike, the fabliau uses speech to characterize its actors. Although "Tehee" may be Alisoun's most famous utterance (I.3740), her earthy directness and shrewdness are apparent in all her words, just as the dim credulousness of John is confirmed every time he opens his mouth. The poet is also skilled enough to distinguish Nicholas's artful appropriation of courtly language to soften the directness of his wooing ("Lemman, love me al atones, / Or I wol dyen, also God me save!" [I.3280–81]) from Absolon's ludicrous incompetence with the same idiom, such as his description of himself as a sweaty animal yearning for its mother's milk (I.3700–3704).

The only extended speech in the Miller's Tale—Nicholas's warning to John of the new flood (I.3501–3600)—though just as long as some of the monologues in the Knight's Tale, is very different from their abstract, rhetorically elevated style. Nicholas's exposition is broken up by questions and answers, by constant reminders (as almost never occur in the romance) that one person is actually speaking to another (for example, "as I have seyd" [I.3567] or "be wel avysed" [I.3584]), and even by a quotation of what will be said in the future (I.3577–80). The actual monologue on the flood is dramatically introduced by a lively dialogue between John and Nicholas in which the student excites both his landlord and the reader with a dramatic opening statement ("Allas! / Shal al the world be lost eftsoones now?" [I.3488–89]) and with his promise to tell secrets

(I.3493–95). Indeed, in his vivacious fabrication of the apocalyptic flood, Nicholas proves that his powers of storytelling equal those of the Miller-poet himself.

Allusions, Imagery, and Vocabulary

The artistic dialectic of the first two Canterbury tales occurs through-out and on all levels: smaller elements, such as learned allusions, imagery, and vocabulary, further demonstrate the extent and consistency of the contrasting poetic voices. In one of the few literary, as opposed to dramatic, comparisons that have been attempted between the *Knight's Tale* and the *Miller's Tale*, Christopher Dean shows that the imagery in each has different functions and almost never uses the same objects. For example, Dean notes that animal imagery in the fabliau draws on the familiar beasts of the English countryside in contrast to the exotic lions, tigers, griffins, and eagles of the romance. These findings accord with what we have previously learned about the poets of each tale: imagery in the *Miller's Tale* serves primarily to "describe people from the outside" and then "the physical world in which they live," whereas imagery in the *Knight's Tale* "deals primarily with abstract ideas and people's emotions."[30] Dean's conclusions are especially valuable because they are based on such detailed comparisons, but other elements in the first two tales are equally revealing.

Neither the *Knight's Tale* nor the *Miller's* is as bookish as many of Chaucer's other works, yet their use of learned and literary allusion, even within these limits, is significantly different. Given the subject of the *Knight's Tale*, we are not surprised that it contains mythological stories, classical figures like Fortune and Phoebus, and frequent mention of the pagan gods, often as planetary deities. Despite this degree of ancient coloring, however, Chaucer has severely reduced the amount of classical material and allusions he found in Boccaccio's *Teseida*.[31] The poet's interests are not particularly literary. Aside from a long, unacknowledged use of Boethius's *Consolation of Philosophy* in Theseus's First Mover speech, which adds philosophical weight to the tale whatever its limitations, most of the learning in the poem is historical and factual (at least by medieval standards): in addition to mythological stories (see also a reference to Hector at I.2832), the poem contains some exotic classical lore, such as the "opie of Thebes fyn" (I.1472), and details of ancient religious and funeral rites. For all its genuine interest in the past, references in the *Knight's Tale* to other literary texts are perfunctory. A quotation on the lawlessness of lovers is identified only as an "olde clerkes sawe" (I.1163), though many manuscripts note in the margin that it is actually from Boethius, and no specific source is mentioned for the story of Perotheus except for a vague reference to "olde bookes" (I.1191–1200; see also I.859 and 1463). The only specific mention of Statius's Thebaid, which is the ultimate source of the entire story, cites the Latin epic, along with "thise bookes olde" (I.2294), merely as an authority on pagan religious practices.

Allusions in the Miller's Tale are more frequent and employed to very different effect: though less historical, they are more contemporary and literary than those in the first tale. The narrator refers to a saying of Cato (I.3227) and to a mystery play about Herod (I.3384). John gives the story of the clerk who fell into a pit (I.3457–61)—which betrays no sign of its classical origin in his retelling—and recites a night-spell (I.3483–86). Nicholas quotes one of Solomon's proverbs (I.3529–30), and the tale as a whole explicitly uses the story of Noah and includes casual citations of several saints. Just as trickery and deceit propel the plot of the Miller's Tale, scholars have discovered its most significant learned references are a series of submerged allusions to popular romances, mystery plays, the Canticum Canticorum, and the story of the Annunciation.[32] Because these allusions are parodic as well as hidden, they (unlike the unacknowledged use of Boethius in the Knight's Tale) must be recognized to be effective and then demand interpretation by the reader.

As we have found with other literary contrasts, genre alone cannot account for the different use of allusions in the first two tales. In writing the Knight's Tale, Chaucer eliminated many of the classical references he found in the Teseida, but his practice is exactly the reverse in his other ancient romance, Troilus and Criseyde, which has many more allusions than its Boccaccian original. Correspondingly, allusions in Chaucer's later fabliaux are very different from those in the Miller's Tale: the Reeve's Tale and the Shipman's have none at all, while those in the Merchant's Tale are much more frequent and more learned, including many that are classical.

Vocabulary is the basic element of any poem, and here also we find a deliberate and sustained contrast between the first two Canterbury tales. Some of the difference is obviously determined by genre, although the purity of each word list can be striking: noble chivalric words like pitee, honour, adventure, roial, victorie, glorie, chivalrie, conquerour, destynee, and pride occur frequently in the romance, but not once in the fabliau; conversely, words of pleasure and deceit like joly, gay, derne, solas, and sleigh are relatively common in the fabliau, but are absent from the romance.

Even more revealing, and further proof that Chaucer has given each poem its own special vocabulary, are words that appear in both tales with radically different meanings. Lord, for example, is an important term in the Knight's Tale; it occurs twenty-three times, often to describe Theseus and his authority.[33] Lord is found three times in the Miller's Tale: once in reference to the Christian God during Nicholas's attempts to convince

John of a second flood (I.3535); once in Absolon's ludicrous description
of himself as a "lord at alle degrees" (I.3724), as he vengefully tries to get
Alisoun to offer a second kiss; and once (the only time it approaches its
primary meaning in the *Knight's Tale*) at the end of Alisoun's portrait when
we are cynically told she is the right sort to marry a yeoman or "for any
lord to leggen in his bedde" (I.3269). It is easy to imagine that the deceitful, comic, and sexual contexts in which *lord* appears in the *Miller's Tale*
were deliberately chosen because they so accurately define how the second tale differs from the first. Similarly, the word *degree*, which reflects the
central concern of the *Knight's Tale* with order and harmony, appears fif-
teen times in the romance; its single, comic use in the *Miller's Tale* is by
Absolon when he describes himself as a "lord at alle degrees" (I.3724).
Mercy is another key concept in the *Knight's Tale*; the word occurs twelve
times, referring both to the noble virtue (for example, "Fy / Upon a lord
that wol have no mercy" [I.1773–74]) and, less frequently, to what the
courtly lover asks from his lady. Its one appearance in the *Miller's Tale*,
however, is during Nicholas's outrageous parody of courtly speech as he
holds Alisoun hard by the haunchbones (I.3288).

Chaucer's careful use of vocabulary to develop the fundamental literary conflict between the first two tales is shown by two words that have
an abstract, idealistic meaning in the romance, but a physical, reductive
one in the fabliau. *Olde* appears seventeen times in the *Knight's Tale*, often
to suggest the dignity of the story and its characters by emphasizing their
venerable age (for example, I.859, 1880, and 2838); the single occurrence
of the word in the *Miller's Tale*, by contrast, stresses the sexual incapacity of
old John, which makes Alisoun available and initiates the plot (I.3225;
see the similar use of *elde* at 3230). A second such word is *noble*, one of the
most important terms in the *Knight's Tale*, which has itself been described
as a pageant of the noble life. *Noble* appears twelve times in the body of
the romance, which is then called a "noble storie" in the following link
(I.3111), during which the Miller declares that he, too, will tell a "noble
tale" (I.3126). The single appearance of *noble* in the *Miller's Tale*, however,
perfectly defines its artistic and thematic differences from the romance:
in the virtuosic portrait of Alisoun, we are told that her hue was brighter
"than in the Tour the noble yforged newe" (I.3256).[34] A reference to the
Tower of London in another context might well suggest chivalry, but
here, especially when we remember the use of the word in the first tale,
noble exposes the contemporary and ruthlessly materialistic world of the
fabliau. Although Alisoun's portrait is a comic achievement of great artistic skill, the values it expresses, like the shining appeal of the coin, are
directly opposed to the philosophical nobility of the *Knight's Tale*.[35]

The Thematic Dialectic of the First Two Tales

Impressive as both the Knight's Tale and the Miller's Tale are as individual works, they achieve their fullest meaning when read together, as the previous discussion of their contrasting poetics has attempted to show. Chaucer's artistic dialectic makes each of the pair a tool by which to understand better the particular achievements (and limitations) of the other: in Pandarus's terms, each is at once a whetstone and a carving instrument. When the Knight's Tale is read in the light of the very different art of the Miller's Tale, we see more clearly how the idealism of its characterization, the nobility of its imagery and vocabulary, and the philosophical dignity of its speeches all contribute to a straightforward but abstract poetic capable of asking important personal, political, and religious questions. Similarly, the deft comedy and perfection of form that distinguish the Miller's Tale, based on such elements as racy speech, swift transitions, and satiric characterization, stand out all the sharper in contrast to the long and somewhat ponderous Knight's Tale.

The artistic dialectic of the Knight's Tale and the Miller's Tale is more than a literary exercise in stylistic variety, for it leads us to the thematic dialectic between the two tales. Their contrasting, though equally successful, kinds of poetry force the reader to confront two very different visions of the world. The philosophical seriousness of the Knight's Tale is clear enough. Without denying the complexities of this life and despite a few passages that some have taken as comic, the romance is an idealistic epic of ancient heroism that advocates chivalric ideals among men in imitation of a divine Chain of Love. For all its concern with human suffering, the Knight's Tale finds value in the world and order in the universe. The greatest achievement of the Miller's Tale is undoubtedly the delightful perfection of its comedy (whose ability to make readers laugh seems undiminished after nearly six hundred years), yet it, too, offers a vision of the world—and a daring one at that. Modern critics sometimes argue that the Miller's Tale is advocating either rampant sexuality or orthodox Christian doctrine, though it is hard to know which view Chaucer would find more surprising: that he approved of the values of the fabliau or that they are, in fact, essentially religious.[36] Both interpretations minimize the shock of the Miller's Tale by ignoring the questions of morality and taste inevitably raised by juxtaposing such a scurrilous poem to the noble Knight's Tale. That Chaucer himself was aware of the problem is indicated by his two long defenses (I.725–46 and 3167–86), which, amidst much characteristic irony, make the serious point that unless he, as poet, includes every word of every kind of story, he must "telle his tale untrewe, / Or feyne thyng" (I.735–36) and so "falsen som of my mateere"

(I.3175). Chaucer has slyly turned against itself the standard medieval accusation that poetry is nothing but lies; he insists that truth goes beyond the philosophical idealism of the Knight's Tale and must include even the low doings of the fabliau.

The thematic dialectic of the first two Canterbury tales reveals many things about each that would not be so apparent if the tales were read separately. By placing the Miller's Tale after the Knight's Tale, Chaucer makes us aware of how much has been left out of the romance. The Knight's Tale is a celebration of the possibilities of this life and the achievements of human beings—both appropriate to the pagan setting of the poem. Although he is a mortal man, the admirable Theseus aspires to imitate the divine Chain of Love on earth. The other characters in the poem are similarly shown to be essentially good and capable of moral growth. Hippolyta comes to love and marry her conqueror, while Arcite and Palamon, despite their Theban background, never lose a fundamental chivalric idealism even when their rivalry seems most deadly, and so are capable of final reconciliation.

Attractive as this vision of human nobility is, the Miller's Tale calls it sharply into question. In contrast to the first tale, the second has a shrewd understanding of human appetites and ambition—from an old man's passion for his young wife to a clerk's itch to fool his lewed landlord. Ignoring the urges of the body altogether, the Knight's Tale often sees only the highest potential of men, and so it is left to the Miller's Tale to remind us that, though human beings may aspire to the heavens, they often act basely. By its rustic and animalistic imagery and by speech that is colloquial and deceptive rather than formal and philosophical, the second tale shows us how far from the idealism of romance much of actual life is led. In contrast to the honorable love of Palamon and Arcite, who spend untold years in faithful devotion to the chaste Emelye, the rival truth of the Miller's Tale is perhaps best summed up in a characteristically witty and cruel proverb that explains why Nicholas succeeds with Alisoun while Absolon fails: "Alwey the nye slye / Maketh the ferre leeve to be looth" (I.3392–93).

In addition to making us laugh, the fabliau forcefully reminds us how stupid and unfeeling human beings can be and fully illustrates their capacity for self-deception and self-destruction. The Miller's Tale offers a pessimistic view of human rationality in contrast to the Knight's Tale: all of its characters are driven by passion rather than reason, and the only thinking in the tale that is not merely wishful is deceitful. As the special artistry of the Miller's Tale also forces us to recognize, characterization in the Knight's Tale is vague, and its speeches, along with much of the action, abstract. Its noble poet, like Theseus, wants to bring order to the complexities of life, but his solutions, like the symmetrical stadium, are often too neat and simple to be completely satisfying. If the first tale inspires us by expressing the human capacity for heroism and generosity, the second speaks to our fear that men are nothing more than creatures of duplicity and selfish desire, who, for all their cleverness, are incapable of self-control or self-knowledge. After the fabliau, the faith in human achievement and goodness advocated by the romance seems naive indeed.

Of course the dialectic works both ways. If the Miller's Tale exposes limits in the Knight's Tale, the reverse is equally true. The fabliau demonstrates what it would be like if the nobility celebrated by the romance were completely absent—a cruel, harsh world almost totally devoid of kindness or affection, let alone love.[37] For all the brilliance of its narrative surface, its characters reveal the emptiness of a life that is pure appetite. The tale is full of wit and jokes, but its distant narrator, deceitful speech, and mocking laughter, if taken seriously at all, can frighten as well as amuse. As the strict plotting and animalistic imagery make clear, the vision of the Miller's Tale is excessively mechanical and reductive. Attempts to soften its harsh view of life by finding poetic justice in the tale are misleading, for it is the heartlessness of the story, in which a foolish old man is humiliated while his lecherous wife escapes punishment entirely, that makes us laugh. If the Miller's Tale appeared by itself, as is often the case with French fabliaux, the horribleness of its world and people would probably never become a real issue, for the reader would be content to accept the humor for itself. After the idealism of the Knight's Tale, however, it is hard not to ask more serious questions.

In the dialectic between the Knight's Tale and the Miller's Tale, Chaucer trains us to be good readers of poetry. He shows us that we are not to choose between the tales but to learn from both, for each has both moral and aesthetic value. The reader need not try to explain away the immorality of the Miller's Tale or find the stiff idealism of the Knight's Tale more agreeable by detecting an underlying vein of satire; rather, he should explore the achievement and limits of each work as it stands, using the other to help him. Neither of the first two tales is absolutely good or bad in theme or style; each is a provisional work, trying out one approach to art and life, and thus the reader cannot be completely satisfied with either. Because Chaucer is a serious artist as well as a Christian, he avoids pat morals and poems with obvious lessons. Like his contemporaries William Langland and the Gawain-poet, Chaucer is more concerned with intelligent moral instruction than indoctrination. Through the variety and contrast of the Canterbury Tales, he asks more questions than he provides answers and clearly aims for plenitude and possibility rather than certainty. The method is very exciting, but asks a great deal from us. Chaucer supplies the many different tales, but we must work out their relationships. The first two Canterbury tales announce the impossibility of completely accepting any single tale, any single theme, or any single artist as final. Instead, we are to learn from all the poets of the *Canterbury Tales*.

CHAPTER V ❧ VARIETY AND CONTRAST IN CHAUCER'S FABLIAUX

haucer's drama of style in the *Canterbury Tales* takes place not only between obviously contrasting works (the satiric *Sir Thopas* followed by the serious *Melibee* or the noble *Knight's Tale* followed by the bawdy *Miller's Tale*), but also between tales of the same kind. In addition to opposing one genre to another, Chaucer explores the stylistic possibilities within a single genre.[1] Although rarely discussed by critics and then only generally, these fundamental literary differences among apparently similar works are the strongest and most interesting evidence for my argument that Chaucer creates an individual poetic for each of the Canterbury tales. In these last two chapters, I wish to explore the artistic variety that occurs within two equally important but opposite genres: the fabliaux, in which Chaucer best shows his skill for comedy and deft narration, and the religious tales, in which his art is directly committed to his Christian faith.

The fabliau is one of the commonest forms in the *Canterbury Tales* and also perhaps the one in which Chaucer breaks the most new artistic ground.[2] Because of the flexibility of the genre (Bédier's standard definition is no more specific than "des contes à rire en vers"), the list of fabliaux in the *Canterbury Tales* varies from critic to critic, but I shall discuss the four tales that most agree on: the *Miller's Tale, Reeve's Tale, Shipman's Tale*, and *Merchant's Tale*. I exclude the *Cook's Tale* because it is only a fragment and the *Summoner's Tale* and the *Friar's Tale* because, although humorous, they are works of a different sort—more overtly moral and anticlerical, for instance. I want to demonstrate that even within a single genre each Canterbury tale has its own unique poetic, and my argument will be strongest if made with works that seem most obviously alike. The essential situation of the four fabliaux I shall compare is remarkably similar: in each a husband is cuckolded by a younger man whom he himself has introduced into the household. All four stories take place in a restricted setting, and the culminating events happen in a space inside another space—an enclosed garden or a bedroom. Within these narrow confines, the most significant differences are created not so much by plot or action, as by the individual styles of the separate fabliaux poets that Chaucer has created.

Even when critics have recognized some differences among the fabliaux, discussion is usually limited either to generalities or to analysis of only a pair of tales (almost inevitably the Miller's Tale and the Reeve's Tale because of their dramatic relationship). Detailed comparative criticism within the entire genre is much needed. One result may be that each of Chaucer's fabliaux will finally be given its due. Too often the Miller's Tale is the standard by which the others, especially the Reeve's Tale and the Shipman's Tale, are judged and found wanting. Unquestionably, the Miller's Tale is a magnificent work whose narrative energy and effortless wit reveal Chaucer at his most playful, but the other fabliaux have their own skills and achievements as well. Each is an outstanding work in its own terms. For instance, the Reeve's Tale reveals a dazzling command of vocabulary and regional dialect, the Shipman's Tale is built on sophisticated dialogue, and the Merchant's Tale challenges every reader with its mix of the beautiful and the ugly. No one before or after Chaucer comes close to equaling the brilliant and varied results he achieves with this low comic form.

The Miller's Tale and the Reeve's Tale

The Miller's Tale and the Reeve's Tale are the two Chaucerian fabliaux most often discussed as if they were identical works. Thomas Warton's two-hundred-year-old judgment has been frequently echoed and is still often the received opinion today: "The REVES TALE . . . is much in the same style [as the Miller's], but with less humour."[3] In fact, nothing could be further from the truth. Whatever their superficial similarity, Chaucer's first two fabliaux are not essentially alike in any important stylistic category; from the smallest details of vocabulary to general narrative tone, the tales are radically and consistently different. The Reeve's Tale is not an inferior copy of the Miller's Tale, but a fully successful work in a style all its own.

My previous chapter discussed the dialectical relationship between the Knight's Tale and the Miller's Tale, and I will need to refer to some of my conclusions in comparing the Miller's Tale with the Reeve's Tale. It is an indication of the extent of Chaucer's art of juxtaposition that the contrast between the second and third Canterbury tales, though different, is no less complex than the contrast between the second and first tales. The literary relationships created by Chaucer in Fragment I are perhaps too subtle for criticism to cope with fully, and the comparisons I am undertaking in this study only suggest, but by no means exhaust, the possibilities.

Critics who have recognized differences between the Miller's Tale and the *Reeve's Tale* usually attribute them to the personal characteristics of the two pilgrims and to their bitter quarrel. The confident robustness of the Miller and the calculating puritanism of the Reeve are frequently cited to explain the change from an exuberant first fabliau to a nastier second.[4] Such readings are perfectly sound as far as they go, but, as with so many dramatic interpretations, the result is necessarily limited to a general comparison of tone and effect that tells us nothing very specific. If we ignore the pilgrims, however, much can be said about the poetic styles of each tale. The frame offers some warrant for this approach, because it presents the quarrel between the Miller and Reeve as essentially literary. The Reeve claims that his objection is not to the person of the Miller, but to his "lewed dronken harlotrye" (I.3144–49). Oswald never intends to respond physically to Robin, which would certainly be dangerous, but he instead answers with a new tale: he promises to "hym quite anoon" by means of a story "in his cherles termes" (I.3916–17). In the first two fabliaux, as throughout the *Canterbury Tales*, the most interesting action is not the dramatic confrontation of pilgrims, but the literary variety and drama of their tales.

Contrasting Passages

As we have seen with other Canterbury tales, the different poetics of the *Miller's Tale* and the *Reeve's Tale* are clear from their opening lines. The beginning of the first fabliau has already been discussed in the previous chapter, but it will be useful to see the lines again:

> Whilom ther was dwellynge at Oxenford
> A riche gnof, that gestes heeld to bord,
> And of his craft he was a carpenter.
> With hym ther was dwellynge a poure scoler,
> Hadde lerned art, but al his fantasye. . . .
>   (I.3187–91)

The opening of the *Reeve's Tale* introduces a poet as distinctly different from that in the *Miller's Tale* as we found him to be from the poet of the *Knight's Tale*:

> At Trumpyngtoun, nat fer fro Cantebrigge,
> Ther gooth a brook, and over that a brigge,
> Upon the whiche brook ther stant a melle;
> And this is verray sooth that I yow telle:
> A millere was ther dwellynge many a day.
>   (I.3921–25)

The most striking quality of the second passage is its insistence on locating the physical scene with absolute precision. In contrast to the beginning of the Miller's Tale, which refers to the general locale only in passing and whose main interest is in the complex personal associations of its characters, the Reeve's Tale provides a detailed, almost pedantic, focusing in on the mill by the bridge near the stream in Trumpington not far from Cambridge. Even more consistently than the first fabliau, the Reeve's Tale pays careful attention to the realities and relationships of the tangible world, as in the wonderful donnybrook at the end whose flamboyant action is supported by exact description. When the poet finally introduces a human character in the fifth line, the attention, here as elsewhere, is squarely on a single figure—Symkyn the miller. Thus the Reeve's Tale begins more like the Knight's Tale than the Miller's, though to the opposite effect, for the central character of the second fabliau, far from being ennobled like Theseus, is soon to be made utterly ridiculous. The language of the passage is plain and straightforward, lacking not only the noble terms of the Knight's Tale, but even the simple descriptive words at the beginning of the Miller's Tale ("riche" and "poure"); nevertheless, although the numerous physical details are listed without comment or valuation, the poet offers more than just an objective recording of fact. A final artistic difference from the opening of the Miller's Tale is the distinct, involved narrative voice heard in the fourth line ("And this is verray sooth that I yow telle"), which plays such an important role at the beginning and end of the tale.

The contrasting literary sensibilities of the first two fabliaux are equally apparent in other comparable episodes, such as the way each poet describes the wooing of his lovers. The initial meeting of Nicholas and Alisoun (I.3271–3306), already discussed in the previous chapter, is a magnificent example of the poem's narrative energy and wit, offering such pleasures as the wordplay on queynte, the tension between Nicholas's elevated language and uncourtly gropes, and the profusion of animal images associated with Alisoun.

The wooings in the Reeve's Tale are the product of a very different poet. The most obvious change is that the lovers of the second fabliau are portrayed as more limited and less attractive. Instead of clever Nicholas or flamboyant Absolon, we have the bumpkins Aleyn and John, and instead of the alluring Alisoun, the passive daughter and mother. The Cambridge clerks show no interest in amorous dalliance until they see it as a way to assuage their economic humiliation by the miller; but once conceived, the thought leads directly to Aleyn's violent coupling with Malyne, which lacks any of the wit or charm of the wooing in the Miller's Tale:

And up he rist, and by the wenche he crepte.
This wenche lay uprighte, and faste slepte,
Til he so ny was, er she myghte espie,
That it had been to late for to crie,
And shortly for to seyn, they were aton.
                              (I.4193–97)

Instead of the ingenious wordplay found in the parallel scene of the *Miller's Tale*, the poet describes events with the paratactic attention to physical detail already noted in the opening lines. Indeed, there is some question whether we should consider this to be wooing at all; if Nicholas accomplishes a rapid seduction of a willing partner, Aleyn seems little more than a rapist. In sharp contrast to the vague geniality with which the eventual union of Nicholas and Alisoun is described ("the revel and the melodye" [I.3652]), the poet of the *Reeve's Tale* insists on brutal particularities.

The difference between wooing scenes in the first two fabliaux comes not so much from their stories as from a deliberate change in style. In most of the analogues, the Aleyn-figure wins the girl with clever patter and a trick with a ring, but the student in the *Reeve's Tale* is given neither brains nor imagination, and so he must depend on force alone.[5] The poet's objective description does not allow us to know whether the miller's daughter goes along with Aleyn out of desire or mere resignation. The subsequent "wooing" of the miller's wife by John is equally direct and physical (I.4228–31), and just as devoid of the clerkly cleverness that runs throughout the *Miller's Tale*. The single trick the poet allows his students (John's moving the cradle next to his own bed) is curiously passive. In the analogues, this character moves the cradle after the wife is already up, and he then pulls the baby's ear to ensure that the child's location will be noticed by its mother.[6] In contrast, John's action seems done entirely on speculation, as it were, merely in the hope that the wife will first get up and then discover the new position of the cradle.

Portraits and Narrator

As critics have long recognized, the elaborate portraits in the *Miller's Tale* are Chaucer's most obvious additions to a genre that when written by almost any other hand scorns such interruptions of pure narrative. In this respect, the *Reeve's Tale* may at first seem quite like the *Miller's Tale*; both begin with a series of formal portraits whose details set up much of the action that follows. Closer comparison, however, reveals fundamentally different literary strategies even here. Whereas the three principal characters in the Miller's Tale (Alisoun and her two lovers) are each described as individuals in separate passages, the three in the Reeve's Tale (the miller, his wife, and their daughter) are presented together as a family unit with special emphasis on their relationship to one another and to their world (I.3925–86).

Just as the Reeve's Tale is always careful to get the physical particulars of a scene right, its portraits offer a more detailed and realistic picture of society than those in the first fabliau and tell us more about the past history of each character. The poet traces what one critic calls "social ramifications in depth," for he is ever alert to such aspects of practical life as class, status, marital alliance, place of origin, and reputation.[7] Whereas the Miller's Tale tells us almost nothing about the marriage of his couple except to note the dissimilarity of their ages, the Reeve's Tale is much more forthcoming, explaining the special situation and influence of the woman's father (he is a priest!), the miller's requirements for a wife, the size (and necessity) of a dowry, and the hope the couple has for their daughter.[8] The reader also learns in some detail about Symkyn's sense of his estate, his wife's pride, the posture both strike as they parade on holidays, and the priest's marital maneuverings unto a third generation. As for the students, although they are not given formal portraits, we know the area of their birth, the name of their college and its past difficulties with the miller, the manciple's present illness, and something about the warden. Of course, the Miller's Tale provides no such detail about Nicholas, and, though we are told of Absolon's clothing and recreations, we learn nothing about his background or professional relationships.[9]

In addition to their greater understanding of the realities of the social world, the most distinctive quality of the portraits in the Reeve's Tale is the hostile, sarcastic style of narration, which directly attacks the characters—calling the miller a thief, the wife a bastard, and the daughter an ugly wench. Although this distinctive voice is largely absent in the body of the tale until it reappears at the very end, it dominates the opening descriptions and adds a tone of nastiness to the entire work. We have already seen how the cool narrative of the Miller's Tale, in contrast to the friendlier accents of the Knight's Tale, remains detached from its characters and becomes an identifiable voice only in a few smug comments (for example, I.3227–32). The mode of narration in the Reeve's Tale is different—and as different—again; the voice we hear so clearly in the opening portraits, far from being distant and impersonal, is involved and angry. Its opinions are definite and supported by the number of tags that insist on their truth: these include the first direct statement in the tale ("And this is verray sooth that I yow telle" [I.3924]), as well as others, such as "A theef he was for sothe" (I.3939) and the sarcastic "But right fair was hire heer, I wol nat lye" (I.3976).

The intrusive, scornful narrator of the opening portraits may be identified generally with the pilgrim Reeve, but there is no necessity to do so. The mode of narrative is fully defined within the tale itself and does not much resemble the elaborate, self-pitying accents of the pilgrim in the *Reeve's Prologue*. That voice is defensive and uses imagery extensively; this one is more aggressive in temper and plainer of speech—more like the pilgrim Miller, in fact, than the pilgrim Reeve. The narrator of the *Reeve's Tale* is most like the nominal teller in his tendency to preach, however, as in the bitter attack on priests for dishonoring "hooly chirche" (I.3983–86). Such a direct, emotional outburst is unimaginable in the *Miller's Tale*, just as instead of the cruel but cool summary of events at the end of the first fabliau, the second concludes with an explicit lesson charged with gloating hostility toward Symkyn, who has been the principal target throughout (I.4313–24).

The severity so many Chaucerians have found in the *Reeve's Tale* begins with the eagerness in these opening portraits to record the social and physical defects of the miller's family. The characters in the *Miller's Tale* are satirized—lightly and deftly—but they are also enjoyed. If Alisoun is finally an amoral wench, a flower no finer than a "piggesnye," the energy and almost metaphysical imagery with which she is portrayed also make her attractive. Physical description in the *Miller's Tale* is often magnifying ("Hir mouth was sweete as bragot or the meeth" [I.3261] or "Crul was his heer, and as the gold it shoon, / And strouted as a fanne large and brode" [I.3314–15]). In striking contrast, comparable references to the body in the portraits of the *Reeve's Tale* are simpler in rhetoric, more physically exact, and unmistakably reductive ("Round was his face, and camus was his nose; / As piled as an ape was his skulle" [I.3934–35] or "This wenche thikke and wel ygrowen was" [I.3973]). The same Swiftian note of disgust with the body is heard again in the description of the miller and his wife as they stagger drunkenly off to bed and fall into noisy unconsciousness (I.4149–67).

The formal portraits in the *Reeve's Tale* record not only the physical limitations of its characters, but also their social failures—in keeping with its careful attention to the realities of the world. Pretentiousness quickly attracts the poet's attention. He suggests that the miller, for all his weaponry, may not be as dangerous as he likes to appear: "For jalous folk ben perilous everemo; / Algate they wolde hire wyves wenden so" (I.3961–62). The wife's absurd social pride is similarly mocked; not only does she demand to be called "dame" (I.3956), but also "for she was somdel smoterlich, / She was as digne as water in a dich" (I.3963–64). The poet also enjoys quoting the characters' own words to make them look ridiculous. He records the miller's demands for a wife ("For Symkyn wolde no wyf, as he sayde, / But she were wel ynorissed and a mayde" [I.3947–

48]—no matter that she is illegitimate), and notes the wife's equally absurd ideas of her exalted station: "Hir thoughte that a lady sholde hire spare, / What for hire kynrede and hir nortelrie" (I.3966–67).

Imagery and Literary Allusion

The bleak and narrow world of the Reeve's Tale is the result of much more than the hostility of the narrative voice. It is also produced by other aspects of the individual poetic Chaucer has created for this tale, such as the particular use of imagery and allusion. Although the literary and religious allusions in the Miller's Tale are taken from popular rather than learned sources, their number and range are impressive; they include the mystery play, English romances, contemporary songs, familiar stories like Noah's flood, and the sayings of standard authorities like Solomon and Cato. In contrast, the Reeve's Tale contains not a single genuine borrowing from a literary work, learned authority, or religious story.[10] A few saints are invoked in oaths (for instance, Cuthbert at I.4127 and James at I.4264), but the only narrative mentioned in the tale—a fleeting reference to the story of the wolf and the clerk (I.4055)—is not a real literary work at all, but simply a proverbial tale with an anti-intellectual message. Similarly, the mention of Bayard (I.4115) is probably not a literary association, however remote, as this was a common name at the time for a mare.[11] Robert Kaske has detected "a parody of the aube" in the speeches of Aleyn and Malyne as they part (I.4234–48), but these lines might more properly be seen as an anti-aube, the deliberate negation of the real thing, rather than true parody.[12] Unlike Nicholas's deft handling of the courtly idiom to win Alisoun in the Miller's Tale or Absolon's elaborate incompetence, Aleyn's leave-taking is typical of this poet's unliterary verbal plainness: "Fare weel, Malyne, sweete wight! / The day is come, I may no lenger byde" (I.4236–37). Malyne's response also echoes ordinary rather than courtly speech. She begins, "Now, deere lemman, . . . go, far weel!" and concludes, "And, goode lemman, God thee save and kepe!" (I.4240–47). Between which commonplace sentiments, Malyne precisely and practically explains where Aleyn can find the meal, "Which that I heelp my sire for to stele." In contrast to the extensive parodic misuse of courtly conventions in the first fabliau, the second fabliau provides the occasion for further parody, only to prove how completely ignorant its characters are of such discourse. Once again, the deliberate lack of literary reference in the Reeve's Tale is emphasized.

The striking difference between the use of allusion in the Miller's Tale and the Reeve's Tale cannot be attributed primarily to their nominal tellers (judged by their prologues, the pilgrim Reeve is more learned and rhetorically accomplished—not to mention more sober—than the pilgrim

Miller); instead, the contrast reflects the different artistry of each tale. Although Chaucer is correctly regarded as one of the most bookish of poets, he completely abandons that aspect of his art to create the unique poet of the *Reeve's Tale*.

In place of genuine literary allusions or other evidence of learning, the *Reeve's Tale* contains significantly more proverbs than the *Miller's Tale*, a kind of expression that perfectly accords with its sour, deflating artistry.[13] The Cambridge student John, the antitype of the clever Nicholas, uses five himself and the miller one; none in any way suggests the great events (like the new Flood) so often evoked by the allusions in the first fabliau, but instead they all, in the usual manner of proverbs, stress the limits and harsh necessities of the everyday world. John's proverbs draw the depressing lessons that (1) need has no peer (I.4026), (2) one must help oneself in need (I.4027–28), (3) one can use only what one has or finds (I.4129–30), (4) an empty purse gets no attention (I.4134), and (5) nothing ventured is nothing gained (I.4210). But it is the miller's single proverb that most successfully captures the anti-intellectual tone of the poem in which human reason so often miscarries: "The gretteste clerkes been noght wisest men" (I.4054).[14]

When the students return wet and weary from chasing their horse in the fens and request lodging for the night, the miller ridicules their supposed learning:

> Myn hous is streit, but ye han lerned art;
> Ye konne by argumentes make a place
> A myle brood of twenty foot of space.
> (I.4122–24)

Although this is a common jibe against students and appropriate to the sarcastic tone of the *Reeve's Tale*, the lines may seem instead to describe the flamboyant art of the very different *Miller's Tale*, especially its sense of scope and possibility as seen in Nicholas's imaginative stories and the poet's many diverse allusions. In contrast, the poet of the *Reeve's Tale* chooses to create his art out of the narrow dimensions of the real and everyday.

Instead of the concentrated imagery found in the first fabliau and, indeed, in the *Reeve's Prologue*, the *Reeve's Tale* contains only a few images of limited variety.[15] Many of these are animalistic and, unlike the noble beasts of the *Knight's Tale* or the lively ones of the *Miller's*, further contribute to the nasty effect of the poem because their primary function is to belittle.[16] Symkyn is compared to a peacock (I.3926) and an ape (I.3935), his wife to a magpie (I.3950) and a jay (I.4154). Similarly insulting is the description of the students as beasts in the rain (I.4107) and the nonanimalistic but equally rustic image likening the wife's pride to water in a ditch (I.3964). The characters themselves also use aggressive, demeaning imagery: Aleyn says that he counts the miller as less than a fly (I.4192) and calls John a swine's head (I.4262), whereas John accuses himself of being an ape (I.4202). Perhaps the one line that best represents the animal imagery of the *Reeve's Tale* is the description of Aleyn and the miller in the climactic fight scene: "They walwe as doon two pigges in a poke" (I.4278).

The narrow range of imagery in the *Reeve's Tale*, which is used primarily to attack its characters, is in sharp contrast to the variety and vivacity of imagery in the *Miller's Tale*, the most spectacular example of which is the blizzard of metaphors that describe Alisoun.[17] Even the fart Nicholas directs at the poker-wielding Absolon becomes more than just a nasty smell and is made to seem almost magnificent because of the poet's imagery: "As greet as it had been a thonder-dent" (I.3807). A similar explosion in the *Reeve's Tale*, however, is simply disgusting because of its poet's demeaning simile:

> This millere hath so wisely bibbed ale
> That as an hors he fnorteth in his sleep,
> Ne of his tayl bihynde he took no keep.
> (I.4162–64)

Language

Although the artistry of the *Reeve's Tale* is different from that of the *Miller's Tale*, it is by no means inferior. In addition to a powerful sense of the realities of the world on which he builds his comedy, the poet of the second fabliau is especially accomplished in his use of language, as seen most obviously in his skillful creation of a special dialect for the two Cambridge students. John and Aleyn, who are said to have been born in a certain Strother ("Fer in the north, I kan nat telle where" [I.4015]), employ a complex northern vocabulary, including *heythen* (I.4033), *ille* (I.4045, 4174, and 4184), and *ymel* (I.4171), as well as distinct northern forms such as *banes* (I.4073, for *bones*), *swa* (I.4030, 4040, and 4239, for *so*), and -*s* or -*es* for southern -*eth* or -*th* in the third personal singular of the present indicative. Such a sophisticated use of regional speech is without parallel in any of Chaucer's other works, as it is almost nonexistent elsewhere in Middle English.[18] Yet, although Chaucer uses dialect only once in his career, he does it masterfully. No less a philologist than J. R. R. Tolkien, who had scant regard for the literary value of the *Reeve's Tale*, testified to the "considerable skill and judgment" used in creating the students' northern speech. The poet does not rely on extreme or out-

landish forms but demonstrates a deep and remarkably accurate knowledge of northern practices that could not have been acquired casually
in London.[19] Even if Tolkien may overrate Chaucer's accomplishment
somewhat (and his remains the only full study of the subject), it seems
certain, as another scholar notes, that "Chaucer is the first literary writer
in English to attempt to reproduce a dialect other than his normal
one."[20] His achievement was recognized by some of his earliest readers,
the scribes, who often added northern forms of their own to the text of
the poem.[21] For this one tale, and to define its special poetry, Chaucer
created a remarkable and sophisticated literary device he was never to
use again.

The *Reeve*-poet's particular skill with language is also seen in his distinct
vocabulary. The poet deploys what R. W. Frank in his excellent study of
the tale calls a "glorious glossary," which serves "the demands of low style
while charging it with a crude, demonic energy."[22] Both Frank and the
Spearings note the great number of words in the tale that appear nowhere else in Chaucer's writings. Indeed, it has recently been shown that
the work contains a higher percentage of nonce words than any other
Canterbury tale, a proportion that remains impressive even when we
subtract northern forms.[23] These unique words and phrases often have a
particular appropriateness to the poetry of the *Reeve's Tale*, for they include precise terms for physical objects such as *panade* (I.3929), *poppere*
(I.3931), *thwitel* (I.3933), *camus* (I.3934 and 3974), and *throte-bolle* (I.4273);
examples of excited speech by both man and animal, such as *wehee*
(I.4066), *step on thy feet* (I.4074), and *jossa* (I.4101); and a wonderful array of
insulting terms that contribute to the nasty tone of the poem such as
market-betere (I.3936), *smoterlich* (I.3963), *hoker* and *bisemare* (I.3965), *draf-sak*
(I.4206), *toty* (I.4253), and *swynes-heed* (I.4262). The special glossary of the
Reeve's Tale cannot be explained by personal differences between pilgrim
Reeve and pilgrim Miller. If anything we would expect the drunken,
door-demolishing Miller to use such vigorous and violent words, not the
sly Reeve. In the *Reeve's Prologue*, the pilgrim employs a different and more
elevated (though equally vigorous) vocabulary and speaking style, which
the Host suggests is similar to that of a preacher, full of moral terms,
biblical echoes, and complex imagery, none of which appears in the tale
itself.

Direct Speech and Dialogue

The special use of language in the *Reeve's Tale* is equally evident in its
direct speech and dialogue, which contribute both to the robust comedy
and to our sense of the bleak, narrow lives of the characters. The very

first exchange in the tale, between the miller and the two students, brilliantly characterizes the world of the *Reeve's Tale* by capturing the tedium of everyday speech:

> Aleyn spak first, "Al hayl, Symond, y-fayth!
> Hou fares thy faire doghter and thy wyf?"
>
> "Aleyn, welcome," quod Symkyn, "by my lyf!
> And John also, how now, what do ye heer?"
>
> "Symond," quod John, "by God, nede has na peer.
> Hym boes serve hymself that has na swayn,
> Or elles he is a fool, as clerkes sayn.
> Oure manciple, I hope he wil be deed.
> Swa werkes ay the wanges in his heed;
> And forthy is I come, and eek Alayn,
> To grynde oure corn and carie it ham agayn;
> I pray yow spede us heythen that ye may."
>   (I.4022–33)

All three voices speak in the flat conversational tones of real life. The courtly parody, puns, fantasies, and wit of the *Miller's Tale* have been replaced by conventional greetings and familiar proverbs. John's exposition of his plans is nothing if not obvious, and the most striking literary device in the lines (the northern dialect) reveals the cleverness of the poet at the expense of his characters, whom we laugh at rather than with (especially because of the misuse, to southern ears, of "hope" at I.4029). It is as if the *lewed* language of the carpenter in the *Miller's Tale* has taken over the second fabliau, though even silly old John can be more articulate and imaginative than this (as when he expresses his fears about Nicholas's condition at I.3449–67 and 3477–86). Clerks in fabliaux are often clever with words, like Nicholas, or at least glib, like Absolon, but not the pair from Cambridge; it is impossible to imagine either of them playing Herod or inventing the story of a new Flood.

Nicholas's education is always evident in his speech, and even the foolish Absolon reveals a wide, if confused, knowledge of courtly and biblical idioms, but the *Reeve's Tale*, whose view of human achievement is not high, never allows John and Aleyn to reveal any evidence of their academic training. When the foolish pair return from chasing their horse and are mocked by the miller for their supposed learning (I.4120–26), their only response is meek praise of their tormentor (I.4128) and a resort to common proverbs instead of educated wit (I.4129–34). Similarly, Aleyn's later citation of a supposed legal principle (I.4179–82) is really only a perversion of the law that excuses his desire for revenge.[24] Verbal skill is certainly not the students' strongest asset, and they finally gain advantage over the miller only in the second half of the tale, when they abandon speech altogether and resort to action. The Cambridge clerks are not capable of manipulating language for their own benefit; on the contrary, it is a power they fear may be used by others to ridicule them (I.4207–8). Neither man bothers to waste a single syllable on wooing his respective sexual partner, but each wisely depends on more direct methods. When Aleyn subsequently lapses into speech (bragging of his conquest to the miller, whom he mistakenly believes is John), he only causes more trouble for himself, which once again must be remedied by physical force.

In keeping with poetry based on the ordinary and tangible materials of everyday life, the art of the *Reeve's Tale* is especially skilled at producing comedy by mixing realistic, colloquial speech with violent action. The climactic fight in the miller's bedroom, which begins with Aleyn's unwitting confession to Symkyn just mentioned and the miller's heated response (I.4262–72), is given a new direction by the wife's fearful prayer for help (I.4286–91) and concludes with the miller's pitiful cry, "Harrow! I dye!" (I.4307). Perhaps the most delightful example of the poet's facility in combining chaotic words and deeds is the earlier collection of cries and alarms (some of which barely qualify as articulate speech) given to the clerks as they desperately try to recapture their runaway horse, a fine sample of which is John's initial outburst:

> And [he] gan to crie "Harrow!" and "Weylaway!
> Oure hors is lorn, Alayn, for Goddes banes,
> Step on thy feet! Com of, man, al atanes!
> Allas, our wardeyn has his palfrey lorn."
> (I.4072–75)

These lines deftly and humorously portray John's shock ("Harrow!" and "Weylaway!") and confusion ("Step on thy feet!"), along with his efforts to avoid blame for what has happened by first involving Aleyn (I.4074) and then phrasing the loss so that it seems to be the warden's problem rather than the students' responsibility (I.4075).

Literary and Thematic Contrasts in
Chaucer's First Two Fabliaux

My comparison of the styles of the first two fabliaux has attempted to show that the *Reeve's Tale* is not merely a pale imitation of the *Miller's Tale*, but the product of a totally different, though equally skilled, poet. If the world of the second fabliau is bleak and limited, its literary skill is anything but. A reader who comes to the *Reeve's Tale* expecting to find the delights of the *Miller's Tale* will be dissatisfied because much that is most successful in the first work (its imagery, allusions, and witty dialogue, for instance) is absent in the second. In compensation, however, are the special virtues of the *Reeve's Tale*—its comedy of action rather than of cleverness, careful delineation of social relationships and pressures, and special use of dialect, direct speech, and vocabulary. But even if we are willing to accept that the first two fabliaux are fundamentally different, which is the main burden of my argument, we may still wonder why Chaucer went to all that trouble. Delight in variety for its own sake is certainly part of the answer. As he does elsewhere throughout his career, Chaucer is trying different ways of presenting the same basic material. The *Miller's Tale* and the *Reeve's Tale*, along with the *Shipman's Tale* and the *Merchant's Tale*, are experiments that explore the dynamic potential of the fabliau.

The contrasting styles of the *Miller's Tale* and the *Reeve's Tale* may also contribute, however indirectly, to some of the more serious themes raised in the *Canterbury Tales*. I am reluctant to see the first two fabliaux as disguised religious allegory or even the working out of some sort of "poetic" justice; Robert K. Root's Victorian regret that Chaucer ever wrote such works is a truer response to the dangerous power of the fabliaux than more modern attempts to housebreak them into conventional Christian sermons or exempla of reason and justice.[25] The apology Chaucer offers before the *Miller's Tale* for telling such churlish stories cannot be dismissed as only ironic; he recognized, and so should we, that along with its ability to delight, the fabliau could also shock and unsettle by subverting the values that high medieval culture took most seriously. Nevertheless, because it appears in the context of the *Canterbury Tales*, the moral anarchy of the fabliau must strike a reader differently than if such tales were read by themselves. As we have seen in the previous chapter, the literary dialectic of the *Knight's Tale* and the *Miller's Tale* offers the reader two contrasting visions of the world; another philosophical opposition exists between the superficially similar tales of the Miller and the Reeve.

If nothing else, the *Reeve's Tale* offers a sobering corrective to the surface attractiveness of the *Miller's Tale*. As an attack on the fabliau from within, it describes the limits and even the sordidness of the natural world, thus suggesting that the *Miller's Tale* is as much a fantasy as the *Knight's Tale*. The delights and playfulness of the *Miller's Tale* are deflated by the greater awareness in the second fabliau of the constraints of physical and social reality and by its understanding of the pettiness of man. Although the *Miller's Tale* is emotionally cool and lacks the nobility of the *Knight's Tale*, its view of life is optimistic and even generous. The bedding of Nicholas and Alisoun is described almost sweetly, and the pain various characters suffer does not seem to hurt for very long. The language used by the poet magnifies his silliest creations, while hope is characteristic of the men. Even old John, the humblest and least rewarded figure in the tale, has dared to marry the young Alisoun and can imagine himself lord of all he surveys.

This is all changed in the second fabliau, which offers a powerful vision of the harsh necessities of human existence. Although the second fabliau is less exuberant and fanciful than the first, it does have its own virtues, as we have seen, principally a shrewd knowledge of how things actually work in the world—an insight that echoes the physical precision of its narrative. Nothing is free or easy in the *Reeve's Tale*. The priest had to spend money to marry his illegitimate daughter (I.3944–45) and will have to do the same for his granddaughter (I.3977–86), just as the students have to pay out for lodging, as they well know (I.4119 and 4135). Throughout the tale the cruel realities of the fallen world are insisted upon in the plot and the proverbs. The miller unhesitatingly steals the students' corn when he has a chance, and John and Aleyn obtain "esement" (I.4179) by pure force. An untied horse inevitably runs away, and the miller finds his wife and daughter violated because his sleeping quarters are one small room.

The claustrophobia of the poem extends beyond the physical to the social and psychological, as the characters try to maintain their ridiculous self-respect before the eyes of others. Worries about status and reputation, familiar enough in ordinary life but totally absent from the more innocent *Miller's Tale*, are central in the *Reeve's Tale*. The absurd social pretensions of the miller and his wife culminate when the former, on being informed that his daughter has been *swyved* three times by Aleyn, seems outraged principally because the violation has occurred to one "that is come of swich lynage" (I.4272). Similarly, the Cambridge clerks' fondest hope is not so much to succeed at something new, but simply to maintain their tatty dignity in the world. When John realizes that he and Aleyn have been tricked by Symkyn, he does not, like Absolon, get honestly angry, but instead begins to worry about being mocked by the miller, the warden, and his fellows back at college (I.4109–13). Likewise, his seduction of the wife is not the result of lust or even revenge, but is undertaken only so that he will not look like such a fool to others: "And when this jape is tald another day, / I sal been halde a daf, a cokenay!" (I.4207–8). The poet's acute understanding of some of the meaner aspects of human psychology is an important part of his bleak art. Beneath its slapstick comedy, the *Reeve's Tale* contains a powerful vision of the depths to which humans—without morals, manners, intelligence, or joy—can sink. The tale offers us much comedy, but also a criticism of the values of the fabliau from within the form itself.

The Shipman's Tale

That the Shipman's Tale is sharply different from Chaucer's first two fabliaux is clear from its opening lines. Immediately we find ourselves in a
grander, more exotic setting than those of the Miller's Tale and the Reeve's
Tale. The Shipman's Tale takes place near the capital city of a foreign country, instead of a provincial English university town, and its actors are not
laborers and clerks, but a rich mercantile couple and an influential
monk. The greater sophistication of the characters, and of their sur-
roundings and relationships, soon becomes apparent. In contrast to the
limited physical confines of the first two fabliaux, this is a world of
"festes" and "daunces" (VII.7), and of high finance involving several nations (France, Flanders, and the Lombards in Paris), in which even the
nominally cloistered monk moves about with ease and freedom. The
merchant does not take in paying guests, as both the carpenter and the
miller do, but instead offers generous, almost chivalric hospitality, especially to the elegant monk, "ful of curteisye" (VII.69), who he believes is
his cousin.

The new kinds of people and places are signals of the stylistic individuality of the Shipman's Tale. Different as the Reeve's Tale is from the Miller's
Tale, the Shipman's Tale is equally different from what they have in common, though the reader may at first be struck and even disappointed by
what is missing. The Shipman's Tale contains almost no detailed description of place, for instance, and thus we never understand the arrangement of the merchant's house as we do that of the carpenter's and miller's. Physical action and the comedy it produces are also virtually nonexistent. The calm respectability that dominates the surface of the tale is
never violated by the howls, blows, insults, and falls that mark the first
two fabliaux. Formal portraits of the main characters, which are among
Chaucer's greatest achievements in the Miller's Tale and the Reeve's Tale, are
also absent from the Shipman's Tale, whose equally skilled characterization
is achieved otherwise, as we shall see.

A more subtle change in the Shipman's Tale is the colorlessness of its
imagery, language, and literary allusions. In contrast to the Miller's Tale's
lavish use of literary and biblical references and to the humble proverbial
sayings, vigorous vocabulary, and dialect of the Reeve's Tale, the only obvious literary decoration in the Shipman's Tale is the brief evocation of a few
saints (VII.148, 151, 227, 259, 355, and 402). The poet never once indulges in a learned allusion, and there is not a single reference to another
literary work anywhere in the tale. In keeping with the polite narrative
surface of the tale, the use of formal metaphorical imagery is restrained,
consisting of fewer than a dozen phrases remarkable only for their
blandness.[26] For example, the monk assures the wife that the merchant
is no more cousin to him than "this leef that hangeth on the tree"

(VII.150), and the wife says her husband is not worth "the value of a flye" (VII.171). Perhaps most revealing of the poet's indifference to stylistic vividness is his repetition of virtually the same image within a few lines. The merchant's alliance with the monk is said to make him "as glad therof as fowel of day" (VII.38); less than twenty lines later the monk's arrival makes the entire household "as glad of his comyng / As fowel is fayn whan that the sonne up riseth" (VII.50–51). In addition to being trite phrases, the bird similes replace the active, even violent animal imagery of the first two fabliaux and thus further indicate a different artistic sensibility.

Although the *Shipman's Tale* has recently acquired a few able defenders, its differences from the *Miller's Tale* and the *Reeve's Tale* have generally been taken as signs of failure. The tale is often thought to be Chaucer's least distinctive fabliau, the one closest to the standard continental model, and thus, as one critic puts it speaking for many, no more than a "successful trifle."[27] Such conclusions badly misjudge the *Shipman's Tale*. Its individuality in no way indicates inferiority; if the work lacks many of the most successful literary elements of Chaucer's first two fabliaux that is because its achievement is to be found elsewhere.[28]

The Artistry of Business

For all the lack of literary decoration in the *Shipman's Tale*, the events of the story are far from unsophisticated. The characters manipulate each other skillfully and succeed in the affairs of the world. Instead of complex imagery, wide-ranging allusions, or a deeply involved narrator, the poem provides business talk between husband and wife, monk and merchant, and even the adulterous lovers, which results in the various contracts and transactions that are executed with such deftness in the course of the story. The special achievement of the *Shipman's Tale* can best be appreciated if we see its poet, like each of its characters, as a successful man of business. As such, he is practical, detached, and skillful. Innocent of learning and indifferent to literary elaboration of any sort, he knows what he wants to achieve and is efficient in accomplishing it—never more so than in his no-nonsense description of the merchant's progress from his counting house to table:

> And with that word his countour-dore he shette,
> And doun he gooth, no lenger wolde he lette.
> But hastily a messe was ther seyd,
> And spedily the tables were yleyd,
> And to the dyner faste they hem spedde,
> And richely this monk the chapman fedde.
> (VII.249–54)

The businesslike poet does not, of course, much resemble the two pilgrims usually associated with the tale: the Shipman himself and the Wife of Bath. He lacks their energetic physicality, and, in contrast to the poets of the first two fabliaux, he does not waste much time on the passions of sex or revenge. He cannot afford to be bothered with his characters' inner lives and motivations; instead, his interest is almost entirely absorbed by commercial transactions. Business dealings are repeatedly given much more space and attention than demanded by the plot (for example, VII.53–56, 75–88, 299–306, 325–34, and 365–72), and we even hear the merchant's pseudo-philosophical speeches on the "curious bisynesse" of "chapmen" to his wife (VII.224–38) and to the monk (VII.287–92).

Unlike the *Reeve's Tale*, the *Shipman's Tale* contains few nonce words and almost no unusual vocabulary—except for business terms. McGalliard counted "forty different terms with commercial associations" in the tale.[29] For instance, *chevyssaunce*, which is used three times in the tale (VII.329, 347, and 391), occurs only twice more in Chaucer's work. *Chapman* or *chapmanhode* appears five times in the tale, but, excluding the *Romaunt of the Rose*, is used in only three other places in Chaucer, two of which are at the beginning of the *Man of Law's Tale*. The technical commercial terms *reconyssaunce* (VII.330) and *creaunce* (VII.289)—also in the forms *creaunceth* (VII.303) and *creanced* (VII.366)—are unique to the *Shipman's Tale*, though versions of the latter, meaning belief, occur elsewhere.

The poet describes in great detail not only the business dealings of the merchant, but also those hardly less complicated ones of the other two characters. We are told of the arrangement the monk has with his abbot to supervise their monastic estates (VII.62–66) and hear at length about a supposed livestock purchase for which he requests a loan (VII.269–80). Similarly, the wife's need for money to pay a debt due "Sonday next" (VII.180) initiates the whole plot, and the tale is then largely concerned with the financial deals that she strikes first with the monk and then with her own husband, both of which depend on a loan between merchant and monk. All of these arrangements, even the non-erotic ones, have the secrecy usually associated with sexual relationships.

The central importance of money in the *Shipman's Tale* is in strong contrast to its peripheral role in the first two fabliaux. Money appears in the *Miller's Tale* only as a minor detail of characterization: Alisoun's hue is said to be brighter than a newly forged noble (I.3255–56) and "meede" is one method Absolon tries in his incompetent wooing (I.3380–82). Money is a revealing but nevertheless small part of the social realism of the *Reeve's Tale*: we are told that the priest must pay to marry his daughter (I.3944) and granddaughter (I.3977–86) and that it will cost the clerks to spend the night at the miller's (I.4133–35).

In the *Shipman's Tale*, by contrast, money pervades the story and is the basis of every relationship. The narrator's early comment ("But wo is hym that payen moot for al!" [VII.10]) is not just applicable to silly husbands; who pays and for what determines every single action in the tale. The merchant's riches cause him to be considered wise (VII.2), and his "largesse" (VII.22), along with his fair wife, attracts visitors to his house; at the end of the tale his sexual potency appears to depend entirely on his balance sheet (VII.375–76). The wife, who eventually finds a new way of defining and collecting the Christian "debt of the body" by transforming her tail into a tally, is motivated throughout by the need to pay, as we see in her attempts to meet her dress bill and to avoid refunding the monk's money. The monk, who is beloved by the household in large measure because he is "free" and "namely of dispence" (VII.43), so skillfully becomes a borrower and lender that he secures the wife's favors for nothing.

The reader is continually reminded that money rules all in the *Shipman's Tale*. Preparing for his business trip to Flanders, the merchant speaks to his wife of material things. He implores her to protect "oure good" and assures her that she has enough food, clothing, and silver (VII.243–48). At the end of the tale, whatever he suspects about his wife's conduct, the merchant's expressed concern remains only about his possessions, as he urges that she "keep bet my good" (VII.432). Perhaps most significant of all is the repetition of forms of *paye(n)* in the tale. The word is used thirty-nine times in all of the *Canterbury Tales*; fourteen of these appearances, or more than one-third of the total, are in the relatively brief *Shipman's Tale*, whereas only one other tale (the *Canon's Yeoman's Tale*) contains as many as four.[30]

The Play of Speech

Beyond its businesslike efficiency and vocabulary, the most distinctive and impressive literary element of the *Shipman's Tale* is the dialogue between its characters. The poet develops his story not through action, as in the first two fabliaux, but almost entirely through the spoken word. Over half of the lines in the tale are dialogue, resulting in a medieval version of a theatrical comedy of manners.[31] As on the stage, we get to know the characters principally through what they say.[32] The importance of speech in the *Shipman's Tale* is not always recognized, and, even when it is, the poet's achievement is often undervalued. T. W. Craik, for example, discusses the speeches at length, but sees them as no more than partial compensation for the absence of action in the tale—another instance in which the assumption that Chaucer's fabliaux are all alike and aiming for the same effect produces distorted readings of individual works.[33]

The poet's most impressive achievement in speech is unquestionably the long dialogue during which the merchant's wife and monk agree to trade franks for flanks. None of Chaucer's other fabliaux has anything like this complex, sophisticated, and indirect wooing scene, which accomplishes its immoral purposes through language that never violates the proprieties. The substantive result is the same as that of the brief opening dialogue between Nicholas and Alisoun in the Miller's Tale (the couple agrees on a future amorous rendezvous), but, in contrast to the quick, parodic exchanges of the first fabliau, the Shipman's Tale contains an extended and subtle dialogue in which an adulterous agreement takes place under the guise of respectable conversation. As happens in none of Chaucer's other fabliaux, we witness the actual seduction—in fact, a mutual seduction or, even more accurately, the tale's ultimate business deal. It is as if Chaucer has taken the witty couplet from the Miller's Tale ("And spak so faire, and profred him so faste, / That she hir love hym graunted atte laste" [I.3289–90]) and, after raising the characters in status and making their desires less animalistically sensual, if equally urgent, extended two lines into one hundred (out of 434 lines for the entire tale). The poet's skill in using speech may remind us of similar, if greater, achievements in Troilus and Criseyde, especially the dialogue between Pandarus and Criseyde in Book Two during which each attempts to outmaneuver the other. Of course, the Shipman-poet does not provide the richness of psychological insight found in the Troilus, nor does he aim to, but his skill at sophisticated dramatic dialogue is equally developed.

The subtlety of the central dialogue between wife and monk has been noted by others, but it has not been analyzed in detail, nor has its absolute difference from speech in other Chaucerian fabliaux been sufficiently emphasized. None of the other fabliaux contains such extended, calculated, and equal exchanges between two characters. The characteristic speech of the Merchant's Tale is monologue; of the Miller's Tale monologue or brief, rapid dialogue; and of the Reeve's Tale flat, proverbial statements or inarticulate noises. In contrast, the intricate dialogue between monk and wife in the Shipman's Tale, suggesting a complex modern business deal, perfectly defines the rich, clever, vicious world of the fabliau.

After she comes upon the monk in the garden, it is the wife, whose verbal aggression is markedly different from the passivity of the women of the first two fabliaux, who first begins the central dialogue: "What eyleth yow so rathe for to ryse?" (VII.99). For all its apparent innocence, the question is actually quite personal, indirectly concerns the bedroom, and hints that the monk may have a problem that she can solve. The monk responds in kind to this sexual innuendo by suggesting that the wife is pale because her husband has "yow laboured sith the nyght bigan" (VII.108). Although the statement causes the monk to blush, apparently at his own audacity (VII.111), the wife is in no way abashed. She quickly goes on to indicate her receptivity to such suggestions by complaining that no wife in France gets less enjoyment from such "sory pley" (VII.117), adding melodramatically that, because she has no one to tell her troubles to, she is thinking of doing away with herself. The wife also takes the initiative in beginning the dialogue again after the ambiguous kiss at line VII.141 and is the first to move from formal to more personal address: "'My deere love,' quod she, 'O my daun John'" (VII.158).

Despite the wife's aggression and occasional extravagances, the most surprising quality of this dialogue, as with speech in the entire tale, is how carefully appearances are maintained by both parties. After the wife's threat of suicide, the monk suggests that he may be able to "conseille or helpe" and solemnly swears that all she says will be kept secret (VII.128–33). Although the form of the words indicates a concerned friend, even a religious adviser (his vow of secrecy suggests the seal of the confessional), the effect of the monk's words is to signal the wife that he too desires a deep intimacy. Her response is quite as respectable. She swears that she will also keep his secrets (though her motive obviously cannot be religious), not because of "cosynage" or "alliance" but from "love and affiance" (VII.139–40). It is not the words themselves, which might elsewhere have an innocent interpretation, but rather the context that reveals the wife's real intent. Although desire for an amorous relationship has been indicated by both parties, no explicit statement has been made, and the "mayde child," who apparently is a witness to the entire exchange (VII.95–97), would have no reasons for suspicion, as she would if witnessing the initial dialogue between the lovers in the *Miller's Tale.*

The polite shamelessness of the dealings between monk and wife is summed up by the kiss they share in the middle of the dialogue (VII.141). There is nothing necessarily wicked in such a greeting between cousins (it might be only an example of the gracious, courtly manners all the characters in the tale like to exhibit), but in this context it is clearly a hint of further exchanges to come. The delicacy with which wife and monk speak to each other is unparalleled in Chaucer's other fabliaux. The lovers in the *Miller's Tale* and the *Merchant's Tale* also use deceptive speech, but only to fool the husband and not each other, whereas the *Reeve's Tale* contains no preliminary wooing words at all, just action. Nicholas's initial words to Alisoun may be more courteous than his hands, but his ultimate purpose is expressed clearly enough: "Lemman, love me al atones, / Or I wol dyen" (I.3280–81). The carefully calculated indirection of the dialogue between the lovers in the *Shipman's Tale* is a distinguishing mark of its unique poet.

The skill of the poet with this kind of speech is seen most clearly in the longest single utterance of the central dialogue (VII.158–94). The wife, encouraged by the monk's surprising claim that the merchant is not really his cousin, denigrates her husband while claiming not to and finally comes to the point of the whole scene—her request for one hundred franks. Despite its length, the speech is highly dramatic and never becomes just a formal monologue: the wife's voice is clearly heard throughout, as when she addresses the monk directly (VII.169), even urgently ("Daun John, I seye, lene me thise hundred frankes" [VII.187]), and when she concludes with an extravagant oath (VII.193–94). The cleverness of the speech lies in the way it stretches the tension between ostensible propriety and ignoble intent to the limit. Although the wife insists it would not be fitting to reveal the "privetee" of her marital relationship (VII.163–65), she has already said that the merchant is the worst man who ever lived (VII.161–62), and will add only this: he is worth less than a fly, acts niggardly, and, by implication, is incompetent in bed (VII.170–77). Not only are these terrible things for a wife to say about her husband, but the rest of the story suggests that none of them is true.

The height of the wife's hypocrisy is her insistence that she wants the franks to uphold her husband's "honour" (VII.179).[34] In essence, she claims that it is only to avoid "sclaundre or vileynye" (VII.183), which would result from not paying the dress bill, that she is willing to commit adultery with the monk for money. Of course, the truth of what she is proposing is never so crudely stated. All she does is ask the monk for a loan and conscientiously promise to pay it back "at a certeyn day" by doing "what plesance and service / That I may doon, right as yow list devise" (VII.187–92).

The carefully disguised wickedness of the wife's plan is brilliantly carried off, and the end of the long dialogue is equally skillful. The monk suavely expresses his "routhe" (VII.197) and vows to deliver the wife from her "care" when her husband is away (VII.200). Only now do we see the first and only physical act of seduction as the monk promises the wife one hundred franks and then catches "hire by the flankes, / And hire embraceth harde, and kiste hire ofte" (VII.202–3). The frankes/flankes rhyme is reminiscent of the queynte/queynte rhyme in the Miller's Tale, yet it is significant that the rhyme in the Shipman's Tale, in addition to being more commercial, occurs only at the end of the wooing scene when all is settled. Although the monk's embraces might alarm the young maid if she is still present, the mood of strong sexual passion is quickly undercut by the last speech in the dialogue in which the monk sends the wife away because of another physical appetite—it is past the time for them to dine (VII.204–6). The monk concludes this amazing dialogue with wonderful impudence: "Gooth now, and beeth as trewe as I shal be" (VII.207). These are noble words to end such sleazy dealings; for just as honor was only a convenient word with which the wife justified her dishonor, so the monk is true only to himself.

The Doubleness of Language

The hypocritical dialogue between monk and wife is one part of the deliberate use of imprecise language throughout the tale.[35] In direct contrast to the first two fabliaux, and especially the *Reeve's Tale*, the *Shipman's Tale* contains almost no purely sexual or vulgar word, but its ostensibly proper surface conceals a pervasive verbal doubleness. Words in the *Shipman's Tale* shift their meanings with disconcerting ease, and all is expressed by insinuation and indirection. The ugliness of the characters' actions is only hinted at by what they say, just as the speculative danger of the merchant's deals is concealed by a show of calm confidence (VII.230–34). Nicholson notes the "many euphemisms" in this poem, a sharp difference from the relative frankness of Chaucer's first two fabliaux.[36]

The poet's consistent use of calculatingly imprecise language begins with a sly narrative voice, which is more involved than that in the *Miller's Tale*, without the animus of that in the *Reeve's Tale*. The direct comments of this voice occur most frequently at the beginning of the tale; after setting the three characters in their proper places (VII.85–94), it then withdraws to allow the all-important speeches to proceed without comment, as in a play. The first line and one-half of the *Shipman's Tale* reads much like the beginning of the *Miller's Tale* ("Whilom ther was dwellynge at Oxenford / A riche gnof "), but the sly accents of the narrator are heard in the second half of line two:

> A marchant whilom dwelled at Seint-Denys,
> That riche was, for which men helde hym wys.
> (VII.1–2)

Quietly, but unmistakably, we have been introduced to a central theme of the tale: the difference between appearance and reality. Just as the merchant's wealth may not necessarily betoken wisdom, so none of the characters will be exactly what he seems. A similar doubleness requiring alertness in the reader is then used to describe the wife:

> A wyf he hadde of excellent beautee;
> And compaignable and revelous was she.
> (VII.3–4)

On the surface, these lines might easily be read as conventional praise, except for the darker suggestion of the last term: *revelous*. Although this word often indicates nothing more than innocent fun (see "revelrye" in line I.4005 of the *Reeve's Tale*), it is also capable of less attractive connotations (see "revelour" in lines I.4371 and 4391 of the *Cook's Tale*). Once alerted, the reader may then wonder if the words *compaignable* and even *beautee* are also meant to reveal dishonorable things about the wife's character, a suspicion that the tale soon proves to be justified.

The subsequent adulterous relationship between wife and monk is foreshadowed by a similar technique. The narrator says that many come to the merchant's house because of its owner's largess, "and for his wyf was fair" (VII.22). Already this common and generally positive adjective (*fair*) seems, in association with what we have learned of her before, to suggest someone other than an ideal wife, and our doubts are increased when similar terms are used to describe the monk. He also is fair, and more: "a fair man *and a boold*" (VII.25, my emphasis). Here as elsewhere the poet makes no direct accusation, but enough unmonkly qualities are implied to make the reader take a careful look at the rest of the passage. The insistence on the monk's youth and the information that he "was so fair of face" now seem to stand out as especially meaningful, and we may well wonder just how "famulier" a "freend" he will turn out to be (VII.26–32).

A final example of deliberate imprecision in language by the narrative voice occurs when the monk is described walking early one morning in the garden:

> . . . And hath his thynges seyd ful curteisly.
> This goode wyf cam walkynge pryvely
> Into the gardyn, there he walketh softe,
> And hym saleweth, as she hath doon ofte.
> (VII.91–94)

As always in this tale, the surface proprieties are maintained, but the words that end each of the first three quoted lines must raise suspicions in the reader and demand interpretation. What does it mean that the monk is saying the Divine Office (his "thynges") "curteisly"? It certainly might indicate something other than a fully devout attitude. Similarly, what is the poet trying to tell us by noting that the "goode" wife is walking "pryvely" and the monk "softe"? No direct accusations are made and no conclusive evidence is offered, but the implications of unseemly or even immoral intent are strong and prepare us for the seduction dialogue to come.

Because so much of the *Shipman's Tale* is dialogue, its most frequent perversions and evasions of language are to be found in the words of the characters themselves. We have already analyzed examples of such doubleness in the seduction dialogue between monk and wife, and all that need be added here are two later and especially striking examples of the monk's concealed impudence. In asking to borrow the one hundred franks from his "cousin," which he then uses to cuckold the lender, the monk explains that it is for "certein beestes that I moste beye" (VII.272). It is hard to imagine how a statement could appear more innocuous on the surface while being, in fact, more insulting to both wife and husband. Finally, after he has both had sex with the wife and then caused her potential trouble by telling the merchant he has repaid the borrowed money to her, the monk's last words in the tale are "Grete wel oure dame, myn owene nece sweete, / And fare wel, deere cosyn, til we meete!" (VII.363–64). Once again the form is perfectly polite (the sentiments of a friendly relative), but, after all that has happened, the greeting conceals a stunning combination of the shameless and the nasty.

The poet's double use of language culminates in the widely recognized punning on *tail* in the wife's long final speech, which equates sex and money.[37] A similar play on the word *cousin* (to cheat as well as the family relationship) has also been claimed.[38] The puns of the *Shipman's Tale* are more central to its art than those scattered through the *Miller's Tale*. Instead of being an incidental, if witty, aspect of the comedy as in the first fabliau, they are part of a larger pattern of doublespeak, in which the dishonorable and disgusting occur without being directly named. Charles Owen notes that the respectability of the tale is maintained to the very end, for, unlike most fabliaux, the *Shipman's Tale* does not conclude with any sort of "violent or decisive exposure."[39] The climax of the *Shipman's Tale* is purely verbal (the dialogue between husband and wife), and leaves us with an additional possible pun when the husband forgives his wife but begs her not to be so "large" in the future: "Keep bet my good, this yeve I thee in charge" (VII.432). The reader cannot be sure how much the husband has guessed of his wife's conduct and thus does not know if "good" is a final reference to both sex and money.

Thematic Doubleness

The deliberate imprecision of language in the *Shipman's Tale*, seen especially in its puns and the astonishing gap between what the characters say and what they mean, leads the reader to the thematic doubleness at the heart of the tale. Nothing is quite what it seems to be in the *Shipman's Tale* and there is great confusion in roles. The merchant, shut up in his counting house "cell" and meditating on the insecurity of the world, appears more cloistered than the outriding, gift-giving monk, just as the wife and monk prove themselves better at business than the merchant.[40] Other reversals occur: the woman is the aggressor in the garden scene, and the "routhe" (VII.197) offered her by the monk is more properly a female gift.[41] Family and social norms are overturned when the wife betrays her

marriage with one the merchant had considered both a friend and relation. She then turns sexual relations with her husband into a purely commercial transaction, so that her prostitution with the monk becomes the
model for her marriage. The climactic confusion in the tale is the equa-
tion of sex and money: the wife sells her body for one hundred franks,
and the merchant is virile only after his business transactions have gone
well. The wife's play on the word *wedde* ("Ye shal my joly body have to
wedde" [VII.423]) is in keeping with the other puns of her last speech: it
shows that the sacrament of marriage has become just another business
contract, another money-making opportunity.

By exploiting the treacherous ambiguities of seemingly proper language, the *Shipman's Tale* puts the reader on his guard and trains him in
intellectual and moral judgment. Neither the narrative voice nor any of
the characters can ever be fully trusted, and the reader must continually
weigh the difference between appearance and reality. Certainly we enjoy
the tale as a fabliau and delight in its cleverness and wit, but the constant
and revealing imprecision of language also suggests a more literary lesson: the need to attend well to words and to interpret them carefully.
Not to do so is to risk being deceived like the merchant.

To many critics, the *Shipman's Tale* seems nothing more than a delightful
and pleasant comedy. Nevill Coghill groups the *Shipman's Tale* with others
that exist "in a world of comedy and happy endings" and claims that
together they create "a golden world."[42] Copland insists that the reader's
response is not meant to be disapproval because the tale is a "holiday,"
and Ruggiers argues that through all the irony of the work there shines
"something quite genial, warm, and amiable."[43] Presumably these critics,
and others like them, are responding primarily to the pleasant surface of
the tale with its absence of crudeness and pain. But the particular art of
the *Shipman's Tale* demands more. Throughout, the reader is shown how
difficult it is to know what to believe. Are the monk and merchant really
cousins? Has the monk always loved the wife or does he just say he has
to gain an advantage? Does the wife have genuine complaints against her
husband or is she only pretending to have? How much does the merchant know or guess about his wife's infidelity? The gap between reality
and appearance, which is merely a comic device in other fabliaux, is here
a key to deeper questions that lie beneath the tale's surface attractiveness.

Christian significance has been claimed for all Chaucer's fabliaux, but
the number and seriousness of such elements in the *Shipman's Tale* are far
greater than in the first two examples of the genre.[44] Robert Kaske, for
one, has argued that echoes of the *Canticum Canticorum* in the *Miller's Tale*
give it a "moral edge."[45] Some passages in that tale seem to support such
an approach, most obviously the way its narrator ends his description of
the sexual melody between Nicholas and Alisoun with reference to an-

other kind of music: "Til that the belle of laudes gan to rynge, / And freres in the chauncel gonne synge" (I.3655–56). But suggestive as such hints may be, they occur only infrequently in the first two fabliaux and inevitably seem more significant to modern readers unaccustomed to casual references to religion as part of normal life. The *Shipman's Tale*, however, is quite different. Christian duties and ideals are explicitly and continually shown to be abused, while their empty forms are retained—a gap between surface and substance that the literary style of the tale has trained us to recognize. The wife swears on God and the breviary that she will not betray the monk's secrets (VII.135), makes an astonishingly blasphemous rhyme when she insists that wives want husbands "fressh abedde. / But by that ilke Lord that for us bledde . . ." (VII.177–78), and asks that "God take on me vengeance" (VII.193) if she does not do pleasance and service to the monk—thus invoking the justice of God to sanction the breaking of her marriage vows. Whereas the physical world of the *Shipman's Tale* is more refined and delicate than that in either the *Miller's Tale* or the *Reeve's Tale*, the moral world is much more vicious because money dominates so completely and all is for sale.

Appropriately enough in this tale of doubleness and reversals, the worst abuser of Christianity is the monk. The clerks in the first two fabliaux are certainly not devout, but none holds such a responsible position as the outrider Daun John, and none so constantly and flagrantly perverts his profession. The monk apparently subverts the seal of the confessional by swearing on his breviary to keep the wife's secrets (VII.128–33), just as he somewhat later swears "on my professioun" (VII.155) that he loves the wife above all other women. He also calls on God and Saint Augustine to guide the merchant on the ride that will leave the coast clear for cuckolding (VII.259), commits his adultery on a Sunday (VII.307), and arrives with not only his beard but also his symbol of office, the tonsure, "al fressh and newe yshave" (VII.309).[46] The fabliau genre is based on trickery and deceit, but the monk's wickedness is more vicious and extensive than anything in either the *Miller's Tale* or the *Reeve's Tale*: the monk not only betrays his Christian profession, but also his host, his friend, his cousin, his benefactor, and his lover.

In Boccaccio's analogue to the *Shipman's Tale* in the *Decameron* (the first story of the eighth day), the character who corresponds to Chaucer's monk is outraged when he learns that the woman he loves is prepared to offer herself for money. Such disgust at shameless behavior is the kind of healthy response completely missing from Chaucer's tale, in which crimes are committed and accepted by all with politeness. Any indignation must be supplied by the reader. The contrast with the artistry of the *Prioress's Tale*, the tale which immediately follows the *Shipman's Tale*, is instructive here and reveals another aspect of the literary variety of the

Canterbury Tales. If the *Prioress's Tale* is too sentimentally childish, as we shall see, the *Shipman's Tale* is too cold-bloodedly adult. Together, they provide more evidence of Chaucer's art of contrast. The special achievement of the *Shipman's Tale* is certainly apparent when it is compared with Chaucer's other fabliaux, as we have just done, but much would also be learned if it were compared in detail with the religious tale that comes immediately after. Once again we must acknowledge that criticism cannot easily keep up with the full complexity of Chaucer's drama of style.

One important line of development from the *Miller's Tale* to the *Shipman's Tale* is now apparent: each successive poet, in addition to providing entertainment, raises more serious questions about the values implicit in any fabliau. The *Miller's Tale* is almost totally delightful, but the *Reeve's Tale* begins to expose the limits of the physical appetites celebrated by the genre. It is one thing for a yeoman or lord to bed the frisky Alisoun, but quite another to do the same with the lumpish daughter of Symkyn or with his drunken, smelly wife. The *Shipman's Tale* offers an even more frightening picture: a world that pays lip service to love, friendship, and faith, but is actually devoid of any concern except material self-interest. So cold and heartless is the "civilized" ending of the tale that even the brute animality of the *Reeve's Tale* would be a welcome relief. But the most vicious world and most serious use of the art of the fabliau is still to come in the *Merchant's Tale*, whose complex poet shows just how horrible a happy ending can be.

The Merchant's Tale

I have not left the *Merchant's Tale* until last because that is necessarily its order in the *Canterbury Tales.* Although we can only guess at what the final arrangement of the tales would have been, the *Merchant's Tale* regularly comes before the *Shipman's Tale* in the extant manuscripts. Nevertheless, the *Merchant's Tale* appropriately ends our discussion of the fabliaux because it is the most complex and powerful of Chaucer's experiments in the genre and is generally regarded as one of his greatest works.

Chaucer's drama of style is so complex in the *Canterbury Tales* that the story of January and May might profitably be compared with several other tales (with its austere predecessor, the *Clerk's Tale*, for example, with the romances, or with the equally varied though more benign *Nun's Priest's Tale*). Nevertheless, the *Merchant's Tale* belongs in this chapter because its essential plot is that of a fabliau, though that plot has been adorned with an unprecedented variety of additions drawn from a wide range of genres. The basic story is exactly that of Chaucer's other fabliaux—a husband is cuckolded by a younger man whom he himself has introduced into the household—and the tale contains other familiar elements. It is like the Miller's Tale in its emphasis on the difference in age between husband and wife and in its many allusions, like the Reeve's Tale in its often nasty narrative tone and disgust with the physical, and like the Shipman's Tale in its rich, foreign setting and intricate use of speech; but these echoes of Chaucer's other comic tales are here transformed into something more verbally complex and thematically profound. The virtuosity of this poet in many different styles—from noble rhetorical flourish to gross physical description—is matched only by the moral ferocity with which he employs his literary flair. Christian values only hinted at in the earlier fabliaux dominate the Merchant's Tale, as materials previously used primarily for comedy now expose sin and corruption. The Merchant's Tale is both truly a fabliau and a great deal more.

As noted in my first chapter, the Merchant's Tale has been the subject of a spirited debate between dramatic and nondramatic critics. Put most briefly, dramatic critics see the tale as a dark work reflecting its teller's disillusionment with marriage and life, while nondramatic critics, reading the tale apart from the teller whom they insist it does not much fit, see it as essentially comic and merry—nothing more than good fabliau fun.[47] I suggest a synthesis of these positions that recognizes the seriousness of the tale, but locates it in the poetry itself rather than in the imagined personality of the Merchant. Nondramatic critics are right to ignore the shadowy, inconsistent teller—not because the Merchant's Tale is merely another amusing fabliau, as they claim, but because the painful bitterness in the poem, so well described by dramatic critics, is trivialized by being attributed only to the domestic frustrations of a disappointed husband. The harrowing virtuosity of the tale is instead the product of Chaucer's most demanding poet, whose unremitting excoriation of wickedness goes so far beyond the usual heartlessness of the fabliau that the reader must struggle to avoid being overwhelmed by its bitter pessimism. In Helen Corsa's phrase, the Merchant's Tale is "an ugly tale brilliantly told," and the reader is challenged as much by its ugliness as by its brilliance.[48] Yet for all its malignancy, the Merchant's Tale contains passages of genuine beauty and idealism, which must also be part of any full interpretation of the tale. The art of the Merchant's Tale not only differs in essential ways from that of Chaucer's other fabliaux, it is also in fundamental and valuable conflict with itself.

The stylistic variety and moral intensity that distinguish the Merchant's Tale are present from its opening lines:

Whilom ther was dwellynge in Lumbardye
A worthy knyght, that born was of Pavye,
In which he lyved in greet prosperitee;

And sixty yeer a wyflees man was hee,
And folwed ay his bodily delyt
On wommen, ther as was his appetyt,
As doon thise fooles that been seculeer.
(IV.1245–51)

The first three lines are blandly attractive and read more like the beginning of a romance than a fabliau. The "worthy" foreign knight living in
"greet prosperitee" is grander than the meaner characters of the first two
fabliaux or the explicitly commercial figures of the *Shipman's Tale*. As so
often with this tale, however, the attractive is a foil for the sordid. Thus
in the fifth line the poet abruptly confronts the reader with January's
"bodily delyt" practiced "on wommen." The run-on line not only puts
special emphasis on the last phrase, making the knight's "appetyt" seem
especially promiscuous; it also interrupts the smooth rhythm of the
opening two couplets. By the last line of the passage, a distinct narrative
voice calling for moral judgment ("thise fooles") has clearly announced
itself. Within the first seven lines of the tale, then, the potentially noble
world of knighthood is reduced to be the low fabliau world of gross
physical appetite—foreshadowing many other contrasts to come.

Words, Allusion, and Symbol

Although the *Merchant's Tale* has greater literary range and is more explicitly moralistic than Chaucer's other works in the genre, many of its
effects are achieved through transforming fabliau techniques rather than
abandoning them. A common device in Chaucer's other fabliaux is the
introduction of an apparently innocent but actually loaded word or
phrase, whose full significance becomes clear only later in the plot: for
instance, the information that Absolon is "somdeel squaymous / Of
fartyng" (I.3337–38) or the casual mention of a child in cradle when
Symkyn's family is described in the *Reeve's Tale*. Similar verbal time bombs
in the *Merchant's Tale* go beyond comedy to become vehicles for moral
exposure. Well-known examples include January's assertion that the un-
married life is not worth a "bene" (IV.1263)—the exact image May will
use to denigrate his lovemaking on their wedding night (IV.1854)—and
his belief that a young wife can be molded like "warm wex" (IV.1430)—
the same material with which she makes a key that allows Damyan into
the garden (IV.2117). When the full implications of these charged words
are finally revealed, the reader laughs as in the other fabliaux, but he is
also being instructed about the extent of January's vain and foolish ignorance. A similarly didactic adaptation of fabliau wordplay is the epithet
fresshe for May. In the *Miller's Tale*, the repeated label of *hende* for Nicholas

at first seems merely conventional, but then its literal meanings "good with one's hands" and "at hand" emerge with comic effect.[49] The device is precisely reversed in the *Merchant's Tale*; we see how inaccurate the epithet is. As her behavior becomes more and more shameless, the fourteen occurrences of *fresshe* to describe May produce an increasingly sharp indictment.[50]

The extraordinary profusion of learned allusions in the *Merchant's Tale*—what Coghill calls the poem's "heap of learning" and Sedgewick its "dense mosaic of references, allusions, quotations"—is unmatched in the *Reeve's Tale* and the *Shipman's Tale*, which have virtually none, and even in the *Miller's Tale*, whose several are drawn from a narrow slice of popular culture.[51] The many allusions in the *Merchant's Tale* define its unique kind of poetry while introducing new standards of judgment. By linking January with the Bridegroom in the *Canticum Canticorum* (IV.2138–48) or May and Damyan with Pyramus and Thisbe (IV.2128), the poet forces us to recognize how far these characters and their values are from their biblical and classical models in order to deepen his criticism, rather like the ironic use of allusion in T. S. Eliot's *Waste Land* to mark the decline of the modern world from its nobler past. Apparently similar juxtapositions in the *Miller's Tale* (references to the Flood or courtly love conventions, for example) exploit the difference between the ideal and real for purely comic purposes; in the more ambitious *Merchant's Tale*, the result is moral condemnation.[52]

The *Merchant's Tale* further transforms its genre by developing images that occur naturally in the fabliau plot into powerful thematic symbols. The word *blind*, for example, first appears as no more than a proverbial tag about love ("love is blynd alday" [IV.1598]), but in its eight subsequent occurrences (the most in any of the Canterbury tales), we discover that the term not only applies to January's loss of physical sight, which is essential to the fabliau denouement, but also perfectly defines his spiritual condition. The central image of this kind is January's garden. The word *garden* is used eleven times within 300 lines (IV.2029–2321), by far the greatest number of appearances in any Canterbury tale, and the poet's art makes sure that we see the setting, unlike its counterpart in the *Shipman's Tale*, as more than just an appropriate meeting place for lovers. January's specially built enclosure is the necessary locale for the climax of the fabliau plot, but it is also loaded with a great variety of literary, mythological, and courtly associations that must be sorted out and interpreted by the reader. In his initial description, the poet refers to the *Roman de la Rose* (IV.2032), Priapus (IV.2034), and Pluto and Proserpina (IV.2038–39), and he later links the garden with Ovid's story of Pyramus and Thisbe (IV.2125–28). Of even more significance are the explicitly Christian allusions. January invites May into the garden with words that echo the

Canticum Canticorum (IV.2138–48), and echoes of the Fall, which have been developed throughout the tale, are now reinforced by specific images like tree (IV.2210, 2257, 2360, 2374, and 2411) and fruyt (IV.2211 and 2336) to reveal that the garden—with its married couple, fruit desired by a woman, and tempter in the tree—is not a paradise of delights but the appropriate stage for a reenactment of the first biblical drama.[53] We need not here unravel and explicate all the many references associated with January's garden; it is enough for our purposes to recognize that the poet gives the conventional setting a thematic depth unimagined in any of Chaucer's other fabliaux.

The Complexity of Moral Speech

Direct speech in the Merchant's Tale reveals more about the way the poet uses literary variety to explore moral questions. Chaucer's other fabliaux tend to rely on one characteristic mode of speech—quick, witty exchanges in the Miller's Tale; flat, often inarticulate utterance in the Reeve's Tale; and subtle, ostensibly proper dialogue at length in the Shipman's Tale. Although monologue can be considered its own special form, speech in the Merchant's Tale is restricted to no single pattern, but ranges from coarse obscenity to allegorical debate, from intimate sexual musings to lively argument between classical gods. Even though the characters of the Merchant's Tale parallel those in other fabliaux, the greater complexity of speech in the tale forces us to judge them by stricter standards.

The first two speeches given May (the only times we hear her before the dialogue at the end) condemn her not only because they contradict one another, but also because they juxtapose the fabliau world to nobler values. Her first speech finds May talking to herself after Damyan has declared his love:

> "Certeyn," thoghte she, "whom that this thyng displese,
> I rekke noght, for heere I hym assure
> To love hym best of any creature,
> Though he namoore hadde than his sherte."
> (IV.1982–85)

Although this is the most explicitly sexual talk we have yet heard from a woman in Chaucer's fabliaux, the sentiments are perfectly appropriate to the genre. The real shock is that the willful vulgarity of May's first words flatly contradict the image of young virtuous beauty we have been shown through January's eyes, a contrast the poet further emphasizes by the ironic courtly statement in the following line: "Lo, pitee renneth soone in gentil herte!" (IV.1986).

May's second speech is as apparently noble as the first was crude, but the moral effect is even worse. In the garden, she responds weepingly in the accents of a good wife to January's pitiful demand that she be true to him: "'I have,' quod she, 'a soule for to kepe / As wel as ye, and also myn honour ...'" (IV.2188–89). Her touching claims of innocence, which continue in an extended monologue worthy of a Griselda or a Custance, are impossible for the reader who has heard her private words to believe, and their noble sentiments are further subverted by the shameless body language she addresses to her waiting lover (IV.2207–16). In contrast to her first speech, now her actions are appropriate to a fabliau, while her speech is piously virtuous. The gap between fair words and foul deeds, which was so comic when practiced by Nicholas on Alisoun in the *Miller's Tale*, has become thoroughly nasty and corrupt.

Speech in the *Merchant's Tale* is not primarily witty or used to advance the plot, as in Chaucer's other fabliaux; instead, it operates more deeply to expose the inner corruption of its characters.[54] As we might expect, January is the character we hear speak most frequently. His many kinds of utterance include formal address (IV.1400–68), ill-tempered bullying (IV.1566–71), apparently gracious praise of another (IV.1907–15), love talk that is both boastful and self-pitying (IV.1828–41 and 2160–84), and squeals of outrage when his sight suddenly returns (IV.2366ff.). Perhaps the most significant speech in the tale is the series of private musings that float through January's mind, especially concerning May. January's interior monologue begins with the very first speech (IV.1263–65) and is found throughout the tale, especially in the long opening encomium, which, even if filtered through the narrator's scorn, clearly represents the old knight's foolish expectations of marriage. Such personal soliloquy, which takes us into January's very soul, is more ambitious morally than speech in any of the other fabliaux and reveals the full extent of the knight's foolish fantasies.

The unrelenting exposure of sin and error through speech in the *Merchant's Tale* is often conducted in explicitly Christian terms. January's long public monologue announcing his intention to wed, in which he characteristically asks for assent rather than real advice, carefully spells out the proper reasons given by the Church for marriage—to produce children, avoid lechery, pay the debt of the body, or live together in chastity (IV.1441–55). But after defining the good, the old knight deliberately spurns it by boasting, with ironic thanksgiving to God, that he is still sexually active and that his motives are far from Christian: "But sires, by youre leve, that am nat I. / For, God be thanked! I dar make avaunt ..." (IV.1456–57).[55] Deception is a common motive for speech in the fabliau, but such blatant self-deception is something altogether more serious. The *Merchant's Tale* shows us a conventional fabliau character from the inside and thus forces us to treat him as a genuine moral being. Christian doctrine declares that no one is guilty of sin unless he is fully conscious of his action, and speech in the Merchant's Tale seems often designed to fulfill this condition. If the characters, and especially January, are morally blind, it is a blindness they have chosen with their eyes wide open, as they themselves assure us.

Inner Characterization and January's Wooing

The Merchant's Tale is a fabliau with the victim at the center of the narration. Although January is a familiar comic type, the senex amans, the Merchant-poet analyzes his character in unprecedented depth and, as we have just seen, explicitly judges him by moral standards only implicit, if present at all, in Chaucer's other fabliaux. In the three other examples of the genre in the Canterbury Tales, the deceived husband is always a subordinate figure, but the focus in the Merchant's Tale is squarely on the Lombard knight. In contrast to the series of exterior portraits that were such a rich addition to the genre in Chaucer's first two fabliaux, the Merchant's Tale contains what might be called inner characterization. As happens to no one else in all of Chaucer's fabliaux, the mind and soul of January are repeatedly explored to reveal the full horror of his self-deluding blindness—from the knight's opening praises of the joys of marriage to his final fantasy in the garden when he refuses to accept the evidence of his own eyes and instead believes what he wishes were true: "This Januarie, who is glad but he?" (IV.2412).[56]

The inner characterization of January is most prominent during his extended courting of May, which, as with comparable wooing scenes in Chaucer's other fabliaux, well defines the special artistry of the work. The poet takes the familiar fabliau situation in which an old man wishes to marry a young wife and finds there, in addition to comedy, further opportunities for the psychological and moral analysis of his central figure. In the Miller's Tale a similar union is the given that begins the comedy, but the Merchant's Tale carefully traces every detail of January's marriage from his first plans to the wedding night itself. Unlike the Shipman's Tale, however, which also makes wooing the center of its story, the Merchant's Tale is not so much interested in the outward forms of courtship as in the inner working of January's mind and will. Indeed, the poet presents the wooing in two, characteristically contrasting ways: first a long account of January's mental wooing and then a briefer view of the physical act itself. As so often in this tale, an imagined heaven is juxtaposed to a hellish reality.

January's mental wooing begins during the long opening encomium, which to some degree reflects his foolish views on the unalloyed joys of marriage, and continues as he indulgently parades the potential candidates through his imagination:

Heigh fantasye and curious bisynesse
Fro day to day gan in the soule impresse
Of Januarie aboute his mariage.
Many fair shap and many a fair visage
Ther passeth thurgh his herte nyght by nyght,
As whoso tooke a mirour, polisshed bryght,
And sette it in a commune market-place,
Thanne sholde he se ful many a figure pace
By his mirour; and in the same wyse
Gan Januarie inwith his thoght devyse
Of maydens whiche that dwelten hym bisyde.
He wiste nat wher that he myghte abyde.
(IV.1577–88)

Although such lust of the mind is not unprecedented in Chaucer's other fabliaux, the style and perspective of this passage are totally original. In none of the other comic tales are actual events ignored so completely in order that we might instead enter deeply into a character ("inwith his thoght") and begin to understand why he acts as he does. In addition to exploring January's most private thoughts, these lines also contain a subtle but clear level of moral criticism. The word "fantasye," which also occurs later in a similar interior description of January's final choice of May (IV.1610), suggests the delusion, willfulness, and near auto-eroticism of the knight's passion, just as the words "mirour" and "market-place" point to his self-absorption and cupidity.

The moral intensity of the poet's inner characterization of January continues after the old knight has decided on the one whom he will marry and takes to his bed to imagine her:

He purtreyed in his herte and in his thoght
Hir fresshe beautee and hir age tendre,
Hir myddel smal, hire armes longe and sklendre,
Hir wise governaunce, hir gentillesse,
Hir wommanly berynge, and hire sadnesse.
(IV.1600–1604)

Although, as Mary Schroeder shrewdly notes, this is the only physical account of May in the entire tale, we do not really see the woman herself, but instead the foolish delusions of January.[57] The poet has refashioned the techniques of exterior description found in the Miller's Tale and the Reeve's Tale to support his deeper, more psychological portrait. The characterization of January by means of his mental wooing of May continues right up to the wedding night as the new husband, "ravysshed in a traunce" (IV.1750), imagines the sexual vigor he will soon practice on

May: "Now wolde God ye myghte wel endure / Al my corage, it is so sharp and keene!" (IV.1758–59).

January can assert such illusions of potency only so long as his passion remains in the imagination, however. The reality behind his fantasies is therefore brutally exposed during the second, more physical part of the wooing episode, in which the poet first shows us the couple in bed together. We now learn that the knight's "corage" requires aphrodisiacs (IV.1807–12), and that he who had rejected "old boef" for "tendre veel" (IV.1420) has himself an unpleasant beard "lyk to the skyn of houndfyssh, sharp as brere" (IV.1824). In very different and more graphic poetry than that used to describe his mental wooing, January is revealed as an old, ugly, and apparently incompetent lover:

> He was al coltissh, ful of ragerye,
> And ful of jargon as a flekked pye.
> The slakke skyn aboute his nekke shaketh,
> Whil that he sang, so chaunteth he and craketh.
> But God woot what that May thoughte in hir herte,
> Whan she hym saugh up sittynge in his sherte,
> In his nyght-cappe, and with his nekke lene;
> She preyseth nat his pleyyng worth a bene.
> (IV.1847–54)

Neither the detailed physical description of this passage nor the mention of May's thoughts means that the poet has abandoned his inner characterization of January. In contrast to the comic snapshots of sexuality in Chaucer's other fabliaux, the pitiless account of January's slack skin and lean neck as he crows over his sorry performance is like a moral X-ray that forces our condemnation. As in other explicit accounts of the horrors of the body found in Middle English religious works like Hali Meidenhad or Piers Plowman, to see appetite this unsparingly is to strip it of all glamour and appeal. Moreover, the sudden, brief switch to May's perspective at the end of the quoted lines once again tells us less about her than about January. As he sings merrily away, the old knight is completely deluded about his appearance and appeal to May. In addition to being a spiritual renegade, January is now also revealed as a practical fool because, despite the vigor of his amorous imagination, when it comes to performance, he proves incompetent at the lechery for which he has sold his soul.

The Narrator

The stylistic virtuosity and moral ferocity of the Merchant's Tale find their fullest expression in its complex and endlessly manipulative narrative voice. Once again I want to distinguish between the overarching "poet" of the tale and the more limited "narrative voice" that directly addresses the reader, but the insinuating pervasiveness of the latter in the *Merchant's Tale* makes such an absolute division difficult to maintain. The voice is busier, more brilliant and obtrusive, and nastier than its counterpart in any of Chaucer's other fabliaux. Charles Muscatine properly compares it with the narrator in the *Reeve's Tale*, noting that both are "prominent and unsympathetic," and yet the difference between these two voices is even more significant.[58] In contrast to the *Reeve*-narrator's single weapon of sarcasm, the *Merchant*-narrator employs a range of strategies that attack from every angle. Chaucer has once again taken a device from another fabliau and extended it for his more complex purposes in the *Merchant's Tale*.

The voice that first announces itself, as we have seen, in the seventh line of the tale never allows the action to unfold unaided, as generally happens in Chaucer's other fabliaux, but incessantly manipulates the reader throughout the tale.[59] Mocking and subverting everyone and everything, its principal target is January, whose fantasies about marriage and whose faith in his own judgment and powers are ridiculed throughout. An early effect of such a narrative style is to poison the long opening encomium on marriage (IV.1267–1392).[60] Although the ostensibly optimistic sentiments of the encomium must ultimately derive from January's inner soliloquies, they are narrated through a filter of scorn to emphasize the knight's fatuity ("How myghte a man han any adversitee / That hath a wyf?" [IV.1338–39]), ignorance (citing Eve, Rebekka, Judith, Abigail, and Esther as women helpful to men), and self-contradiction—one passage begins with a wistful fantasy of complete male control ("She seith nat ones 'nay,' whan he seith 'ye'" [IV.1345]) only to end in abject submission ("Do alwey so as wommen wol thee rede" [IV.1361]). The narrative voice is particularly active during January's wedding, which ends with the mock heroic insistence that the pen of Martianus Capella is too small to describe the "myrthe" when "tendre youthe hath wedded stoupyng age" (IV.1738–39).

Although the principal target of this style of narration is January, all the characters are reduced. An especially sly example is the impudent *occupatio* that concludes an account of Damyan's sudden passion for May on her wedding day:

> Namoore of hym at this tyme speke I,
> But there I lete hym wepe ynogh and pleyne,
> Til fresshe May wol rewen on his peyne.
>   (IV.1780–82)

The first two lines are conventional enough, but the third deliberately removes any suspense about Damyan's ultimate success and thus compromises January's "blissful" marriage before it is even consummated.

The liaison between May and Damyan, a sort of second courtship scene in the tale, might have been presented as comic, exciting, or even romantic, but several careful narrative intrusions ensure that it is instead disgusting. For instance, just before the two first meet, the narrative voice elaborately expresses concern for poor, "sely Damyan" because "fresshe" May will obviously reject his adulterous advances and, like a good wife, probably betray him to her husband (IV.1869–74). Of course, the lament is mock praise more insulting than direct criticism because, as we quickly see, May is only too eager to break her marriage vows. Space does not permit detailed analysis of the many other narrative tricks in this scene, except to mention the extraordinary manipulation of the story when May returns to her bedroom with Damyan's love letter (IV.1946–54). The actions that follow are unpleasant in themselves, but it is the particular way they are told that makes the effect as repulsive as it is. We are first shown January eagerly welcoming the embraces of his bride ("He taketh hire, and kisseth hire ful ofte"), but this quickly ends in limp anticlimax as the old knight rolls over and goes to sleep. The narrative then resorts to one of its leering euphemisms ("She feyned hire as that she moste gon / Ther as ye woot that every wight moot neede") to describe the singularly inappropriate place May chooses to read her love "bille," before brilliantly using a potentially attractive adverb ("softely") to produce a final effect of total disgust as May disposes of her letter: "She rente it al to cloutes atte laste, / And in the pryvee softely it caste."[61] Indeed, throughout the Merchant's Tale, the style of narration often seems to tear to pieces all that it touches and consign it to the privy.

Some of the nastiest effects of the special mode of narration are saved for the last scene in the tale. The description of May and Damyan's arboreal coupling in a tree is anything but romantic and brutally gives the lie to all their courtly posturing: "And sodeynly anon this Damyan / Gan pullen up the smok, and in he throng" (IV.2352–53). The direct narrative voice makes things even worse with a smarmy apology beforehand for being so direct ("Ladyes, I prey yow that ye be nat wrooth; / I kan nat glose, I am a rude man" [IV.2350–51]), whose insincerity is compounded by the claim not to "speke uncurteisly" after having just done so (IV.2363). To actions that are themselves appalling enough, such a style of narrative adds hypocrisy and a nasty prurience, both of which are missing from Chaucer's other fabliaux. Equally shocking, as Tatlock pointed out long ago, is the simile that compares January's cry when he sees what his wife is up to in the tree with a mother crying over her dead child.[62] The final lines of the tale, which show January's doting love conquering the evidence of his eyes and conclude with a cheery narrative farewell ("Now, goode men, I pray yow to be glad" [IV.2416]), produce a crueler effect than even the relish with which victims are counted up at the end of the *Miller's Tale* and the *Reeve's Tale.*

Morality and Judgment in the Merchant's Tale

Because the *Merchant's Tale* contains more explicitly moralistic elements than any of Chaucer's other fabliaux, its purpose would seem to be clear: an unrelenting exposure of spiritual corruption, especially in January, whose actions and motives are examined to a depth unprecedented in the genre. Leading the crusade is a pitiless narrative voice, whose constant and varied attacks transform the heartlessness that is central to the form into a more engaged and corrosive criticism. The narrative frequently pretends to the objectivity common in other fabliaux: for example, "Were it for hoolynesse or for dotage" (IV.1253), "But God woot what that May thoughte in hir herte" (IV.1851), or "How that he wroghte, I dar nat to yow telle; / Or wheither hire thoughte it paradys or helle" (IV.1963–64). But, of course, the answer to these pseudo questions is clear from their formulation—and it is never a generous one. The *Merchant's Tale* offers a consistently negative exemplum on the wages of sin and delusion that is more direct and powerful than the moral criticism occasionally implicit in Chaucer's other fabliaux. But this is still only part of what the tale has to tell us.

The lessons of the *Merchant's Tale* are as complex as its artistry. Although the flamboyant narrative style seems to offer moral certainty, it is anything but a reliable guide. For all its energy and dark brilliance, the narrative voice speaks in such a range of contradictory styles (from direct attack to mock praise and from coarse obscenity to overheated rhetorical set pieces) that we often have trouble getting our bearings and, while impressed, may also be overwhelmed and numbed.[63] The moral ferocity of the narrative is often too extreme. The danger is not, as it is with some other fabliaux, that the pleasures of the world are portrayed too attractively, but rather that the continual jeers at the foolish wickedness of human life may cause despair.

But darkness is not all in the *Merchant's Tale*. In addition to describing a world of depraved appetite and vain delusion far more horrible than anything in Chaucer's other fabliaux, the poet also offers a series of images that assert the possibility of love, beauty, and salvation. We have previously noted that the many references to classical and Christian figures in the *Merchant's Tale* expose the comparative pettiness of January and May. At the same time, there is another, positive side to such allusions: these evocations of the great and good counter the nastiness of the tale and offer hope. We are reminded that all women are not May and all men not January or Damyan; others have been saints and heroes who achieved true love and real faith.[64]

An even more complex effect is produced by three narrative set pieces that establish the time of a scene with great rhetorical skill: the coming of night (IV.1795–1801), the passing of several days (IV.1885–91), and the coming of morning (IV.2219–25). Read alone, each of these passages is an accomplished and attractive piece of poetry, and none more so than the first:

> Parfourned hath the sonne his ark diurne;
> No lenger may the body of hym sojurne
> On th'orisonte, as in that latitude.
> Night with his mantel, that is derk and rude,
> Gan oversprede the hemysperie aboute;
> For which departed is this lusty route
> Fro Januarie, with thank on every syde.
>   (IV.1795–1801)

In the context of the story, however, the lines are one more example of the poet's fierce attacks on his chief character. To give such a lovely introduction to January's pitiful haste to bed May emphasizes how far the *Merchant's Tale* is from a truly noble tale, like the *Knight's Tale* or even *Troilus and Criseyde*, in which such an elegant passage would be appropriate. But despite the clear narrative intent, the reader cannot entirely dismiss the inherent beauty of the poetry, which exists along with the mockery and serves to ameliorate it by demonstrating that evil and ugliness are not everything.

The *Merchant's Tale* contains more of the truly disgusting than Chaucer's other fabliaux, but also more that is potentially attractive and noble. Speech is frequently used in the poem to reveal the wickedness of January and May, as we have seen, but it is also capable of commending the good. Even though May's long speech in defense of her wifely virtue is delivered while she is arranging an assignation with Damyan (IV.2188–2206), it nevertheless expresses a powerful ideal of marital fidelity and moral responsibility completely foreign to the other three fabliaux—assuming that the reader responds to the meaning of the words themselves and not to the intent of the speaker.

As we would expect, even more of these mixtures of good and bad are found in the speeches of January. His frequent praises of the cleanliness and ease of marriage are undoubtedly meant selfishly, and yet the ideals themselves offer a model of compassion and service, but only if practiced by husbands as well as by wives.[65] The most striking appearance of the beautiful and true amidst the muck of the *Merchant's Tale* occurs in

January's long, and in itself quite lyrical, speech of love to May derived from the *Canticum Canticorum* (IV.2138–48). In context, the speech well deserves the narrator's sharp rebuke: "Swiche olde lewed wordes used he" (IV.2149). January is using holy words from the Bible that were believed to describe the love between Christ and his Church to gild his own nasty and senile lechery. And yet, on another level, the literary beauty and divine love so many medieval thinkers found in these words remain despite the sordid setting. Even January cannot make us forget St. Bernard's commentary; indeed, the old knight's foolishness makes Bernard's vision of ascetic love all the more attractive. Part of the reason that May's infidelity and January's lust seem uglier than anything in Chaucer's other fabliaux is that we are forced to measure them against much higher standards. In the course of the tale we witness a repetition of the original Fall, but we are also allowed glimpses of Paradise.

The artistic and thematic variety of the *Merchant's Tale* puts great demands on the judgment of its readers. The result of faulty judgment is always before us in January, who remains trapped in fantasy and self-delusion. At the end of the tale he does not even believe the horrible evidence of his own eyes because May convinces him that things are not always what they seem: "He that mysconceyveth, he mysdemeth" (IV.2410). As happens often in this subtle, paradoxical tale, although the words themselves are intended only to deceive, they point to the truth. Neither *mysconceyveth* nor *mysdemeth* occurs elsewhere in the *Canterbury Tales*, but together in this proverbial formulation they neatly summarize the tale as a whole, which is all about the need to see accurately and then to judge well. Even the dominating narrative voice admits this. The mock praise of January's wedding, into which is packed a dizzying array of styles and allusions, concludes with a direct statement to the reader: "Assayeth it youreself, thanne may ye witen / If that I lye or noon in this matiere" (IV.1740–41). The constant challenge of the *Merchant's Tale* is to grapple with and properly assess its extraordinary mixture of true and false. The tale is a powerful illustration of the central lesson taught by the literary variety of the *Canterbury Tales*: the reader should never simply accept the truths (or lies) of any one kind of poem, however skillful. He must always "assayeth it" himself.

The *Merchant's Tale* is a daring experiment mirroring the poetic and thematic complexity of the *Canterbury Tales* as a whole. The longest of Chaucer's fabliaux is also his most morally challenging work in the genre, offering both a positive and negative exemplum of the truths of Christianity. Negatively, the tale adapts fabliau conventions and other devices to provide an analysis of corruption in body and mind that is harrowing to the point of despair. No other Canterbury tale exposes evil more relentlessly. And yet, at the same time, the fabliau repeatedly offers visions of faith and love, both human and divine, that promise hope to the reader. This disgusting and bitter tale is also a compelling advocate for the highest Christian values, and therefore its extraordinary poet needs all the range and virtuosity we have discovered in him to contain such extremes of good and bad. Not only does the *Merchant's Tale* differ radically from Chaucer's other fabliaux, but its unique artist is also one of the most difficult, though ultimately rewarding, Christian poets in Middle English literature.

CHAPTER VI  THE CONTRASTING RELIGIOUS TALES OF THE PRIORESS AND SECOND NUN

he radical stylistic individuality we have seen in the fabliaux is also found in the two other major genres of the *Canterbury Tales*: the romance, which I shall not discuss here, and, perhaps more surprisingly, the religious tale. In technique and intent, the religious tale is, of course, the very opposite of the fabliau, and yet, even when writing such holy stories, Chaucer continues to experiment with the possibilities of literary diversity and conflict. He does not cease being a complex poet even when he is most directly Christian. The stylistic drama of the religious tales, an example of which (the contrast between the *Prioress's Tale* and the *Second Nun's Tale*) I shall use to conclude my study, shows that the principle of artistic variety operates everywhere in the *Canterbury Tales*, even among its most devout works.

Although the *Prioress's Tale*, which tells of a pious boy miraculously able to sing the *Alma redemptoris* even after his foul murder by Jews, is strictly a miracle of the Virgin, whereas the *Second Nun's Tale* of St. Cecile, a woman whose purity and faith are compromised by neither Roman persecution nor human marriage, is a saint's life proper, their form and basic stories are even more alike than those of the four fabliaux just studied.[1] Both tales are short, begin with a formal prologue, and employ Chaucer's most elevated metrical form, rhyme royal; both are set in a distant place and tell of the martyrdom of a pious virgin whose death, however physically gruesome, is a triumph of faith. Out of this similar material, Chaucer constructs two very different kinds of religious poetry: the *Prioress's Tale* is a lyrical exercise in affective piety in contrast to the more intellectually challenging *Second Nun's Tale*.

Dramatic critics usually compare only tales that are physically juxtaposed or those whose pilgrims refer directly to one another (as the Clerk does to the Wife of Bath), and thus even though both the *Prioress's Tale* and the *Second Nun's Tale* have been discussed with contiguous works (the *Shipman's Tale* and the *Canon's Yeoman's Tale*, respectively), their own relationship has not attracted much attention.[2] The few comparisons that have been attempted between the two are usually quite brief and strongly favor one tale over the other.[3] Yet the *Prioress's Tale* and the *Second Nun's Tale* are an important addition to the stylistic variety of the *Canterbury Tales*. Although the tales have no dramatic connection, their superficial resemblance encourages us to compare the different way each treats similar material. Only when the two works are read closely together in this way will the reader be able to understand the individual strengths and limitations of each.

Two common, though contradictory, problems with the dramatic approach are illustrated by the nuns and their tales: we are often given either too much or too little information about a pilgrim to be useful in interpreting the tale. As already discussed in the first chapter, the portrait of the Prioress is one of the most delicately ambiguous in the entire *General Prologue*; as a consequence, it has frequently attracted attention away from the tale itself and inspired views of Madame Eglentyne that range from the strongly sympathetic to the utterly damning. The story of the death of the little clergeon is generally appropriate to the sentimental Prioress (though it reflects nothing of her courtliness or taste for fine living), but it is impossible to have confidence that any of the psychological judgments of her character can be reliably used to interpret her tale: they are simply too contradictory and too subjective.[4] Dramatic readings of the *Second Nun's Tale*, of which there are naturally few, would be suspect for the opposite reason. Whereas the reader is able to speculate endlessly, if uncertainly, about the intriguing Prioress, he knows virtually nothing about the Second Nun. She has no portrait in the *General Prologue* and never addresses a personal word to any of the pilgrims.[5]

In large part because of such problematic tellers, dramatic readings often fail to take either religious tale very seriously. The complete lack of characterization of the Second Nun is one of several reasons that critics have assumed the tale is an early and unrevised work, which can therefore be dismissed as immature.[6] Some of the best recent criticism of the tale has disputed this, however, by showing how carefully the tale anticipates and contradicts the highly dramatic, and presumably quite late, *Canon's Yeoman's Tale*. The *Prioress's Tale* is undervalued for a different reason: many dramatic critics read the tale ironically as Chaucer's attack on the Prioress's anti-Semitism. It is surely to our credit that we are disturbed by the negative portrayal of the Jews in the *Prioress's Tale*; but attempts to find comfort in the argument that Chaucer could not possibly be a bigot, as we understand the term, are almost certainly anachronistic distortions of medieval attitudes. The Jews in the *Prioress's Tale* are conventional and rather vaguely described enemies of Christianity, little different from the Roman authorities in the *Second Nun's Tale* or the Muslims of the *Man of Law's Tale*.[7] Much as we might wish it, the achievement of the *Prioress's Tale* is not its exposure of medieval prejudice. If we ignore the tellers and instead look carefully at the tales, which, unlike the elusive nuns, can be analyzed with confidence and in detail, we shall see that Chaucer is once again experimenting with the possibilities of a literary genre.

Contrasting Literary Prologues

The prologues to the *Prioress's Tale* and the *Second Nun's Tale* are literary statements rather than dramatic scenes; neither contributes to the Roadside Drama of the Canterbury pilgrimage, but instead each expresses a distinct view of art that defines the poetic of the tale it prefaces. At one point both prologues even draw on the same source (St. Bernard's prayer to the Virgin from Canto XXXIII of Dante's *Paradiso*), though the material is used in revealingly different ways. In the *Prioress's Prologue*, the Bernardine passage is incorporated into a strongly emotional prayer, whereas in the *Second Nun's Prologue* it is one link in a learned exposition that instructs as well as inspires. The lyricism of the first prologue is in contrast to the homiletic and intellectual style of the second, as each announces the special artistry of the tale to follow.

The *Prioress's Prologue* has been justly valued as a high achievement of aureate diction and a "gem of construction."[8] Its art is powerfully devotional. The brief and often intense prayer begins with a paraphrase of Psalm 8, a song to God, and echoes the liturgy throughout, especially the Office and Little Office of the Blessed Virgin.[9] The prologue is a magnificent hymn of praise that powerfully restates the central paradoxes of Mary ("O mooder Mayde! o mayde Mooder free! / O bussh unbrent, brennynge in Moyses sighte" [VII.467–68]), prays directly to her ("Lady, thy bountee, thy magnificence, / Thy vertu, and thy grete humylitee" [VII.474–75]), and celebrates her ability to intercede on behalf of mankind. In addition to elevated diction and impassioned rhetoric, the prologue contains a striking image of the Virgin's role in the Incarnation worthy of *Piers Plowman*: "That ravyshedest doun fro the Deitee, / Thurgh thyn humblesse, the Goost that in th'alighte" (VII.469–70).

In contrast to this perfectly unified prayer, the much longer *Second Nun's Prologue* (119 lines as opposed to 34) is formally divided into three stylistically different sections: an opening exposition on the dangers of Idleness (VIII.1–28), praise of the Virgin (VIII.29–84), and several different etymological explanations of the name Cecile (VIII.85–119).[10] The first and third sections, especially, are significantly more intellectual than anything in the prologue to the *Prioress's Tale*. The initial warning against "roten slogardye," with its periodic syntax and complex image of the Devil waiting to bind mankind, reads like a homily, whereas the detailed etymologies of Cecile, including "the wey to blynde" and "wantynge of blyndnesse," suggest a learning that is the very opposite of fervent prayer.[11]

The deliberate artistic differences between the two prologues are clearest in the lines where they are superficially most alike: the direct address each offers to the Virgin, which takes up the entire *Prioress's Prologue* but only the middle section, the *Invocacio ad Mariam*, of the *Second Nun's Prologue*.

Although both prayers echo the liturgy and Dante, as already noted, the prologue to the *Second Nun's Tale* also uses a wide variety of other sources, possibly including Jean de Meun, Cato, Alanus de Insulis, Macrobius, and Statius, to produce an effect that is more learned than devotional.[12] The *Second Nun's Prologue* further indicates its distance from the direct, emotional prayer of the *Prioress's Prologue* by citing an authoritative source at the beginning of its address to the Virgin ("Of whom that Bernard list so wel to write" [VIII.30]) and by concluding with the assertion that the "wordes and sentence" of the written original will be faithfully translated (VIII.78–84).[13] G. H. Russell has shown how well the *Prioress's Prologue* expresses conventional Christian paradoxes, but these are characteristically extended and made more intellectually complex in the *Second Nun's Prologue*.[14]

The contrasting artistries of the two prologues suggest two different conceptions of religious poetry and of the relationship between human beings and God. The previously mentioned image in the *Prioress's Prologue* that describes Mary's role in the Incarnation reveals a skill at creating striking devotional poetry based on ordinary human experience, as well as a view of the divine that leaves little room for human accomplishment: "That ravyshedest doun fro the Deitee, / Thurgh thyn humblesse, the Goost that in th'alighte" (VII.469–70). The Virgin has attracted the Godhead not through direct action or appeal, but through their opposite: her humility. If even the mother of God is portrayed as the passive receptacle of divine favor, we may be sure that ordinary humans are more powerless still; and, indeed, the prologue uses an entire stanza to emphasize man's inability to express or understand Mary's qualities and acts (VII.474–80). The speaking voice in the prologue, which is nominally that of the Prioress, expresses a particular sense of inadequacy. It doubts its own ability to tell of Mary and Jesus ("as I best kan or may" [VII.460]), and its admission that no story is capable of increasing the Virgin's honor (VII.464) culminates in the self-abnegation of the last stanza. Opening with an extreme statement of worthlessness ("My konnyng is so wayk"), the voice continues with a comparison of itself to a child of a year or less ("That kan unnethes any word expresse"), and concludes with a prayer to Mary to guide "my song" (VII.481–87).

Before dismissing these sentiments as conventionally modest and inevitable in such a context, we should note that nothing like them, but rather their opposite, occurs in the *Second Nun's Prologue*, which celebrates human accomplishment and proclaims a less subservient relationship with the divine. Whereas the prologue to the *Prioress's Tale* shows the holy ravishing of the Virgin, the comparable image in the prologue to the *Second Nun's Tale* insists on Mary's own contribution: "Withinne the cloistre blisful of thy sydis / Took mannes shap the eterneel love and pees"

(VIII.43–44). If less poetically striking, the Second Nun's formulation replaces the Prioress's passive and erotic view of the Incarnation (seen especially in such terms as "ravyshedest" and "alighte") with an allusion to the active religious life of the cloister.[15] In contrast to the extreme condescension implied by the Deity's coming "doun" to earth in the first image, the monastic life referred to in the second was thought to allow mortals to transcend this world and achieve spiritual states approaching the divine. The praises of God and Mary for the unmerited favor they shower on lowly mankind in the *Prioress's Prologue* give way to assertions of what humans can accomplish through their own efforts. From its opening denunciation of Idleness, the *Second Nun's Prologue* stresses the importance of human labor—forms of the word *werk* occur often here, but not at all in the *Prioress's Prologue*.[16] In addition to a more active Mary, the prologue also celebrates a heroine, St. Cecile, whose own effects have earned her heaven: "Thy maydens deeth, that wan thurgh hire merite / The eterneel lyf, and of the feend victorie" (VIII.33–34).

The speaking voice in the *Second Nun's Prologue* boasts of its literary accomplishment and proudly declares, "I have heer doon my feithful bisynesse / After the legende" (VIII.24–25). In contrast to the *Prioress's Prologue*, which avoids personal responsibility for its art by declaring that without Mary's help its expression is only that of a year-old child, the *Second Nun's Prologue*, while asking for assistance, also insists on its own efforts: "Now help, for to my werk I wol me dresse" (VIII.77). In the next stanza, moreover, while requesting amendment and denying that what it has written is in any way subtle, the voice does claim the ability to reproduce both the words and *sentence* of its source (VIII.79–84), just as it concludes the entire prologue with satisfaction over the etymologies: "Now have I yow declared what she highte" (VIII.119). The respect for human intellect and achievement in the *Second Nun's Prologue* and the passionate, emotional intensity of the *Prioress's Prologue* prepare us for the contrasting kinds of religious poetry in the tales that follow.

Contrasting Narrators and Speech

Despite the essential similarity of their subjects, the *Prioress's Tale* and the *Second Nun's Tale* continue the artistic differences announced in their prologues. As in all of the tales we have examined, both narrative voice and direct speech are key elements through which Chaucer creates an individual poetic for each work. The frequently intrusive narrative voice of the *Prioress's Tale* is prominent from the beginning of the tale to the end.[17] As early as the fourth stanza, the tale echoes the prologue in calling on divine help, this time from St. Nicholas: "But ay, when I remembre on this mateere, / Seint Nicholas stant evere in my presence" (VII.513–14). And the tale concludes with a characteristically passionate address to the dead little boy ("Ther he is now, God leve us for to meete!" [VII.683]), followed by a request for God's mercy through the prayers of another young martyr, Hugh of Lincoln (VII.684–90). The urgent voice of the narrator repeatedly calls attention to its telling of the story and demands our attention: for example, "As I have seyd" (VII.551), "I seye that in a wardrobe they hym threwe" (VII.572), and "This hooly monk, this abbot, hym meene I" (VII.670). A clear sense of good and evil, as well as a depth of emotional involvement, is evident throughout. The voice condemns the sin of "foule usure and lucre of vileynye" (VII.491) in the first stanza and later denounces both "Oure firste foo, the serpent Sathanas" (VII.558) and the "cursed folk" (VII.574) who committed the "cursed dede" of murder (VII.578). At the opposite emotional extreme, it sweetly consoles the martyred child (VII.579–85) and identifies with the mother's desperate search for her lost boy (VII.586–606).[18]

A bloody struggle between extremes of good and evil also takes place in the Second Nun's Tale, but its narrator is as cool and objective as the other is warm and committed.[19] The few times we hear a narrative voice at all, it is purely objective and functional, without the impassioned empathy or judgments of the narrator in the Prioress's Tale.[20] Even when the first person is used in the Second Nun's Tale, we find no passionate voice trying to involve us emotionally, but instead the accents of authority assuring us that we are being given the truth, as in the first such phrase in the tale: "as I writen fynde" (VIII.124).[21] Much of the Second Nun's Tale consists of intellectual argument spoken by the characters, which the narrator presents without color or comment. Even the debate between St. Cecile and her Roman persecutor Almachius during the climactic trial scene is allowed to unfold without obvious rooting for one side.

The contrast in these two tales between emotional and austere religious poetry is also apparent in their different use of speech. Although the Second Nun's Tale contains extensive dialogue, as just noted, its characters never address each other intimately or with ordinary human affection. Instead, the spoken words in the tale are almost always intellectual and forensic.[22] Speech is often vivacious in the trial scene between the bullying Almachius and the combative St. Cecile, a woman who is not afraid to call an idol a stone or a prince a fool, but their long dialogue does not define two dramatic characters so much as two philosophical positions.[23] Although Cecile's first words to her new husband, Valerian, seem affectionate enough ("O sweete and wel biloved spouse deere" [VIII.144]), their purpose is not to create an intimate romantic relationship, but to prevent one, and, as in the subsequent dialogue between Valerian and his brother, we soon hear formal doctrinal exposition. The sublimation of normal feelings into a higher spiritual vision is characteristic of the poem and its heroine. Cecile's last words to her husband and brother-in-law as they are about to be cruelly martyred betray no trace of human grief (she does not address either by name), but, with "ful stedefast cheere," she echoes St. Paul in assuring "Cristes owene knyghtes leeve and deere" that they have fought a great battle that will win them the "corone of lif that may nat faille" (VIII.382–90).

Although speech in the *Second Nun's Tale* is doctrinal rather than personal, it is nevertheless extremely crucial. The poet firmly believes in the power of words to change, convert, and save. All of the Christian characters use language well: Pope Urban successfully instructs Valerian and Tiburce for baptism, and they, on the point of death, use "prechyng" to convert the Roman officer and "his folk echone" sent to kill them (VIII.372–78). Without recourse to force of any kind, St. Cecile relies entirely on words. She convinces her husband to give up sexual for spiritual love (and on his wedding night!), persuades her brother-in-law Tiburce of the truth of the faith, converts those sent to arrest her, utterly confounds Almachius at her trial, lives on half-dead for three days teaching and preaching, and with her last words recommends the souls of the faithful and successfully urges the building of a church. Efficacious speech indeed![24]

Speech not only occurs much less frequently in the *Prioress's Tale* than in the *Second Nun's Tale*, but the poet is also more suspicious of its effects, which are often shown to be incompetent when not actually evil. In the first speech of the tale, the little boy asks his older fellow to explain the meaning of the song *Alma redemptoris*, but gets little satisfaction. The other student replies that he knows it is in honor of Mary and nothing more: "I lerne song, I kan but smal grammeere" (VII.536). The second speech in the tale is even less admirable—vicious rather than merely ignorant—as Satan, with his usual corruption of logic and rhetoric, incites the Jews against the innocent boy (VII.560–64). Further misuse of speech is implicit in the Jews' conspiracy to murder and their false denial of knowledge about the child after his death (VII.600–603).

This pessimistic view of speech is countered by another, more positive sound in the *Prioress's Tale*: sincere, reverent songs of praise. The words *sing*, *song* (as noun and verb), and *singing* occur eleven, ten, and two times respectively in the tale, in each case more often than in any other Canterbury tale, even though the *Prioress's Tale* is one of the shortest poems in the collection.[25] The devout sincerity of the clergeon's singing of the *Alma redemptoris* is valued much more highly by the poet than knowledge of its precise meaning. Following a long medieval tradition echoed even by the resolutely intellectual *Piers Plowman*, an innocent heart is shown to bring salvation more surely than a learned mind. Indeed, so powerful is the child's song that not even death can stop it. After the boy's throat is cut, the melody that continues from him is precisely the kind of poetry called for in the prologue to the *Prioress's Tale* and exactly characterizes the artistry of the tale. Owing nothing to human thought or ingenuity, the little clergeon's song is a miraculous inspiration from God through the intercession of the Blessed Virgin.

The last and longest speech in the *Prioress's Tale*, the martyr's explanation to the abbot of how he is able to sing with his throat cut, may at first seem exceptional (VII.649–69). This single example of positive speech in the tale has been correctly seen as symbolizing intellectual growth in the child; no longer a beginner struggling with his primer, he refers confidently to learning, "as ye in bookes fynde" (VII.652), and he gives answers to his elders rather than asking questions.[26] Despite its relative sophistication, even this final utterance accords with the poet's conception of the best speech: not only are the clergeon's words about song, but their result is a hymn of praise completely different from the exposition of doctrine found throughout the tale of St. Cecile. Unlike the saint, the boy is not at all argumentative, nor does he seek to persuade rationally or convert (for here as elsewhere in the tale, humans are seen as capable of little on their own); instead, he celebrates the power and mercy of Christ and Mary:

> But Jesu Crist, as ye in bookes fynde,
> Wil that his glorie laste and be in mynde,
> And for the worship of his Mooder deere
> Yet may I synge O *Alma* loude and cleere.
>   (VII.652–55)

The child martyr then concludes with a direct quotation of the words spoken to him by the Virgin—a speech within a speech that offers the emotional warmth and human comfort never found in the *Second Nun's Tale*:

> "My litel child, now wol I fecche thee,
> Whan that the greyn is fro thy tonge ytake.
> Be nat agast, I wol thee nat forsake."
>   (VII.667–69)

Emotional versus Learned Art

After even such a brief comparison, the general differences between the two tales should be clear. The poet of the *Prioress's Tale* is a lyrical, emotional artist whose often lovely poetry is a work of celebration and prayer rather than analysis. For instance, although both prologues borrow from the liturgy, as we have seen, only the *Prioress's Tale* continues such echoes, especially from the Mass for Holy Innocents, into the narrative itself.[27] In contrast to this late Gothic sensibility, the *Second Nun's Tale* seems austerely Romanesque. Its colder, more intellectual poetry describes a learned and active faith that urges us first to know and then to do the work of Christianity.

Once the deliberately opposed artistries of these two tales are recognized, Chaucerians will be less inclined to attribute their individuality to exterior forces—to read the tale of the clergeon as primarily an exposé of the Prioress, for example, or dismiss the tale of St. Cecile as an early and uninspired work. As becomes increasingly apparent when the tales are read together, Chaucer is once again exploring the possibilities of a form. His irrepressible literary virtuosity offers two different kinds of religious poetry: poetry that makes us feel and poetry that makes us think. Each is a genuine accomplishment and plays its part in the artistic variety and complex moral meaning of the *Canterbury Tales*.

In the *Prioress's Tale* all the resources of the poet's art are employed to evoke strong emotions in an audience, especially a close identification with the sufferings of its two main characters (the clergeon and his mother) and indignation at their wicked persecutors. A poor widow and her devout little son are figures that in and of themselves will move all but the most stony-hearted reader, and the poet's method of telling their story is intended to increase our sympathetic response. The lowering of the age of the boy to seven, from ten as it apparently was in Chaucer's source, deliberately reinforces his innocence, and the widow is portrayed so sweetly that she is allowed no other impulses except tender love and concern for her son.[28] While mother and child are shown to be free from stain and even temptation, the Jews appear as thoroughly wicked, easily incited by Satan to kill a child for a song.

Childlike innocence is not only the subject of the *Prioress's Tale*; it also characterizes its artistry. The most obvious example is the poet's vocabulary.[29] Alan Gaylord and others have commented on the frequent use in the tale of words that emphasize sweetness and vulnerability, such as *litel* and *innocent*, as well as *sely*, *yong*, *tendre*, and *smale*.[30] The poet's technique is especially revealing in comparison with the tale of St. Cecile. *Litel* appears twelve times in the *Prioress's Tale*, the highest percentage per line of any tale, whereas its single use in the *Second Nun's Tale* (VIII.437) is an insulting reference to the empty power of Almachius. *Innocent* occurs four times (VII.538, 566, 608, 635), more often than in any other tale; in contrast, though *innocent* is also used twice in the *Second Nun's Tale* (VIII.452, 464), both appearances are in the trial scene with judicial rather than sentimental meaning. Just as revealing as vocabulary is the frequent use of doublets in the Prioress's Tale, especially in the first half of the story—for example, "ride or wende" (VII.493), "free and open" (VII.494), "yeer by yere" (VII.498), and "day by day" (VII.504).[31] This concentrated use of an aspect of oral style does not produce the dignified effect of repetition in the Knight's Tale because the noble vocabulary of the romance is missing, but instead these doublets well represent the slow, modest, and childish style of the Prioress's Tale. Indeed, after the convincingly boyish dialogue between the two students over the Alma redemptoris (VII.525–43),[32] the narration itself becomes syntactically simple and repetitious, as though being told to a child:

> His felawe taughte hym homward prively,
> Fro day to day, til he koude it by rote,
> And thanne he song it wel and boldely,
> Fro word to word, acordynge with the note.
> Twies a day it passed thurgh his throte,
> To scoleward and homward whan he wente;
> On Cristes mooder set was his entente.
>   (VII.544–50)

The emotional artistry of the Prioress's Tale, which often seems overly sentimental to modern, secular readers, is not meant satirically, as some critics have argued, but derives from the long and respected Catholic tradition of "affective piety." Practiced by such as Anselm and Bernard, and surviving in the Church today in such passionate devotions as the Stations of the Cross, affective piety was especially popular in the late Middle Ages. Its literary manifestations generally ignore narrative and intellectual complexity in favor of extreme expressions of love, praise, and gratitude prompted especially by the spectacle of unmerited suffering.[33] In accord with this tradition, the Prioress's Tale makes no effort to instruct the reader intellectually; instead, it aims to make him respond emotionally to God's merciful love for mankind, especially as seen in the tender intercession of Mary. The art of the tale is designed to produce emotion, not thought. Like so many Middle English religious lyrics, particularly those on the Passion, which also inspire affective piety and emphasize Mary, the Prioress's Tale gets its readers to respond to the divine and miraculous by direct appeals to their human sympathy for its characters.[34] That Chaucer need not have treated these themes in this way is shown not only by the Second Nun's Tale but also by the alliterative Pearl, a contemporary poem that also concerns childish innocence and death, which for all its emotionalism—most of which is shown to be misdirected—contains real learning in the service of a complex and paradoxical message. What the poet of the Prioress's Tale offers instead is an intensity of feeling and character identification that is common in lyric poetry or in the mystics, but rarely found in the great Ricardian poets of the fourteenth century.

The different artistry of the Second Nun's Tale is especially clear when read in the light of the Prioress's Tale. The tale of St. Cecile is an austere work that persuades us intellectually like a homily and advocates an almost unreachable ideal of asceticism, thereby violating the normal affections central to the Prioress's Tale. The two principal male characters in the tale are each taught to deny a basic human instinct in order to achieve a higher spiritual state: Valerian, though "ful yong of age" (VIII.128), must put away any thoughts of sexual relations with his wife, while his brother Tiburce is required to overcome his fear of death. The emphasis throughout the Second Nun's Tale is on knowledge that leads to devout action, as the characters come to see things in a new way. The word truth, for example, occurs five times in the tale, always in reference to Christian truth, but not once in the Prioress's Tale. The learning already noted in the prologue is continued in the tale by the insistence that the story follows a written record (VIII.120 and 124) and by the description of Cecile's faith as intellectual: she "bar [Christ's] gospel in hir mynde" (VIII.123). Just as the prologue cites St. Bernard as an authoritative source, the Second Nun's Tale—in contrast to the more emotional liturgical echoes of the Prioress's Tale—has a long citation from Ambrose's preface to the Mass for St. Cecilia's day, clearly identified as such, that explicates the meaning of the crowns of rose and lily (VIII.270–83).[35] Cecile's principal complaint against the pagan idols of Rome is that they are stupid, being only "dombe" and "deve" stones (VIII.286). The poet of the Second Nun's Tale insists that we understand and not just feel.

In contrast to the "litel book lernynge" of the clergeon (VII.516), who knows the Alma redemptoris only by rote (VII.522 and 545), the Second Nun's Tale is full of instances of careful instruction and learning. Cecile begins to convert her husband from physical to spiritual love by offering him "conseil" (VIII.145). When told about the guardian angel, Valerian, quite understandably, does not immediately accept his wife's word, but demands proof before he will agree to forgo his marital rights (VIII.163–66). Cecile replies that knowledge will come only with baptism, the achievement of which sacrament is described in some detail as a mental rather than emotional process: first Valerian is carefully instructed by Cecile on how to find and address Pope Urban (VIII.172–80); then, when Valerian, "taught by his lernynge" (VIII.184), reaches his goal, the Pope praises Cecile for her "conseil" (VIII.192); and finally a mysterious old man reads from a book a summary of the Creed to which Valerian must make formal assent (VIII.207–13). Lengthy as it is, Valerian's conversion is not, of course, a realistic or full account of Christian instruction, but a dramatized version suitable for poetry.[36] Nevertheless, in contrast to the purely emotive faith in the *Prioress's Tale*, or the simpler conversions described in the *Man of Law's Tale*, the poet of the Cecile story emphasizes knowledge, learning, books, and rational agreement. The same intellectual approach to faith is stressed elsewhere in the *Second Nun's Tale*: in the conversions of Tiburce (VIII.319–48 and 353), Maximus (VIII.372 and 375), and the Roman officials (VIII.414), as well as in Cecile's logical, if not physical, mastery over Almachius during her trial.

Emotional versus Learned Faith

The childlike art of the *Prioress's Tale* inevitably produces a simple view of the world and of the power of God in human affairs. Indeed, its archetypically good and bad characters and deliberately sentimental narrative frequently approach melodrama.[37] Even though the tale depends greatly on our warm, emotional response to the human plight of the little boy and his mother, the poet has little faith in the achievements of mankind. As we have seen anticipated in the prologue, the characters in the *Prioress's Tale*, both good and bad, are presented as essentially passive agents whose acts result from supernatural initiative. The widow needs inspiration from Jesus to discover the pit where her child was thrown (VII.603–6), and the martyr's body is finally located only as a result of his divinely instigated song. Even the murder itself comes after a suggestion by Satan (VII.558–66). The only effective human action in the poem—the brutal execution of the Jews who conspired in the murder—is carried out by an outsider, the provost of the Asian city sent for by the "Cristene folk" (VII.614), who, despite his praise of Christ and Mary, is presumably not himself Christian, but one who operates on a simple principle of retributive justice: "Yvele shal have that yvele wol deserve" (VII.632).

The faith of the characters in the *Prioress's Tale* is as limited as their actions. Belief comes from rote learning and intensity of feeling, not rational assent, and genuine religious education or change seems impossible. The poet's frequent references to "Cristene folk" (VII.489, 495, and 614) and "Jewerye" (VII.489 and 551) suggest that one is what one is by birth, even though many analogues of the story end with the conversion of the Jews. In contrast to the doubts of Valerian and Tiburce in the *Second Nun's Tale*, the clergeon is too young and the widow too pure to be anything but perfectly devout. Evil is not a matter for internal struggle in the tale, nor even, apparently, much of a question for the Christian community; instead, it is shown as wholly exterior, practiced only by the Jews and inspired by the promptings of a melodramatic Satan:

Oure firste foo, the serpent Sathanas,
That hath in Jues herte his waspes nest,
Up swal, and seide, "O Hebrayk peple, allas!"
(VII.558–60)

In contrast to this childlike innocence and simplicity in the *Prioress's Tale*, religion in the *Second Nun's Tale* is for adults. The poem shows characters achieving their faith only after detailed instruction and rational acceptance. Although Cecile is an effective public debater against Almachius, the real drama in the tale occurs within the souls of those who respond to her message of a new life. The *Second Nun's Tale* continually celebrates human religious accomplishments. The opening denunciation of Idleness in the prologue introduces a theme of Christian busyness and activity that continues throughout the tale, as the characters try to imitate Christ by using their intellect to produce tangible results: "That Fadres Sone hath alle thyng ywroght, / And al that wroght is with a skilful thoght" (VIII.326–27).[38] Such activity is especially true of Cecile, the "bisy bee" as Urban calls her (VIII.195), who, without even the aid of a sympathetic provost, teaches Christianity under the most difficult circumstances—on her wedding night and with a severed head in a bath of flames. Twice, during the conversion of Tiburce and in Cecile's final agony, a stanza ends by rhyming "preche" with "teche" (VIII.342–43 and 538–39). As the couplet suggests, the learning so often stressed by this poet is not valuable for its own sake, but because it leads to Christian truth and action.

The *Second Nun's Tale* is fundamentally a poem about conversion, not just the exterior conversion from pagan to Christian (though this is important), but the deeper conversion from earthly to spiritual values. Whereas the strong passions in the *Prioress's Tale* remain focused on human events, the *Second Nun's Tale* ignores the values of this world for those of the next, just as its characters transcend the limits of their humanity to become saints. The several uses of the word *love* in the work—it occurs eleven times in the *Second Nun's Prologue* and *Tale* to one appearance of *loved* in the *Prioress's Tale* (VII.657)—illustrate how Christians can learn to transcend earthly *amor* and achieve divine *caritas*. After insisting on Cecile's "love" for God (VIII.125 and 138), the story opens with the normal sensual expectations of Valerian on his wedding night in opposition to the spiritual affection of Cecile's angel, who "loveth" (VIII.152) her with a "greet love" (VIII.153). Although the new bridegroom fleetingly suspects his wife may "love another man" (VIII.167), she eventually teaches him the difference between "love in vileynye" (VIII.156) and "clene love" (VIII.159 and 160). Valerian learns so well that he is able to pass on the same knowledge to his brother, about whom he says "in this world I love no man so" (VIII.236). As Pope Urban makes clear, the chastity of Cecile, far from being sterile, produces an extraordinarily fruitful love, uniting the brothers (VIII.283) with this saintly woman (VIII.295) in a spiritual *menage à trois* that imitates the "eterneel love and pees" of God celebrated in the prologue (VIII.44).

For all its intellectual austerity, the *Second Nun's Tale* is a powerful literary work. A particular skill is its use of complex and varied imagery to illustrate the contrast between physical and spiritual values. Nothing comparable is found in the more lyrical *Prioress's Tale*, whose infrequent imagery is conventional and relatively simple. The prologue to the *Prioress's Tale*, for example, describes Mary as "the white lylye flour" (VII.461) and the "bussh unbrent" (VII.468), and in the tale itself the clergeon is called "This gemme of chastite, this emeraude, / And eek of martirdom the ruby bright" (VII.609–10). None of these brief, conventional images are developed further. The last image in the tale, the "greyn" (VII.665) that allows the boy to sing after his throat has been cut, has been variously interpreted as symbolizing everything from a pearl to the communion host, though the lack of consensus among critics suggests that there may be less here than meets the eye, and that, instead of a genuine symbol, the image is a plot device that permits the child's singing to end.[39] If so, it would be in accord with the *Prioress's Tale* as a whole, which is not an intellectually complex or allegorical work, but instead persuades us through its affecting characters and moving human situations.

The *Second Nun's Tale*, in contrast, is a highly symbolic poem whose intricate imagery demands the active participation of the reader to be understood fully.[40] The most famous image in the tale is the much discussed "corones two" (VIII.221) of rose and lily given to Cecile and Valerian by the angel. The meaning of the crowns is no more difficult to discover than that of the gems in the *Prioress's Tale*; indeed, it is identical: Ambrose is cited as authority that they stand for virginity and martyrdom (VIII.270–83). But instead of being merely an isolated piece of literary decoration, the image of the crowns, as Trevor Whittock has shown, reinforces the poet's pervasive opposition of the things of this world against those of the next (the contrast between the living, fragrant flowers from heaven and the dead stone idols of paganism is particularly effective).[41] Other, equally complex patterns of images, such as those that use fire or war, begin in the prologue and are then developed in the tale to similar thematic effect.[42]

Perhaps the most powerful symbolic imagery in the *Second Nun's Tale* concerns sight.[43] The difference between good and evil is not always easy to recognize in this tale of conversion, for the characters are required to see much in a radically new way, and thus true vision is as necessary as it is difficult. In the etymologies of her name in the prologue, Cecile is described as a corrective of blindness, and the principal action of the tale—the movement from earthly to heavenly values—is often expressed in images of sight. We are repeatedly told that it is only after their conversions that Valerian and Tiburce (and later the Roman officer Maximus) are able to see the angel of God (VIII.170, 268, 300–301, 355–56, 400–403). In contrast to the spiritual insight of the Christians, Almachius's vision remains earthbound and thus blind to spiritual reality. Cecile scornfully declares that though everyone knows that God is in heaven (VIII.507–8), Almachius is forced to search for him among his silly, inert rocks:

> "Ther lakketh no thyng to thyne outter yën
> That thou n'art blynd; for thyng that we seen alle
> That it is stoon,—that men may wel espyen,—
> That ilke stoon a god thow wolt it calle.
> I rede thee, lat thyn hand upon it falle,
> And taste it wel, and stoon thou shalt it fynde,
> Syn that thou seest nat with thyne eyen blynde."
> (VIII.498–504)

Because his sight is confined to his "outter yën," Almachius lacks true vision. He has eyes but cannot see.

The contrast in artistry and therefore in kind of spirituality between the tales of the two nuns continues right to the end of each poem. In keeping with its affective art and faith, the *Prioress's Tale* concludes with a scene that solicits our pity for the martyrdom of the innocent little clergeon. The boy's dying words that tell of the mercy shown to him by Christ and Mary (and mention the Virgin's promise not to forsake him after his song is over) are touching enough, but that which follows is designed to increase our empathetic response. When the boy finally gives up the ghost, the sobbing abbot ("salte teeris trikled doun as reyn") falls flat upon the ground and is imitated by the entire convent: "Wepynge, and heryng Cristes mooder deere" (VII.673–78). For the emotional poet of the *Prioress's Tale*, intensity of reverent feeling alone is the proper response to the divine. Once again, all that is asked from humans is sincere love and devotion, and, in the face of the miracle, the monks can do nothing except weep, praise Mary, and bury the child's remains:

> And in a tombe of marbul stones cleere
> Enclosen they his litel body sweete.
> Ther he is now, God leve us for to meete!
> (VII.681–83)

The sentimental focus of these lines on the "litel body sweete" is reminiscent of so many late medieval poems on the Passion that elicit sympathy for the human sufferings of Christ and Mary. Appropriately, it is the mercy of the Virgin and her son (the word *mercy* is repeated three times within two lines) that is passionately invoked through "yonge Hugh of Lyncoln" in the Prioress's final prayer (VII.684–90). The conclusion of the *Prioress's Tale* is a powerful demonstration of the affective piety that informs the work throughout.

In striking contrast, the *Second Nun's Tale* ends with intellectual instruction and a call to action instead of with tears. Cecile's final speech is not as touching as the clergeon's, but it is more practical. In keeping with the poet's optimism about human accomplishment, Cecile recommends the souls of the faithful to Pope Urban and requests the construction of a church (VIII.541–46). Significantly, the last couplet spoken by this active saint rhymes "werche" and "cherche."[44] Although Cecile's death is even bloodier than the clergeon's, it is not grieved over. The torment of her severed head only makes her preaching that more effective, and the poet describes her burial briefly and unemotionally (VIII.548–49). The destruction of Cecile's body is no tragedy, but a release so that her soul can go to what she had previously called a "bettre lif in oother place" (VIII.323). The man-made structure at the end of each tale tells us much about the difference between the two poems. The pretty "tombe of marbul stones cleere" (VII.681) of the boy martyr expresses the poignancy of human sorrow and mourning in the face of physical death and our helplessness to do anything except seek God's mercy. In contrast, the church of St. Cecile, which the poet insists is still holding Christian services to this day (VIII.552–53), is a more hopeful symbol that asserts both the possibilities of human action and the continuation of the Catholic faith.[45]

Comparison of the *Prioress's Tale* and the *Second Nun's Tale* reveals that the literary and thematic individuality of these two religious tales is as deep and consistent as that within any genre of the *Canterbury Tales*. Chaucer continues to practice his art of literary variety and contrast even in explicitly Christian works. The different poetics of the *Prioress's Tale* and the *Second Nun's Tale* describe two different kinds of faith, and thus the drama of their opposing styles is a further contribution to the complex experience of the *Canterbury Tales*.

hat then have we discovered about Chaucer's drama of style in the *Canterbury Tales*? Perhaps the first lesson is to acknowledge its pervasive intricacy. As has been noted several times in passing, the literary relationships among the different tales are so many, so complex, and so subtle that criticism finds it difficult to describe them adequately. The *Canterbury Tales* opens with a provocative juxtaposition of chivalric romance (the *Knight's Tale*) and low comedy (the *Miller's Tale*); but the latter also differs significantly from a second fabliau that immediately follows (the *Reeve's Tale*), as well as from other fabliaux later in the work: the *Shipman's Tale* and the *Merchant's Tale*. That much we have been able to discuss, however tentatively, and yet relationships could be traced in other directions as well. In addition to noting the initial contrast of the *Knight's Tale* to the *Miller's Tale*, one might also compare the long opening secular romance with the long religious romance in the second fragment (the *Man of Law's Tale*), as well as with several other chivalric poems in the *Canterbury Tales*, including perhaps the numerous romance elements in the *Merchant's Tale*. And for its part, the *Merchant's Tale*, in addition to its connections with the *Knight's Tale* and Chaucer's other fabliaux, might profitably be discussed with the preceding *Clerk's Tale*, which itself is one of several different religious tales, one of which, the emotional, devout *Prioress's Tale*, follows the cold, knowing *Shipman's Tale*, a contrast in genre and style as extreme as that in the first two Canterbury tales. I could go on.

It has not been possible to discuss in detail all, or even most, of the literary relationships in the *Canterbury Tales*, but I have tried to choose some representative examples. After examining the tales Chaucer assigns himself (*Thopas* and *Melibee*), I turned to the internal conflict between two kinds of moral poetry in the *Pardoner's Tale*, a work usually read dramatically. Then I analyzed at length the opening contrast of the *Knight's Tale* and the *Miller's Tale* and concluded with two chapters (on the fabliaux and religious tales) that explore the radically different styles to be found even in works of the same genre. Although I stopped here, the same approach could be extended to other tales. The frame itself suggests some of these comparisons. The reader may first think of the relationship between the *Summoner's Tale* and the *Friar's Tale* because of their tellers' extended quarrel, but a potentially more interesting literary contrast exists between the morally insistent, though dull, tragedies of the *Monk's Tale* and the indirect lessons and poetic virtuosity of the following *Nun's Priest's Tale*. Analysis of stylistic differences within a single genre, which most clearly shows the individuality of the separate tales, could also be taken further. Although I chose the Prioress's Tale and the Second Nun's Tale to illustrate Chaucer's artistic experiments with the religious tale, two other works in the same genre might have been compared as well: the Man of Law's Tale and the Clerk's Tale. Both poems contain apparently similar stories of saintly, nobly married women who exhibit extraordinary constancy in repeated trials, but, once again, the artistry of each work differs significantly. The Man of Law's Tale is a religious melodrama full of exciting, often exotic, events told with great rhetorical flamboyance; in contrast, the restrained Clerk's Tale reads more like a parable or masque: its austere but sophisticated poetry frustrates easy emotional identification, while exploring some of the most challenging questions of Christian belief. A third major genre in the Canterbury Tales might also have been examined. In addition to the variety of his fabliaux and religious tales, Chaucer also experiments with different romance styles in the Knight's Tale, Wife of Bath's Tale, Squire's Tale, Franklin's Tale, and Sir Thopas.

My argument throughout has been the need to recognize the stylistic individuality of each of the Canterbury Tales. Readers may disagree with some of my readings of particular works, but I believe that the deep and consistent literary differences for which I have argued are undeniable. None of the Canterbury tales is stylistically much like any other, and none speaks in Chaucer's own voice. Chaucer's art of contrast has often been obscured by the attention given to the personal drama of the pilgrims, with the result that the variety of the collection has often been seen as a function of the fictional characters rather than of Chaucer the poet. The General Prologue and links are magnificent creations, but they are not the principal achievement of the Canterbury Tales. The frame sometimes prepares us for the specific poetic style of the tale to follow or returns us to a more ordinary world after the intensity of the fiction, yet the pilgrims we meet there are almost always less knowable and less interesting than the tales themselves. If we would appreciate the full power of the Canterbury Tales, our attention must be on the poetic range of the different stories and the contribution each makes to the experience of the whole. The genius of the Canterbury Tales is not its definition of particular human beings, but its exploration of the ability of poetry to entertain and instruct the audience.

In the course of this study, I have come to see the drama of style in the Canterbury Tales as Chaucer's attempt to find the best way to combine the sentence and solass he deliberately contrasts in his own two tales—in short, his way of being both a good Christian and a good poet. Many modern critics would deny the possibility of such unity, however, for they insist either that Chaucer renounced poetic fiction for doctrinal truth at the end of the *Canterbury Tales*, or that, conversely, his genius allowed him to transcend the confines of medieval belief and achieve a universal sympathy for the human condition. Attractive as each of these interpretations is, I believe that they distort the achievement of the *Canterbury Tales*. Chaucer's commitment to his art and to his faith are equally strong. As we have seen, the fabliaux, in addition to their witty comedy, raise important moral questions, whereas the religious tales, for all their genuine piety, are skillful literary creations. The *Canterbury Tales* maintains no narrow orthodoxy, but recognizes truth in the appetites of the *Miller's Tale* as well as in the idealism of the *Knight's Tale*, just as the *Pardoner's Tale* acknowledges both the potential corruption and the possible triumph of religious fiction. Paradoxically, Chaucer seems able to indulge in such daring literary experiments precisely because of his faith. He can wander far afield because he always knows where home is. In this he is like the other great English poets of the late fourteenth century, especially William Langland and the *Gawain*-poet, although none of their works, however complex in other ways, equals the literary variety and stylistic contrasts of the *Canterbury Tales*. Chaucer's drama of style proves not only that instruction can be delightful, but also that delight is often the best possible form of instruction. As George Herbert, a later Christian poet, put it at the beginning of his *Temple*: "A verse may find him, who a sermon flies."

NOTES

All citations of Chaucer in this text are from F. N. Robinson, ed., *The Works of Geoffrey Chaucer*, 2nd ed. (Boston: Houghton Mifflin, 1957).

I. Beyond the Dramatic Theory

1. These views are most conveniently found in Derek Brewer, ed., *Chaucer: The Critical Heritage* (London: Routledge and Kegan Paul, 1978), vol. 1: John Lydgate, *The Siege of Thebes*, lines 22–25 (p. 50; see also *Fall of Princes*, Pro. 342–45 [p. 54]); William Caxton, "Prohemye" to *The Canterbury Tales* (p. 76; see also John Skelton, "Phillip Sparrowe," lines 612–15 [p. 83]); John Dryden, "Preface" to the *Fables* (p. 167).

2. George Lyman Kittredge, *Chaucer and His Poetry* (1915; reprint, Cambridge: Harvard University Press, 1972), pp. 151, 154–55.

3. John Livingston Lowes, *Geoffrey Chaucer and the Development of His Genius* (Boston: Houghton Mifflin, 1934), pp. 203, 229.

4. John Speirs, *Chaucer the Maker* (1951; reprint, London: Faber and Faber, 1964), p. 98.

5. Robert Kilburn Root, *The Poetry of Chaucer* (Boston: Houghton Mifflin, 1906), pp. 239–40.

6. Robert M. Lumiansky, *Of Sondry Folk: The Dramatic Principle in the Canterbury Tales* (Austin: University of Texas Press, 1955), p. 4.

7. Kemp Malone, *Chapters on Chaucer* (Baltimore: Johns Hopkins Press, 1951), pp. 163–235; Bertrand H. Bronson, "Chaucer's Art in Relation to His Audience," in *Five Studies in Literature*, University of California Publications in English 8 (Berkeley: University of California Press, 1940), pp. 1–53; Bronson, *In Search of Chaucer* (Toronto: University of Toronto Press, 1960), esp. pp. 77–87; Robert M. Jordan, *Chaucer and the Shape of Creation* (Cambridge: Harvard University Press, 1967), esp. pp. 111–31; Martin Stevens, "Chaucer and Modernism: An Essay in Criticism," in *Chaucer at Albany*, ed. Rossell Hope Robbins (New York: Burt Franklin, 1975), pp. 193–216; Durant W. Robertson, Jr., *A Preface to Chaucer* (Princeton: Princeton University Press, 1963), esp. pp. 248–58, 330–31; Judson Boyce Allen and Theresa Anne Moritz, *A Distinction of Stories* (Columbus: Ohio State University Press, 1981), esp. pp. 11–12; Derek Pearsall, "Chaucer and the Modern Reader: A Question of Approach," *Dutch Quarterly Review* 11 (1981): 258–66; Pearsall, ed., *The Nun's Priest's Tale*, A Variorum Edition of The Works of Geoffrey Chaucer (Norman: University of Oklahoma Press, 1984), pp. 32–42; Helen Cooper, *The Structure of the Canterbury Tales* (London: Duckworth, 1983), esp. chap. 3.

8. Alfred David, *The Strumpet Muse: Art and Morals in Chaucer's Poetry* (Bloomington: Indiana University Press, 1976); Donald R. Howard, *The Idea of the Canterbury Tales* (Berkeley: University of California Press, 1976); Charles A. Owen, Jr., *Pilgrimage and Storytelling in the Canterbury Tales* (Norman: University of Oklahoma Press, 1977); Robert B. Burlin, *Chaucerian Fiction* (Princeton: Princeton University Press, 1977). In his recent *Chaucer and the Imagery of Narrative* (Stanford: Stanford University Press, 1984), V. A. Kolve questions

dramatic readings of the Knight's Tale and Miller's Tale but endorses it for the Reeve's Tale. See also Daniel Kempton, "The Physician's Tale: The Doctor of Physic's Diplomatic 'Cure,' " Chaucer Review 19 (1984): 24–38, esp. n. 5, who calls for a return to dramatic readings.

9. Burlin, Chaucerian Fiction, esp. pp. 268–69.

10. John Matthews Manly, Some New Light on Chaucer (1926; reprint, Gloucester, Mass.: Peter Smith, 1959). This approach was continued by Muriel Bowden, A Commentary on the General Prologue to the Canterbury Tales (New York: Macmillan, 1948).

11. Malone, Chapters on Chaucer, pp. 187–96, has shown that, whether or not the Host refers to the Harry Bailly or Baillif who was a contemporary innkeeper in Southwark, nothing suggests that the resemblance is anything but superficial because both Chaucer's Harry and his wife Godelief are essentially stock characters.

12. Jill Mann, Chaucer and Medieval Estates Satire (Cambridge: Cambridge University Press, 1973), p. 187, esp. n. 1. For a recent expression of the view that Chaucer's characters, while easily allegorized, are also "living" naturalistic figures, see F. Diekstra, "Chaucer's Way with His Sources: Accident into Substance and Substance into Accident," English Studies 62 (1981): 220.

13. For example, Mann, Chaucer and Estates Satire, pp. 15–16.

14. See, for example, Gerald Morgan, "The Universality of the Portraits in the General Prologue to the Canterbury Tales," English Studies 58 (1977): 481–93. Even the unconvincing attempt by Terry Jones to debunk the Knight (Chaucer's Knight [1980; reprint, London: Eyre Methuen, 1982]) turns the pilgrim into an antitype, not a specific individual.

15. See, for example, Edmund Reiss, "The Symbolic Surface of the Canterbury Tales: The Monk's Portrait," Chaucer Review 2 (1968): 254–72; 3 (1968): 12–28.

16. Kittredge, Chaucer and His Poetry, p. 154.

17. Robertson, Preface to Chaucer, esp. pp. 248–50. Of course, Chaucer can create much more complex characterization when he chooses, as in Troilus and Criseyde.

18. Mann, Chaucer and Estates Satire, p. 102.

19. Ibid., p. 197.

20. Both examples were noted by Malone, Chapters on Chaucer, pp. 219–22, 226–28.

21. Manly, Some New Light, p. 291.

22. See the survey of criticism on this point by Susan Gallick, "A Look at Chaucer and His Preachers," Speculum 50 (1975): 474, n. 29.

23. Lumiansky, Of Sondry Folk, p. 107.

24. Ibid., p. 110.

25. For a skeptical review of dramatic criticism of the Nun's Priest's Tale, see Pearsall's Variorum Edition of Chaucer, pp. 32–42.

26. Burlin, Chaucerian Fiction, pp. 195–216; David, Strumpet Muse, pp. 108–17; Owen, Pilgrimage and Storytelling, pp. 139–41; Howard, Idea of the Canterbury Tales, pp. 339–76. See also Kolve's argument for the individuality of the Reeve in Chaucer and Imagery, chap. 5.

27. Lee W. Patterson, "Writing About Writing: The Case of Chaucer," University of Toronto Quarterly 48 (1979): 273. For especially effective attacks on the relationship of teller to tale, see Malone, Chapters on Chaucer, who declares, "If this was actually Chaucer's intention, one can only say that he failed to carry it out. Very few of the tales in the collection have much value for the characterization of their tellers" (p. 211).

28. Those who accept such harmony include Kittredge, Chaucer and His Poetry, pp.

171–72; Howard, *Idea of the Canterbury Tales*, p. 275. Perhaps the nicest assessment is by Lumiansky, usually the most enthusiastic proponent of the dramatic theory: "the story and its teller are not completely unsuited" (*Of Sondry Folk*, p. 71).

29. Thomas Tyrwhitt in his eighteenth-century edition of the *Tales* was the first to suggest a female teller (Eleanor P. Hammond, *Chaucer: A Bibliographical Manual* [1908; reprint, New York: Peter Smith, 1933], p.285). The Wife as original teller has been accepted by many from John S. P. Tatlock (*The Development and Chronology of Chaucer's Works*, Chaucer Society, 2nd ser., 37 [London, 1907], pp. 205–6) to Trevor Whittock (*A Reading of the Canterbury Tales* [Cambridge: Cambridge University Press, 1968], p. 195).

30. For example, Derek Brewer, *Chaucer*, 3rd ed. (London: Longman, 1973), p. 127, notes that the feasts and expense mentioned in the tale are reminiscent of the Wife; and Bernard F. Huppé, *A Reading of the Canterbury Tales*, 2nd rev. ed. (Albany: State University of New York Press, 1967), p. 222, argues that the double entendres in the tale suggest the Wife. William W. Lawrence, "Chaucer's Shipman's Tale," *Speculum* 33 (1958): 56–68, offers the strongest defense of the Wife as teller.

31. Albert H. Silverman, "Sex and Money in Chaucer's *Shipman's Tale*," *Philological Quarterly* 32 (1953): 334.

32. Richard F. Jones, "A Conjecture on the Wife of Bath's Prologue," *Journal of English and Germanic Philology* 24 (1925): 544–45.

33. Malone, *Chapters on Chaucer*, p. 182, notes Kittredge's creativity in claiming the Prioress brought her dogs on the pilgrimage, although no such statement occurs in Chaucer's text (the same detail was also invented by William Blake and recently by Durant W. Robertson, Jr.). The Prioress as a country girl is argued by Whittock, *A Reading of the Canterbury Tales*, p. 206; as a thwarted mother by Kittredge, *Chaucer and His Poetry*, p. 178; and as an anti-Semite most vigorously by E. Talbot Donaldson, ed., *Chaucer's Poetry* (New York: Ronald, 1958), pp. 932–34.

34. For surveys of this debate between dramatic and nondramatic readings, see esp. Norman T. Harrington, "Chaucer's Merchant's Tale: Another Swing of the Pendulum," *Publications of the Modern Language Association* 86 (1971): 25–31; Martin Stevens, "'And Venus Laugheth': An Interpretation of the *Merchant's Tale*," *Chaucer Review* 7 (1972): 118–31; Peter G. Beidler, "Chaucer's Merchant and the Tale of January," *Costerus* 5 (1972): 1–25; Emerson Brown, Jr., "Chaucer, the Merchant, and Their Tale: Getting Beyond Old Controversies," *Chaucer Review* 13 (1978): 141–56, 247–62.

35. Previous nondramatic critics have tended to reduce the tale to no more than a merry jest, a view I shall dispute in my penultimate chapter. See esp. Bertrand H. Bronson, "Afterthoughts on the Merchant's Tale," *Studies in Philology* 58 (1961): 583–96; Robert M. Jordan, "The Non-Dramatic Disunity of the *Merchant's Tale*," *Publications of the Modern Language Association* 78 (1963): 293–99.

36. For the Friar as original teller, see Albert C. Baugh, "The Original Teller of the Merchant's Tale," *Modern Philology* 35 (1937): 15–26; for the Monk, see Thomas J. Garbáty, "The Monk and the *Merchant's Tale*: An Aspect of Chaucer's Building Process in the *Canterbury Tales*," *Modern Philology* 67 (1969): 18–24.

37. Bronson, *In Search of Chaucer*, p. 65.

38. For a survey of views, see Beidler, "Chaucer's Merchant and the Tale of January," pp. 4–13. For a recent defense of the view that the narrator of the tale is indistinguishable from the Merchant of the prologue, see Brown, "Chaucer, the Merchant, and Their Tale," pp. 142–47.

39. The most complete argument against the story of January as the Merchant's autobiography is made by Beidler, "Chaucer's Merchant and the Tale of January," pp. 8–13.

40. Such circular reasoning is noted by Stevens, "'And Venus Laugheth'," pp. 120–21.

41. See Beidler, "Chaucer's Merchant and the Tale of January," pp. 11–12, for a survey of these misconceptions.

42. The quotation is from John R. Elliott, Jr., "The Two Tellers of The Merchant's Tale," *Tennessee Studies in Literature* 9 (1964): 14. The misconception is common: see also Lumiansky, *Of Sondry Folk*, p. 173; Owen, *Pilgrimage and Storytelling*, p. 190.

43. A. I. Doyle and M. B. Parkes, "The Production of Copies of the *Canterbury Tales* and the *Confessio Amantis* in the Early Fifteenth Century," in *Medieval Scribes, Manuscripts and Libraries: Essays Presented to N. R. Ker*, ed. M. B. Parkes and Andrew G. Watson (London: Scolar, 1978), esp. pp. 190–91. John S. P. Tatlock, "The *Canterbury Tales* in 1400," *Publications of the Modern Language Association* 50 (1935): 112, argues, in opposition to Kittredge, that the *Canterbury Tales* in the fifteenth century was not "a dramatic whole," but "chiefly a collection of stories."

44. A description of the miniatures in MS Gg.4.27, as well as those in a less fully illustrated Oxford manuscript, whose miniatures also do not follow the *General Prologue* very closely, is given by Margaret Rickert, *The Text of the Canterbury Tales*, ed. John M. Manly and Edith Rickert (Chicago: University of Chicago Press, 1940), 1:590–605. The miniatures of Cambridge Gg can be seen in *The Poetical Works of Geoffrey Chaucer: A Facsimile of Cambridge University Library MS GG.4.27*, introduced by M. B. Parkes and Richard Beadle (Norman, Okla.: Pilgrim Books, 1979).

45. Moreover, the *Parson's Tale* in MS Gg has several explicitly allegorical illustrations in the same style (Invidia and Charite, Glotenye and Abstinence, and Lecherye and Chastite), with no indication that these were to be regarded as any less believable than the portraits of the pilgrims.

46. R. H. Bowers, "Brathwait's 'Comments' Upon Chaucer," *Notes and Queries* 196 (1951): 558–59.

47. Brewer, *Chaucer: The Critical Heritage*, esp. 1:9–16; see also Brewer's "Some Observations on the Development of Literalism and Verbal Criticism," *Poetica* 2 (1974): 71–95.

48. In Brewer, *Chaucer: The Critical Heritage*, 1:162–63.

49. Ibid., 1:167.

50. William Blake, "A Descriptive Catalogue," in *The Complete Writings of William Blake*, ed. Geoffrey Keynes (London: Nonesuch Press, 1957), pp. 568, 569, 572, and 567. See Betsy Bowden, "The Artistic and Interpretive Context of Blake's 'Canterbury Pilgrims,'" *Blake* 13 (1980): 164–90.

51. For Ogle, see Brewer, *Chaucer: The Critical Heritage*, 1:205. For claims that Chaucer is a poet of realism and nature, see also in Brewer: Ambrose Phillips (?), writing in 1720 (1:175); John Dart and William Thomas, writing in 1721–22 (1:182, 185–86). Thomas Tyrwhitt, *The Canterbury Tales of Chaucer* (London: T. Payne, 1775), 4:116.

52. *Retrospective Review* 9 (1823): 172–206, esp. pp. 200–202.

53. *Retrospective Review* 14 (1826): 305–57, esp. p. 315.

54. Ibid., p. 339.

55. In her *Structure of the Canterbury Tales*, Cooper usefully discusses the variety of kinds of tales in the work and their often startling juxtaposition, but she does not stress the individuality of each tale as much as I think necessary.

56. Brewer, *Chaucer: The Critical Heritage*, 1: 166. See also the suggestive comments of William Hazlitt, *Characters of Shakespear's Plays* (London: 1817), p. 92: "Chaucer's mind was consecutive, rather than discursive . . . Chaucer had great variety of power, but he could do only one thing at once."

57. Brewer, *Chaucer*, p. 108; Lee W. Patterson, "The 'Parson's Tale' and the Quitting of the 'Canterbury Tales,'" *Traditio* 34 (1978): 331–80, 375. I have also profited much from the ideas in Robert O. Payne, *The Key of Remembrance* (1963; reprint, Westport, Conn.: Greenwood Press, 1973). As noted in several of the following chapters, I have often found my analysis of poetic contrast between tales anticipated, though not developed, by Paul G. Ruggiers, in his superb *The Art of the Canterbury Tales* (Madison: University of Wisconsin Press, 1965).

58. A. J. Minnis, "Discussions of 'Authorial Role' and 'Literary Form' in Late-Medieval Scriptural Exegesis," *Beiträge zur Geschichte der deutschen Sprache und Literatur* 99 (1977): 37–65. In his essay, "The Influence of Academic Prologues on the Prologues and Literary Attitudes of Late-Medieval English Writers," *Mediaeval Studies* 43 (1981): esp. p. 348, Minnis demonstrates that medieval commentators well undertood how variety in literary materials and methods could produce a coherent moral intent. See also Minnis, *Medieval Theory of Authorship* (London: Scolar, 1984).

59. On the genre of the story collection, especially in the Middle Ages, see Cooper, *Structure of the Canterbury Tales*, pp. 8–41.

60. See, for example, Winthrop Wetherbee, *Platonism and Poetry in the Twelfth Century* (Princeton: Princeton University Press, 1972), pp. 77–78; Richard A. Dwyer, *Boethian Fictions* (Cambridge, Mass.: Medieval Academy of America, 1976), esp. pp. 22–23.

61. Carol V. Kaske, "Getting Around the *Parson's Tale*: An Alternative to Allegory and Irony," in *Chaucer at Albany*, ed. Rossell Hope Robbins (New York: Burt Franklin, 1975), pp. 151–54, notes that both Boethius and the *Roman* are built on a number of limited perspectives. See also Winthrop Wetherbee, "The Literal and the Allegorical: Jean de Meun and the 'de Planctu Naturae,'" *Mediaeval Studies* 33 (1971): 264–91. Serious misunderstandings arose among later, more literal readers of the *Roman*, like Jean Gerson, who read all of the speeches as direct statements of the poet instead of as interesting but incomplete expressions of a limited perspective.

62. Cooper, *Structure of the Canterbury Tales*, pp. 41–55.

63. See, for example, the last paragraph of Robertson's *Preface to Chaucer*, p. 503.

II. Chaucer the Pilgrim and His Contrasting Tales

1. E. Talbot Donaldson, "Chaucer the Pilgrim," *Publications of the Modern Language Association* 69 (1954): 928–36; quoted here as reprinted in Donaldson, *Speaking of Chaucer* (London: Athlone Press, 1970), pp. 1–12, esp. pp. 4, 7, 8. Many of the same ideas are repeated in the commentary to Donaldson, ed., *Chaucer's Poetry* (New York: Ronald, 1958), pp. 877–81. Donaldson's argument has been generally accepted by all varieties of Chaucerians, though there has been some dissent, most notably by Bertrand H. Bronson, *In Search of Chaucer* (Toronto: University of Toronto Press, 1960), pp. 25–30, who insists that a distinct narrative persona would be impossible for a poet who read his works before an audience. For a discussion of the critical debate favorable to Donaldson's view, see William R. Crawford, *Bibliography of Chaucer 1954–63* (Seattle:

University of Washington Press, 1967), pp. xxiv–xxviii; Thomas J. Garbáty, "The Degradation of Chaucer's 'Geffrey,'" *Publications of the Modern Language Association* 89 (1974); 97–104.

2. John M. Major's description of the narrator of the *General Prologue* ("a marvelously alert, ironic, facetious master of every situation") may not be fully convincing (because it also assumes a unified characterization), but his objections to Donaldson's views have never been fully answered ("The Personality of Chaucer the Pilgrim," *Publications of the Modern Language Association* 75 [1960]: 160–62). Major correctly points out that for the pilgrim Chaucer to encompass the contradictions of the *General Prologue* (praise of both Monk and Plowman and also of both Friar and Parson) "he would have to be credulous to the point of stupidity" (p. 161); thus we are not faced with a believable dramatic character so much as with a calculated rhetorical stance. Although Garbáty generally supports Donaldson over Major, he, too, recognizes that the "naïve Chaucerian pose" is used only intermittently in the *Canterbury Tales* (pp. 98, 103).

3. See Leo Spitzer, "Note on the Poetic and the Empirical 'I' in Medieval Authors," *Traditio* 4 (1946): 414–22. For variety in the narrative voice of the *Canterbury Tales*, see also Ben Kimpel, "The Narrator of the *Canterbury Tales*," ELH 20 (1953): 77–86; Edgar H. Duncan, "Narrator's Points of View in the Portrait-sketches, Prologue to the *Canterbury Tales*," in *Essays in Honor of Walter Clyde Curry* (Nashville: Vanderbilt University Press, 1954), pp. 77–101; Ralph Baldwin, *The Unity of the Canterbury Tales*, Anglistica 5 (Copenhagen: Rosenkilde and Bagger, 1955), pp. 67–74; Rosemary Woolf, "Chaucer as a Satirist in the General Prologue to the Canterbury Tales," *Critical Quarterly* 1 (1959): 150–57.

4. Donaldson, "Chaucer the Pilgrim," p. 5.

5. Ibid., p. 8.

6. Ibid., p. 6.

7. For another view, see Paul G. Ruggiers, *The Art of the Canterbury Tales* (Madison: University of Wisconsin Press, 1965), p. 19. Ruggiers also suggests, however, that Chaucer the pilgrim remains somewhat mysterious (see esp. pp. 17, 22).

8. Bernard F. Huppé, *A Reading of the Canterbury Tales*, 2nd rev. ed. (Albany: State University of New York, 1967), p. 234.

9. Thomas A. Knott, "A Bit of Chaucer Mythology," *Modern Philology* 8 (1910): 135–39; Robert M. Lumiansky, *Of Sondry Folk: The Dramatic Principle in the Canterbury Tales* (Austin: University of Texas Press, 1955), p. 89.

10. Ruggiers, *Art of the Canterbury Tales*, p. 19; Alan T. Gaylord, "Sentence and Solaas in Fragment VII of the *Canterbury Tales*: Harry Bailly as Horseback Editor," *Publications of the Modern Language Association* 82 (1967): 226–35.

11. See Caroline F. E. Spurgeon, *Five Hundred Years of Chaucer Criticism and Allusion*, 3 vols. (1908–17; reprint, New York: Russell & Russell, 1960), 4:10–11; for other early responses to *Thopas*, see Spurgeon, 1:83–84, 185, 422, 427–28; A. Wigfall Green, "Chaucer's 'Sir Thopas': Meter, Rhyme, and Contrast," *University of Mississippi Studies in English* 1 (1960): 2; J. A. Burrow, "Sir Thopas in the Sixteenth Century," in *Middle English Studies Presented to Norman Davis*, ed. Douglas Gray and E. G. Stanley (Oxford: Clarendon Press, 1983), pp. 69–91.

12. J. A. Burrow, *Ricardian Poetry* (London: Routledge & Kegan Paul, 1971), pp. 12–21.

13. Helen S. Corsa, *Chaucer: Poet of Mirth and Morality* (Notre Dame: University of Notre Dame Press, 1964), p. 200; J. A. Burrow, "'Sir Thopas': An Agony in Three Fits," *Review of English Studies* n.s. 22 (1971): 57.

14. Many critics have been dissatisfied with the silly surface of *Thopas* and professed to find weightier themes beneath. John Speirs (*Chaucer the Maker* [1951; reprint, London: Faber and Faber, 1964], p. 181), Stephen Knight (*The Poetry of the Canterbury Tales* [Sydney: Angus and Robertson, 1973], p. 145), and Arthur K. Moore ("Sir *Thopas* as Criticism of Fourteenth-Century Minstrelsy," *Journal of English and Germanic Philology* 53 [1954]: 532–45) see *Thopas* as a work of literary criticism. Although there is certainly some truth to this observation, it runs the risk of treating the tale too solemnly. Lilian Winstanley (ed., *The Prioress's Tale: The Tale of Sir Thopas* [Cambridge: Cambridge University Press, 1922], pp. lxviii-lxxvii), John M. Manly ("Sir Thopas: A Satire," *Essays and Studies* 13 [1928]: 52–73), and F. N. Robinson (ed., *The Works of Geoffrey Chaucer*, 2nd ed. [Boston: Houghton Mifflin, 1957], p. 737) find a political message in the poem, but the inadequacy of this view has been demonstrated by William W. Lawrence, "Satire in Sir *Thopas*," *Publications of the Modern Language Association* 50 (1935): 81–91. A new but equally unconvincing approach finds a pattern of sexual reference in *Thopas*. Some find the secret message to be about homosexuality (George Williams, *A New View of Chaucer* [Durham, N.C.: Duke University Press, 1965], pp. 145–51; John Gardner, *The Poetry of Chaucer* [Carbondale: Southern Illinois University Press, 1977], pp. 307–9); some find more normal postlapsarian lust (Chauncey Wood, "Chaucer and 'Sir Thopas': Irony and Concupiscence," *Texas Studies in Literature and Language* 14 [1972]: 389–403; Mortimer J. Donovan, "Sir Thopas, 772–74," *Neuphilologische Mitteilungen* 57 [1956]: 237–46; Beryl Rowland, "Chaucer's 'Bukke and Hare' [Thop, VII, 756]," *English Language Notes* 2 [1964]: 6–8). The views of both Williams and Rowland have been attacked by Richard L. Greene, "The Hunt Is Up, Sir Thopas: Irony, Pun, and Ritual," *Notes and Queries* 211 (1966): 169–71.

15. G. K. Chesterton, *Chaucer* (1932; reprint, London: Faber and Faber, 1962), p. 21; the passage is quoted with approval by Donaldson, *Chaucer's Poetry*, p. 937.

16. Donald R. Howard, *The Idea of the Canterbury Tales* (Berkeley: University of California Press, 1976), p. 273.

17. For a translation of Boccaccio, see Charles G. Osgood, trans., *Boccaccio on Poetry*, Library of Liberal Arts (1930; reprint, Indianapolis and New York: Bobbs-Merrill, 1956). For Langland's distrust of minstrels, see, for example, *Piers Plowman*, C. Pro. 35–38. For the seriousness of medieval objections to fiction, see the very interesting article by Peter Haidu, "Repetition: Modern Reflections on Medieval Aesthetics," *Modern Language Notes* 92 (1977): 875–87.

18. Anne Middleton, "The *Physician's Tale* and Love's Martyrs: 'Ensamples Mo Than Ten' as a Method in the *Canterbury Tales*," *Chaucer Review* 8 (1973): 13.

19. I agree with Glending Olson, "A Reading of the *Thopas-Melibee* Link," *Chaucer Review* 10 (1975): 147–53, that Chaucer is here comparing his tale with other versions of the story and not suggesting that the *Melibee*, despite its many proverbs, has the same *sentence* as all of the other Canterbury tales. For this latter view, see Durant W. Robertson, Jr., *A Preface to Chaucer* (Princeton: Princeton University Press, 1963), pp. 367–69; Huppé, *A Reading of the Canterbury Tales*, pp. 235–36; Richard L. Hoffman, "Chaucer's Melibee and Tales of Sondry Folk," *Classica et Mediaevalia* 30 (1969): 560–61. The Robertsonian position has been disputed by John W. Clark, " 'This Litel Tretys' Again," *Chaucer Review* 6 (1971): 152–56.

20. See *sentence* in *A Chaucer Glossary*, ed. Norman Davis et al. (Oxford: Clarendon Press, 1979). See also Gaylord, "*Sentence and Solaas*," pp. 229–30. For the argument that

sentence need not have an allegorical significance, see Olson, *"Thopas-Melibee* Link," p. 152, n.5.

21. W. P. Ker, in *English Prose*, ed. Henry Craik (New York: Macmillan, 1916), 1:40. Gardner, *Poetry of Chaucer*, pp. 309–10; Trevor Whittock, *A Reading of the Canterbury Tales* (Cambridge: Cambridge University Press, 1968), pp. 210–17.

22. Donaldson, *Chaucer's Poetry*, p. 937. For some other discussions that take the tale seriously, see William W. Lawrence, "The Tale of Melibeus," in *Essays and Studies in Honor of Carleton Brown* (New York: New York University Press, 1940), pp. 100–110; Raymond Preston, *Chaucer* (London and New York: Sheed and Ward, 1952), pp. 212–13; Constance Woo and William Matthews, "The Spiritual Purpose of the *Canterbury Tales,"* *Comitatus* 1 (1970): 105–6; Paul Strohm, "The Allegory of the Tale of Melibee," *Chaucer Review* 2 (1967): 32–42; Charles A. Owen, Jr., "The Tale of Melibee," *Chaucer Review* 7 (1973): 267–80; Howard, *Idea of the Canterbury Tales*, pp. 309–15; Paul G. Ruggiers, "Serious Chaucer: The *Tale of Melibeus* and the Parson's Tale," in *Chaucerian Problems and Perspectives*, ed. Edward Vasta and Zacharias P. Thundy (Notre Dame: University of Notre Dame Press, 1979), pp. 83–94; Judson B. Allen and Theresa A. Moritz, *A Distinction of Stories* (Columbus: Ohio State University Press, 1981), pp. 215–17.

23. Olson, *"Thopas-Melibee* Link," p. 151.

24. Dolores Palomo, "What Chaucer Really Did to *Le Livre de Melibee," Philological Quarterly* 53 (1974): 306; Donaldson, *Chaucer's Poetry*, p. 937.

25. Gardner, *Poetry of Chaucer*, p. 310.

26. Whittock, *A Reading of the Canterbury Tales*, p. 216.

III. Chaucer's Pardoner: The Man and His Two Tales as a Defense of Christian Poetry

1. Paul G. Ruggiers, *The Art of the Canterbury Tales* (Madison: University of Wisconsin Press, 1965), p. 123; for other examples of this widespread view, see A. C. Spearing, ed., *The Pardoner's Prologue and Tale* (Cambridge: Cambridge University Press, 1965), pp. 1–2; Lee W. Patterson, "The 'Parson's Tale' and the Quitting of the 'Canterbury Tales,' " *Traditio* 34 (1978): 360–61; H. Marshall Leicester, Jr., " 'Synne Horrible': The Pardoner's Exegesis of His Tale, and Chaucer's," in *Acts of Interpretation: . . . Essays on Medieval and Renaissance Literature in Honor of E. Talbot Donaldson*, ed. Mary J. Carruthers and Elizabeth D. Kirk (Norman, Okla.: Pilgrim Books, 1982), p. 25.

2. See, most notably, Paull F. Baum, *Chaucer: A Critical Appreciation* (Durham, N.C.: Duke University Press, 1958), pp. 44–59; Bertrand H. Bronson, *In Search of Chaucer* (Toronto: University of Toronto Press, 1960), pp. 79–87; Durant W. Robertson, Jr., *A Preface to Chaucer* (Princeton: Princeton University Press, 1963), pp. 269–70; Gerald Morgan, "The Self-Revealing Tendencies of Chaucer's Pardoner," *Modern Language Review* 71 (1976): 241–55; Derek Pearsall, "Chaucer's Pardoner: The Death of a Salesman," *Chaucer Review* 17 (1983): 358–65.

3. John Halverson, "Chaucer's Pardoner and the Progress of Criticism," *Chaucer Review* 4 (1970): 196.

4. A summary of some of these different interpretations of the end is provided by Baum, *Chaucer*, pp. 54–57.

5. George Lyman Kittredge, *Chaucer and His Poetry* (1915; reprint, Cambridge: Harvard University Press, 1972), pp. 216–17.

6. Halverson, "Chaucer's Pardoner," pp. 185–86; G. G. Sedgewick, "The Progress of Chaucer's Pardoner, 1880–1940," *Modern Language Quarterly* 1 (1940): 431–58, and reprinted in the form that I shall cite throughout in Richard J. Schoeck and Jerome Taylor, eds., *Chaucer Criticism: The Canterbury Tales* (Notre Dame: University of Notre Dame Press, 1960), 1: 199–201.

7. For the first, see Kittredge, *Chaucer*, p. 180, and Bernard F. Huppé, *A Reading of the Canterbury Tales*, 2nd rev. ed. (Albany: State University of New York Press, 1967), pp. 209–19; for the second, Paul E. Beichner, "Chaucer's Pardoner as Entertainer," *Mediaeval Studies* 25 (1963): 160–72; for the third, Edmund Reiss, "The Final Irony of the Pardoner's Tale," *College English* 25 (1964): 263–66, and Monica E. McAlpine, "The Pardoner's Homosexuality and How It Matters," *Publications of the Modern Language Association* 95 (1980): 8–22.

8. That the Pardoner is after money is argued by Robert M. Lumiansky, *Of Sondry Folk: The Dramatic Principle in the Canterbury Tales* (Austin: University of Texas Press, 1955), p. 201, and by Spearing, *Pardoner's Prologue and Tale*, p. 47; that he is after revenge, by Seymour L. Gross, "Conscious Verbal Repetition in the Pardoner's 'Prologue,'" *Notes and Queries* 198 (1953): 413–14, by Penelope Curtis, "The Pardoner's 'Jape,'" *Critical Review* 11 (1968): 16, and by Donald R. Howard, *The Idea of the Canterbury Tales* (Berkeley: University of California Press, 1976), pp. 353–76; that he is after admiration, by Edward I. Condren, "The Pardoner's Bid for Existence," *Viator* 4 (1973): 177–205, and by Lee W. Patterson, "Chaucerian Confession: Penitential Literature and the Pardoner," *Medievalia et Humanistica* n.s. 7 (1976): 164; that he is after compassion, approval, or love by, for example, James L. Calderwood, "Parody in The Pardoner's Tale," *English Studies* 45 (1964): 305, by Malcolm Pittock, "The Pardoner's Tale and the Quest for Death," *Essays in Criticism* 24 (1974): 121, and by Alfred David, *The Strumpet Muse: Art and Morals in Chaucer's Poetry* (Bloomington: Indiana University Press, 1976), p. 201.

9. That the Pardoner is a *eunuchus ex nativitate* was first argued by Walter C. Curry ("The Secret of Chaucer's Pardoner," *Journal of English and Germanic Philology* 18 [1919]: 593–606; reprinted in *Chaucer and the Mediaeval Sciences*, 2nd ed. [New York: Barnes and Noble, 1960], pp. 54–70) and has since been widely accepted (see Halverson, "Chaucer's Pardoner," p. 190) even by exegetical critics (see esp. Robert P. Miller, "Chaucer's Pardoner, the Scriptural Eunuch, and the *Pardoner's Tale*," *Speculum* 30 [1955]: 180–99). Curry's conclusion has been forcefully attacked by Beryl Rowland, "Chaucer's Idea of the Pardoner," *Chaucer Review* 14 (1979): 141. The Pardoner as homosexual was first suggested tentatively by Muriel Bowden, *A Commentary on the General Prologue to the Canterbury Tales* (New York: Macmillan, 1948), p. 274, and by Gordon H. Gerould, *Chaucerian Essays* (1952; reprint, New York: Russell and Russell, 1968), p. 59; it is now a dominant strain in criticism of the *Pardoner's Tale* (see esp. McAlpine, in n. 7 above, who provides a current bibliography).

10. Eric W. Stockton, "The Deadliest Sin in The Pardoner's Tale," *Tennessee Studies in Literature* 6 (1961): 47; Beryl Rowland, "Animal Imagery and the Pardoner's Abnormality," *Neophilologus* 48 (1964): 58.

11. "Chaucer's Pardoner: His Sexuality and Modern Critics," forthcoming in *Mediaevalia*.

12. On the difference between psychological and moral fiction, see Morgan, "Self-Revealing Tendencies"; and for an argument that the Pardoner is naturalistic, though not wholly so, see Patricia M. Kean, *Chaucer and the Making of English Poetry*, 2 vols. (London: Routledge and Kegan Paul, 1972), 2:96–108.

13. For a summary of the views of older critics who believed the Pardoner is drunk, see Leo F. McNamara, "The Astonishing Performance of Chaucer's Pardoner," *Papers of the Michigan Academy of Science, Arts, and Letters* 46 (1961): 597–98. Recent critics who hold this view include Ruggiers, *Art of the Canterbury Tales*, p. 124; Spearing, *Pardoner's Prologue and Tale*, p. 22; Donald C. Steward, "Chaucer's Perplexing Pardoner," *CEA Critic* 29, iii (December 1966): 5; Trevor Whittock, *A Reading of the Canterbury Tales* (Cambridge: Cambridge University Press, 1968), p. 188; Dewey R. Faulkner, "Introduction," *Twentieth Century Interpretations of The Pardoner's Tale* (Englewood Cliffs, N.J.: Prentice-Hall, 1973), p. 11. Halverson, "Chaucer's Pardoner" (pp. 185–86), argues that the text does not support the "drunken hypothesis."

14. Calderwood, "Parody in The Pardoner's Tale," p. 304; Halverson, "Chaucer's Pardoner," pp. 196–97. See also Howard, *Idea of the Canterbury Tales*, pp. 339–71.

15. E. Talbot Donaldson, "Chaucer's Three 'P's': Pandarus, Pardoner, and Poet," *Michigan Quarterly Review* 14 (1975): 282.

16. Charles Muscatine, "*The Canterbury Tales*: Style of the Man and Style of the Work," in *Chaucer and Chaucerians*, ed. Derek Brewer (University, Ala.: University of Alabama Press, 1966), p. 112. See also Donaldson, "Chaucer's Three 'P's'," p. 283.

17. For example, N. E. Osselton, "Chaucer's 'clumsy transition' in the Pardoner's Tale," *English Studies* 49 (1968): 38, contrasts the "rhetorical tirade of the sermon on the sins of the tavern to the more intimate and often colloquial narrative of the tale of the rioters"; and David, *Strumpet Muse*, p. 194, notes the difference between the "revivalist's art" of the denunciation and the "total objectivity" of the exemplum. W. F. Bolton, "Structural Meaning in The Pardoner's Tale and The Nun's Priest's Tale," *Language and Style* 11 (1978): 202–3, actually calls the two parts "Tale I" and "Tale II," although his concern is with structural signals in the text and not with the stylistic contrast that is my subject. Sedgewick, "Progress of Chaucer's Pardoner," pp. 197–99, notes the concern of several early critics about discrepancies between different parts of the tale; and brief comments about stylistic contrast can be found in Bronson, *In Search of Chaucer*, pp. 86–87; Ralph W. V. Elliott, "Our Host's 'Triacle': Some Observations on Chaucer's 'Pardoner's Tale,'" *Review of English Literature* 7 (1966): 67; Ruggiers, *Art of the Canterbury Tales*, pp. 126–28; Curtis, "Pardoner's 'Jape'," pp. 22–29; Stephen A. Barney, "An Evaluation of the Pardoner's Tale," in *Twentieth Century Interpretations of The Pardoner's Tale*, ed. Dewey R. Faulkner (Englewood Cliffs, N.J.: Prentice-Hall, 1973), p. 87.

18. Quoted from Joachim Walsh, "St. Thomas on Preaching," *Dominicana* 5 (1921): 13; I owe this citation to Harry Caplan, "A Late Mediaeval Tractate on Preaching," in *Of Eloquence*, ed. Anne King and Helen North (Ithaca: Cornell University Press, 1970), p. 41.

19. Elliott, "Our Host's 'Triacle,'" p. 64. Patterson, "The 'Parson's Tale,'" pp. 358–59, while recognizing that the Pardoner is a fraud, says that he "produces a fine instance of one of the great set-pieces of vernacular preaching in Chaucer's day, the attack on the tavern vices."

20. Charles A. Owen, Jr., *Pilgrimage and Storytelling in the Canterbury Tales* (Norman: University of Oklahoma Press, 1977), p. 13; Curtis, "Pardoner's 'Jape'," p. 28.

21. James J. Murphy, *Rhetoric in the Middle Ages* (Berkeley: University of California Press, 1974), p. 334. The food metaphor comes from Gregory according to Murphy and is also found in Guibert de Norgent's discussion of how a sermon ought to be given (in *Readings in Medieval Rhetoric*, ed. Joseph M. Miller, M. H. Prosser, and T. W. Benson [Bloomington: Indiana University Press, 1973], p. 169). The late medieval tract on preaching translated by Caplan (see n. 18 above) similarly warns that "The preacher should with greatest care avoid prolixity in a sermon" (p. 74).

22. For the medieval distrust of empty rhetoric in preaching, see Harry Caplan, "Classical Rhetoric and the Mediaeval Theory of Preaching," in *Of Eloquence*, pp. 119–20; Frank V. Cespedes, "Chaucer's Pardoner and Preaching," *ELH* 44 (1977): 6–7. For Alain and Humbert, see *Readings in Medieval Rhetoric*, pp. 231, 250. Of course, appropriate rhetorical eloquence was often praised; see the translation of Robert of Basevorn's *Forma Praedicandi* in *Three Medieval Rhetorical Arts*, ed. James J. Murphy (Berkeley: University of California Press, 1971), pp. 131–32.

23. There has been much debate over whether the Pardoner's performance is a genuine medieval sermon; for references to previous views, see Susan Gallick, "A Look at Chaucer and His Preachers," *Speculum* 50 (1976): 467n; for some recent views, see also Warren Ginsberg, "Preaching and Avarice in *The Pardoner's Tale*," *Mediaevalia* 2 (1976): 77–79; Siegfried Wenzel, "Chaucer and the Language of Contemporary Preaching," *Studies in Philology* 73 (1976): 139–40; Cespedes, "Chaucer's Pardoner"; Robert P. Merrix, "Sermon Structure in the *Pardoner's Tale*," *Chaucer Review* 17 (1983): 235–49. Even those who believe that the Pardoner does not give a real sermon recognize his debt to medieval preaching theories and practices.

24. For the popularity of dividing a theme into three parts, see Robert of Basevorn in *Three Medieval Rhetorical Arts*, pp. 205–7; G. R. Owst, *Preaching in Medieval England* (Cambridge: Cambridge University Press, 1926), pp. 321–22; Richard H. Rouse and Mary A. Rouse, *Preachers, Florilegia and Sermons* (Toronto: Pontifical Institute, 1979), p. 85.

25. Morton W. Bloomfield, *The Seven Deadly Sins* (1952; reprint, East Lansing: Michigan State University Press, 1967), pp. 74, 95.

26. E. Talbot Donaldson, ed., *Chaucer's Poetry* (New York: Ronald, 1958), p. 929.

27. Robert of Basevorn in *Three Medieval Rhetorical Arts*, pp. 205–6; Sermon 37 in Woodburn O. Ross, ed., *Middle English Sermons*, Early English Text Society OS 209 (London: Oxford University Press, 1940), pp. 206–14.

28. The limitations of the Pardoner's discussion of gluttony become clearer if we look at the *Parson's Tale*. The Parson calls gluttony the sin that "corrumped al this world" through Adam and Eve (X.819), but he also earlier provided a long, complex analysis of the Fall showing it to involve all the senses, the Devil, and man's reason (X.322–36). For a brief account of the seriousness with which the Parson treats the Fall, see Patterson, "The 'Parson's Tale'," pp. 341–42. A similarly complex formulation occurs in a sermon from John Mirk's *Festial*, Early English Text Society ES 96 (London: Kegan Paul, 1905), in which he notes the Devil tempted Eve "of gloteny, of vayne glory, and of couetyce" (p. 83.8–9). See also Leicester, "Synne Horrible," p. 31, who calls the discussion of gluttony an example of the Pardoner's deliberate overliteralization.

29. Similarly, the Pardoner denounces gambling as the root of all evil in a tirade that ends in rather limp and worldly anticlimax (VI.591–96).

30. Sermon 17 in Ross, *Middle English Sermons*, pp. 99–103.

31. For Innocent's influence on the *Pardoner's Tale*, see Robert E. Lewis, ed., *De Miseria Condicionis Humane*, The Chaucer Library (Athens: University of Georgia Press, 1978), pp. 8–11. In the *Parson's Tale*, gluttony, the only capital sin discussed by the Pardoner, is given less space than any of the other seven. The Parson treats swearing and gambling as minor branches of the major sins.

32. See the discussion of swearing (pp. 414–25) and of the tavern sins (pp. 425–49) in G. R. Owst, *Literature and Pulpit in Medieval England*, 2nd rev. ed. (1933; reprint, Oxford: Blackwell, 1966).

33. Ibid., p. 444.

34. Ibid., pp. 428–31; the quotation (p. 427) is from a sermon probably delivered at Worcester.

35. William Langland, *The Vision of Piers Plowman*, ed. A. V. C. Schmidt (London: Dent, 1978), Passus V, 297–385.

36. Spearing, *Pardoner's Prologue and Tale*, p. 30, compares the similar lines in the *Parson's Tale* but notes the different, more worldly emphasis in the *Pardoner's Tale*.

37. *Readings in Medieval Rhetoric*, pp. 175–76.

38. For these two stories, see Owst, *Literature and Pulpit*, pp. 428, 275–76. Ross, *Middle English Sermons*, and John Mirk, from whom the second example comes, provide many other such stories.

39. Spearing, *Pardoner's Prologue and Tale*, p. 30.

40. Pittock, "The Pardoner's Tale," p. 120.

41. Robert Kilburn Root, *The Poetry of Chaucer*, rev. ed. (Boston: Houghton Mifflin, 1922), p. 230.

42. For comparison of the tale to a fabliau, see John William Mackail, as quoted in Derek Brewer, ed., *Chaucer: The Critical Heritage* (London: Routledge and Kegan Paul, 1978), 2:296; Ian Bishop, "The Narrative Art of *The Pardoner's Tale*," *Medium Aevum* 36 (1967): 20–21; Barney, "Evaluation of the *Pardoner's Tale*," pp. 89–90.

43. See N. R. Havely, *The Friar's, Summoner's and Pardoner's Tales from the Canterbury Tales* (London: University of London Press, 1975), p. 35.

44. For discussion of this kind of Christian symbolism in the tale, see esp. Robert E. Nichols, Jr., "The Pardoner's Ale and Cake," *Publications of the Modern Language Association* 82 (1967): 498–504; Rodney Delasanta, "Sacrament and Sacrifice in the *Pardoner's Tale*," *Annuale Mediaevale* 14 (1973): 43–52.

45. The Old Man is seen as Death by Root, *Poetry of Chaucer*, p. 229; as penitent avarice by Ginsberg, "Preaching and Avarice," p. 91; as the Wandering Jew by Carleton Brown, ed., *The Pardoner's Tale* (Oxford: Clarendon Press, 1935), pp. xxix-xxxii; as Old Adam by Miller, "Chaucer's Pardoner"; and as a devil by Alexandra H. Olsen, "'They Shul Desiren to Dye, and Deeth Shal Flee fro Hem': A Reconsideration of the Pardoner's Old Man," *Neuphilologische Mitteilungen* 84 (1983): 367–71.

46. Spearing, *Pardoner's Prologue and Tale*, pp. 38–40; see also Alfred David, "Criticism and the Old Man in Chaucer's *Pardoner's Tale*," *College English* 27 (1965): 39–44; Robert B. Burlin, *Chaucerian Fiction* (Princeton: Princeton University Press, 1977), p. 173.

47. William B. Toole, "Chaucer's Christian Irony: The Relationship of Character and Action in the *Pardoner's Tale*," *Chaucer Review* 3 (1968): 37–43; A. Leigh DeNeef, "Chaucer's *Pardoner's Tale* and the Irony of Misinterpretation," *Journal of Narrative Technique* 3 (1973): 85–96.

48. Joseph R. Millichap, "Transubstantiation in the *Pardoner's Tale*," *Bulletin of the Rocky Mountain MLA* 28 (1974): 102–8.

49. See esp. Barney, "Evaluation of *Pardoner's Tale*," p. 93; Bishop, "Narrative Art," p. 22; Nichols, "Pardoner's Ale and Cake," p. 503; Pittock, "The Pardoner's Tale," pp. 110ff.

50. See, for example, Gerould, *Chaucerian Essays*, pp. 69–70; Ruggiers, *Art of the Canterbury Tales*, p. 128.

51. Janet Adelman, " 'That We May Leere Som Wit,' " in *Twentieth Century Interpretations of The Pardoner's Tale*, ed. Dewey R. Faulkner (Englewood Cliffs, N. J.: Prentice-Hall, 1973), p. 104. See also the interesting discussion, without reference to the *Pardoner's Tale*, in Patterson, "The 'Parson's Tale' ": "The Parson destroys the poem, in other words, in order to release the poet from his fiction-making, to turn him finally from shadows to reality" (p. 376). It is my argument, however, that in the *Pardoner's Tale* Chaucer set out to demonstrate that some truths, some reality, can best be conveyed only through the shadows of poetic fiction.

IV. The First Two Poets of the Canterbury Tales

1. Derek Brewer, *Chaucer*, 3rd ed. (London: Longman, 1973), pp. 117–18.

2. Paul G. Ruggiers, *The Art of the Canterbury Tales* (Madison: University of Wisconsin Press, 1965), p. 60 and also p. 54. See also William C. Stokoe, Jr., "Structure and Intention in the First Fragment of The Canterbury Tales," *University of Toronto Quarterly* 21 (1952): 121–23. Patricia M. Kean (*Chaucer and the Making of English Poetry*, 2 vols. [London: Routledge and Kegan Paul, 1972], 2:95) and Stephen Knight (*The Poetry of the Canterbury Tales* [Sydney: Angus and Robertson, 1973], p. 36) both suggest the poems are different, without precise regard to the dramatic theory, but neither carries the discussion forward in any detail.

3. Robert B. Burlin, *Chaucerian Fiction* (Princeton: Princeton University Press, 1977), p. 156.

4. Those who believe the tale is appropriate to the Knight include E. Talbot Donaldson, ed., *Chaucer's Poetry* (New York: Ronald, 1958), p. 905; Bernard F. Huppé, *A Reading of the Canterbury Tales*, 2nd rev. ed. (Albany: State University of New York Press, 1967), p. 58; and Burlin, *Chaucerian Fiction*, p. 155. Peter G. Beidler, "Chaucer's 'Knight's Tale' and Its Teller," *English Record* 18 (1968): 54–60, finds the tale appropriate and summarizes the views of others. Christopher Watson, "Chaucer's Knight and His Tale," *Critical Review* 22 (1980): 56–64, shows the continuing strength of the dramatic theory. The assumption that the tale was first written before the Canterbury period weakens a dramatic reading, as do the facts that the tale is explicitly adapted to the Knight only at the beginning (esp. I.886–92) and later the story is described as written (I.1201), as Huppé notes. Brewer (*Chaucer*, p. 67) and Knight (*Poetry of the Canterbury Tales*, pp. 19–22) note inconsistencies in the voice, and Donald R. Howard (*The Idea of the Canterbury Tales* [Berkeley: University of California Press, 1976]) calls the tale an example of "unimpersonated artistry" (p. 231).

5. Jill Mann, *Chaucer and Medieval Estates Satire* (Cambridge: Cambridge University Press, 1973), pp. 106–15; Thomas J. Hatton, "Chaucer's Crusading Knight, a Slanted Ideal," *Chaucer Review* 3 (1968): 77–87.

6. Robert E. Kaske, "The Knight's Interruption of the *Monk's Tale*," *ELH* 24 (1957): 249–68, argues that both tale and later speech share Boethian ideas, but the argument is not wholly convincing. See also John M. Fyler, *Chaucer and Ovid* (New Haven: Yale University Press, 1979), pp. 146–47.

7. The disparity between the character of the Miller and the style of the tale has been noted by many, including Burlin, *Chaucerian Fiction*, p. 156; Ruggiers, *Art of the Canterbury Tales*, pp. 56–57; Brewer, *Chaucer*, p. 188; and Howard, *Idea of the Canterbury Tales*, p. 243. For a summary of critical views on the relation of the Miller to his tale, see Thomas W. Ross, ed., *The Miller's Tale*, A Variorum Edition of The Works of Geoffrey Chaucer, vol. 2, pt. 3 (Norman: University of Oklahoma Press, 1983), pp. 26–29.

8. For example, he will not "avalen" hood or hat nor "abyde no man for his curteisie" (I.3121–23).

9. For a discussion of the change in genre from *Knight's Tale* to *Miller's Tale*, see Helen Cooper, *The Structure of the Canterbury Tales* (London: Duckworth, 1983), pp. 110–16.

10. For a brief discussion of elements in the *Miller's Tale* that echo the *Knight's Tale*, see Constance B. Hieatt, ed., *The Miller's Tale* (New York: Odyssey, 1970), pp. 4–5. For a summary of other such parallels, see Ross, *Miller's Tale*, pp. 36–41.

11. As should now be clear, my view of the *Knight's Tale* generally agrees with the dominant critical tradition, most memorably expressed by Charles Muscatine, *Chaucer and the French Tradition* (Berkeley: University of California Press, 1957), pp. 175–90, that regards the tale as a serious expression of noble, chivalric values with Theseus as its hero. Although there is much to be learned from a dissident tradition that reads the tale ironically and denigrates Theseus, the result is often an extreme interpretation that distorts the tone of the work. The tragic and chaotic elements in the *Knight's Tale*, as well as the limitations of Theseus's final success, are, in my view, a measure of the philosophical seriousness of the work, not a sign of its failure. For the argument that Theseus is a failure, see Elizabeth Salter, *Chaucer: The Knight's Tale and the Clerk's Tale* (London: Arnold, 1962), pp. 9–36; that he is a tyrant, see David Aers, *Chaucer, Langland and the Creative Imagination* (London: Routledge, 1980), pp. 174–95; and that the tale is primarily comic, see Richard Neuse, "The Knight: The First Mover in Chaucer's Human Comedy," *University of Toronto Quarterly* 31 (1962): 299–315. For a brief recent discussion of some of the critical problems involved, see V. A. Kolve, *Chaucer and the Imagery of Narrative* (Stanford: Stanford University Press, 1984), p. 408, n. 1.

12. See J. A. W. Bennett, *Chaucer at Oxford and at Cambridge* (Toronto: University of Toronto Press, 1974), p. 26.

13. Muscatine, *Chaucer and the French Tradition*, pp. 175–90; see also Knight, *Poetry of the Canterbury Tales*, pp. 19–29, on the poetic texture of the tale.

14. Robert M. Jordan, *Chaucer and the Shape of Creation* (Cambridge: Harvard University Press, 1967), pp. 152–84, esp. p. 154. See also Ronald B. Herzman, "The Paradox of Form: The Knight's Tale and Chaucerian Aesthetics," *Papers on Language and Literature* 10 (1974): 339–52; Joerg O. Fichte, "Man's Free Will and the Poet's Choice: The Creation of Artistic Order in Chaucer's *Knight's Tale*," *Anglia* 93 (1975): 335–60; Robert W. Hanning, "The Theme of Art and Life in Chaucer's Poetry," in *Geoffrey Chaucer*, ed. George D. Economou (New York: McGraw-Hill, 1975), p. 33; and, most recently, Kolve, *Chaucer and Imagery*, pp. 134–36.

15. Morton W. Bloomfield, "The Miller's Tale—An UnBoethian Interpretation," in *Medieval Literature and Folklore Studies: Essays in Honor of Francis Lee Utley*, ed. Jerome Mandel

and Bruce A. Rosenberg (New Brunswick: Rutgers University Press, 1970), pp. 207–8, has called attention to Nicholas's artistic imagination and suggested that his scheme to sleep with Alisoun displays more delight in creative cleverness than in practical results; the plot he invents is "ingenious in the extreme" but, whatever its outcome, must necessarily put an end to his relations with Alisoun. Donaldson, *Chaucer's Poetry*, p. 909, also notes Nicholas's elaborate plot, and Huppé, *A Reading of the Canterbury Tales*, pp. 79–80, its ingenuity; John Gardner, *The Poetry of Chaucer* (Carbondale: Southern Illinois University Press, 1977), p. 256, mentions Nicholas's "creative brilliance"; and Jordan, *Chaucer and Creation*, p. 192, calls him "an artist, an architect of intrigue."

16. On the importance of the stadium, see Kean, *Chaucer and English Poetry*, 2:21ff.; John Halverson, "Aspects of Order in the Knight's Tale," *Studies in Philology* 57 (1960): 615. In a long, new account, Kolve, *Chaucer and Imagery*, chap. 3, discusses the iconographical importance of the amphitheater.

17. Order is seen as central to the tale by many critics, especially Halverson, "Aspects of Order"; Dale Underwood, "The First of *The Canterbury Tales*," *ELH* 26 (1959): 455–69; and Allen B. Cameron, "The Heroine in *The Knight's Tale*," *Studies in Short Fiction* 5 (1968): 119–27.

18. For examples of clever rhymes, see, in addition to the famous *queynte/queynte* (I.3275–76), *kisse/pisse* (I.3797–98) and *art/fart* (I.3805–6), the last two noted by Jordan, *Chaucer and Creation*, p. 195.

19. See Muscatine, *Chaucer and the French Tradition*, p. 224; Brewer, *Chaucer*, p. 118. The Miller-poet is usually very precise about the physical elements and relationships in his scenes, as in a relatively unimportant episode during Nicholas's tricking of John (I.3496–3500). Notice how much we are told and how exact the information is— where John gets the drink, how big it is and of what kind, who drinks it, who does what to the door, and where Nicholas sits in relationship to John.

20. Muscatine, *Chaucer and the French Tradition*, p. 177; for other examples of *occupatio*, see descriptions of battle (I.2601ff.), of a feast (I.2197–2207), and of funeral rites (I.994–1000). The narrator often asserts that, though he could say more, he must hurry on: for example, I.1029, 1188–90, 1201, 1417, 1935, 1953–54, and 2039–40. David V. Harrington, "Rhetoric and Meaning in Chaucer's *Knight's Tale*," *Papers on Language and Literature* 3, Summer Supplement (1967): 74–75, notes that *occupatio* calls attention to the poet.

21. Other examples of careful transitions include I.1001–2, 1334–36, 1449–50, 1488, 1661–62, 2093–94, 2479–82, 2741–42, and 2816.

22. Although this last comment has been seen by some as odd, the narrative voice of the *Knight's Tale*, in contrast to that of the *Miller's Tale*, repeatedly sympathizes with its characters in happiness (I.1870–74) and in sorrow (I.2652–53), and even feels sympathy for Venus (I.2663–66), each time using a variant of the rhetorical question that begins with "who." When this same formula is used in the *Miller's Tale* after Absolon's misdirected kiss, the effect is not sympathy but superior mockery (I.3747–49). Jonathan Wordsworth, "A Link Between the Knight's Tale and the Miller's," *Medium Aevum* 27 (1958): 21, notes the number of rhetorical questions in the first tale in contrast to his single one in the second.

23. For Emelye as an ideal figure, see E. Talbot Donaldson, "The Masculine Narrator and Four Women of Style," in *Speaking of Chaucer* (London: Athlone Press, 1970), p. 49. The poet's distant view is similar to Theseus's; both respect her as a courtly lady, but

neither sees her as an individual. The duke grants her joint plea that mercy be shown Palamon and Arcite in the grove, but apparently never thinks to consult her about the marriage he plans for her.

24. E. Talbot Donaldson, "Idiom of Popular Poetry in the Miller's Tale," in *Speaking of Chaucer*, p. 25.

25. Kevin S. Kiernan, "The Art of the Descending Catalogue, and a Fresh Look at Alisoun," *Chaucer Review* 10 (1975): 1–16.

26. For Chaucer's changes in characterization in the *Knight's Tale*, see Robert A. Pratt, "Chaucer's Use of the *Teseida*," *Publications of the Modern Language Association* 62 (1947): 615; Cameron, "The Heroine in The *Knight's Tale*." For the *Miller's Tale*, see esp. Paul E. Beichner, "Characterization in The *Miller's Tale*," in *Chaucer Criticism*, ed. R. J. Schoeck and J. Taylor (Notre Dame: University of Notre Dame Press, 1960), 1: 117–29.

27. See Pratt, "Chaucer's Use of *Teseida*," pp. 619–20; Salter, *Chaucer: The Knight's Tale*, pp. 12–13.

28. See Janette Richardson, *Blameth Not Me* (The Hague: Mouton, 1970), p. 165.

29. For a brief, illuminating discussion, see A. C. Spearing, ed., *The Knight's Tale* (Cambridge: Cambridge University Press, 1966), pp. 156–57, note to line 89.

30. Christopher Dean, "Imagery in the *Knight's Tale* and the *Miller's Tale*," *Mediaeval Studies* 31 (1969): 149–63.

31. Pratt, "Chaucer's Use of *Teseida*," pp. 614–16.

32. See Donaldson, "Idiom of Popular Poetry"; Kelsie B. Harder, "Chaucer's Use of the Mystery Plays in the *Miller's Tale*," *Modern Language Quarterly* 17 (1956): 193–98; Robert E. Kaske, "The *Canticum Canticorum* in the *Miller's Tale*," *Studies in Philology* 59 (1962): 479–500; Beryl Rowland, "Chaucer's Blasphemous Churl: A New Interpretation of the Miller's Tale," in *Chaucer and Middle English Studies in Honor of Rossell Hope Robbins* (London: Allen and Unwin, 1974), pp. 44–47; Jesse M. Gellrich, "The Parody of Medieval Music in the *Miller's Tale*," *Journal of English and Germanic Philology* 73 (1974): 176–88.

33. For all its faults, and with the hope that a new one will soon be ready, I have relied on the Tatlock and Kennedy *Concordance* throughout this study.

34. The word also appears once in the plural to refer to the coin at line I.3780, another commercial association.

35. See also the contrasting use of *melodye*. The word appears three times in the *Knight's Tale* (I.872, 2565, and 3097) in association with chivalric display, the last time to describe the wedding of Emelye and Palamon. Its three appearances in the *Miller's Tale* (I.3214, 3306, and 3652) are all strongly sexual. The first two describe Nicholas's music making before and after he propositions Alisoun, and the last the pleasure they both enjoy in bed.

36. For the view that Chaucer approves of the values of the *Miller's Tale*, especially as exemplified in Alisoun, see Alfred David, *The Strumpet Muse: Art and Morals in Chaucer's Poetry* (Bloomington: Indiana University Press, 1976), pp. 97, 105; Trevor Whittock, *A Reading of the Canterbury Tales* (Cambridge: Cambridge University Press, 1968), p. 87. For the view that the *Miller's Tale* supports orthodox Christian values, see, among others, Durant W. Robertson, Jr., *A Preface to Chaucer* (Princeton: Princeton University Press, 1963), pp. 382–86; W. F. Bolton, "The 'Miller's Tale': An Interpretation," *Mediaeval Studies* 34 (1962): 83–94; Thomas J. Hatton, "Absolon, Taste, and Odor in The *Miller's Tale*," *Papers on Language and Literature* 7 (1971): 72–75.

37. John's expression of concern for Alisoun (I.3488–89), sometimes taken as genuine, probably reveals worry over his prize possession rather than real affection.

V. Variety and Contrast in Chaucer's Fabliaux

1. See Robert O. Payne's suggestive comment that within the three genres of fabliau, romance, and religious tale, each of which appears four times by his reckoning in the *Canterbury Tales*, "Chaucer experiments variously with the possibilities of the form" (*The Key of Remembrance* [1963; reprint, Westport, Conn.: Greenwood Press, 1973], pp. 157–70).

2. For example, Derek Brewer, "The Fabliaux," in *Companion to Chaucer Studies*, ed. Beryl Rowland, rev. ed. (New York: Oxford University Press, 1979), p. 296, declares, "It has been reasonably suggested that these indecent anecdotes were Chaucer's greatest interest in his maturity"; Germaine Dempster, *Dramatic Irony in Chaucer* (1932; reprint, New York: Humanities Press, 1959), p. 35, calls attention to techniques Chaucer learned from the fabliaux; and Larry D. Benson and Theodore M. Andersson, eds., *The Literary Context of Chaucer's Fabliaux* (Indianapolis and New York: Bobbs-Merrill, 1971), p. ix, describe the fabliaux as "Chaucer's freshest and most original works."

3. Thomas Warton, *The History of English Poetry* (1774; reprint, London: Thomas Tegg, 1824), 2:267. For more recent echoes of the same view, see, for example, Robert Kilburn Root, *The Poetry of Chaucer*, rev. ed. (Boston: Houghton Mifflin, 1922), p. 174; E. Talbot Donaldson, ed., *Chaucer's Poetry* (New York: Ronald, 1958), pp. 909–10; Bernard F. Huppé, *A Reading of the Canterbury Tales*, 2nd rev. ed. (Albany: State University of New York Press, 1967), pp. 87–88; Stephen Knight, *The Poetry of the Canterbury Tales* (Sydney: Angus and Robertson, 1973), pp. 38–40; Robert B. Burlin, *Chaucerian Fiction* (Princeton: Princeton University Press, 1977), p. 156; Helen Cooper, *The Structure of the Canterbury Tales* (London: Duckworth, 1983), pp. 118–19.

4. For example, Charles Muscatine, *Chaucer and the French Tradition* (Berkeley: University of California Press, 1957), pp. 199–200; Donaldson, *Chaucer's Poetry*, p. 909; Paul G. Ruggiers, *The Art of the Canterbury Tales* (Madison: University of Wisconsin Press, 1965), pp. 66–67.

5. In Jean Bodel's late twelfth-century *De Gombert et des II Clers*, for example, the Aleyn-figure crawls in bed with the daughter, but, rather than taking her by force, he convinces her that she will have a golden ring (it is really from a cooking pan) if she will sleep with him. In *Le Meunier et les II Clers*, the closest known analogue to the tale, the Aleyn-figure persuades the daughter that his ring will restore her virginity. Both poems are most conveniently found in Benson and Andersson, *Literary Context of Chaucer's Fabliaux*, esp. pp. 90–93, 110–11.

6. The lack of any real trickery in both seductions in the *Reeve's Tale* as compared to *Le Meunier* or the *Miller's Tale* is noted by Roger T. Burbridge, "Chaucer's *Reeve's Tale* and the Fabliau 'Le meunier et les .II. clers,'" *Annuale Mediaevale* 12 (1971): 33–35, though his conclusions differ from mine.

7. Murray Copland, *The Reeve's Tale*: Harlotrie or Sermonyng?" *Medium Aevum* 31 (1962): 18. Walter Morris Hart, "The Reeve's Tale: A Comparative Study of Chaucer's

Narrative Art," *Publications of the Modern Language Association* 23 (1908): 12, notes the "complex social setting" Chaucer has added to the tale.

8. At the end of the portrait of Alisoun, the poet gives a typically superior, and very funny, summary of her social standing: he says she would be an appropriate flower "For any lord to leggen in his bedde, / Or yet for any good yeman to wedde" (I.3269–70). In contrast to this dismissive couplet worthy of an Alexander Pope, whose effect is to locate Alisoun's status only very generally, the precise marriage arrangements of the characters in the second fabliau are given in convincing detail.

9. J. A. W. Bennett, *Chaucer at Oxford and at Cambridge* (Toronto: University of Toronto Press, 1974), pp. 92–116, shows just how much we are told about the workings of John and Aleyn's college.

10. The "lawe" of retribution cited by Aleyn (I.4180–82), which echoes a similar sentiment of the Reeve in his prologue (I.3912), has been shown to be no actual part of the English judicial tradition but a perversion of medieval law that wrongly attempts to justify private justice. As such, it reveals no genuine learning. See Paul A. Olson, "The *Reeve's Tale*: Chaucer's Measure for Measure," *Studies in Philology* 59 (1962): 7–12; Joseph L. Baird, "Law and the *Reeve's Tale*," *Neuphilologische Mitteilungen* 70 (1969): 679–83; V. A. Kolve, *Chaucer and the Imagery of Narrative* (Stanford: Stanford University Press, 1984), p. 253 and n. 58.

11. Bennett, *Chaucer at Oxford and Cambridge*, p. 8.

12. R. E. Kaske, "An Aube in the *Reeve's Tale*," *ELH* 26 (1959): 295–310. The argument by Robert M. Correale, "Chaucer's Parody of Compline in the *Reeve's Tale*," *Chaucer Review* 1 (1967): 161–66, that the tale contains a parody of compline depends on very slight evidence.

13. For these proverbs, see R. W. Harvey, "The Reeve's Polemic," *Wascana Review* 2, i (1967): 68; Bartlett Jere Whiting, *Chaucer's Use of Proverbs*, Harvard Studies in Comparative Literature 11 (Cambridge: Harvard University Press, 1934), pp. 86–88.

14. See also Symkyn's similar boast that a miller can always deceive a clerk despite his art (I.4096–97) and the final proverb in the tale, which expresses further distrust of cleverness: "A gylour shal hymself bigyled be" (I.4321).

15. George R. Coffman, "Old Age from Horace to Chaucer: Some Literary Affinities and Adventures of an Idea," *Speculum* 9 (1934): 274–75, likens the imagery in the *Reeve's Prologue* to Shakespeare's. Its complexity is also discussed by A. H. MacLaine, "Chaucer's Wine-Cask Image: Word Play in *The Reeve's Prologue*," *Medium Aevum* 31 (1962): 129–31, and by A. C. Spearing and J. E. Spearing, eds., *The Reeve's Prologue and Tale* (Cambridge: Cambridge University Press, 1979), pp. 57–58.

16. Janette Richardson, *Blameth Nat Me* (The Hague: Mouton, 1970), p. 90, notes that the formal imagery in the tale is primarily animalistic. John B. Friedman, "A Reading of Chaucer's *Reeve's Tale*," *Chaucer Review* 2 (1968): 8, notes how many more animals are mentioned in the tale than in its closest source, *Le Meunier*.

17. Alisoun is associated with, among other things, a weasel, milk, coal, a sloe, a pear tree, a wether, a coin, a swallow, a kid, a calf, apples, hay, a colt, and a flower called a pig's eye (I.3234–68). A similarly benign attitude is created toward Absolon when, after his unfortunate kiss, he is described as weeping "as dooth a child that is ybete" (I.3759). If the image deflates and makes Absolon seem ridiculous, there is also something homey and even affectionate in the comparison—the poet's point of view

is superior but not especially nasty. For a recent discussion of celebratory imagery in the Miller's Tale, see Kolve, Chaucer and Imagery, pp. 173–85.

18. The definitive study is still J. R. R. Tolkien, "Chaucer as a Philologist: The Reeve's Tale," in Transactions of the Philological Society (1934), pp. 1–70; but see also Thomas Jay Garbáty, "Satire and Regionalism: The Reeve and His Tale," Chaucer Review 8 (1973): 1–8; N. F. Blake, "The Northernisms in The Reeve's Tale," Lore and Literature 3, i (1979): 1–8; Spearing and Spearing, Reeve's Tale, pp. 53–56.

19. Tolkien, "Chaucer as Philologist," esp. pp. 6, 46.

20. Blake, "Northernisms," p. 1.

21. Ibid., pp. 5–6.

22. Robert Worth Frank, Jr., "The Reeve's Tale and the Comedy of Limitation," in Directions in Literary Criticism: Contemporary Approaches to Literature, ed. Stanley Weintraub and Philip Young (University Park: Pennsylvania State University Press, 1973), pp. 62–63. See also Spearing and Spearing, Reeve's Tale, pp. 62–63.

23. In an extremely useful article, "Chaucer's Use of Nonce Words, Primarily in the Canterbury Tales," Neuphilologische Mitteilungen 80 (1979): 69–77, Walter Scheps shows that, whereas the frequency of nonce words to lines in the Canterbury Tales as a whole (excluding the links) is 1 to 28.8, and in the Miller's Tale, where many unique words appear in the description of Alisoun, it is 1 to 13.3, in the Reeve's Tale it is an astonishing 1 to 6.1. Some are really nonce "forms" from the northern dialect instead of nonce "words," but even if these "were excluded from consideration, the number of nonce words remaining would still be abnormally high" (pp. 73–74).

24. See n. 10 above.

25. Root, Poetry of Chaucer, p. 176.

26. Janette Richardson, "The Facade of Bawdry: Image Patterns in Chaucer's Shipman's Tale," ELH 32 (1965): 303–13, finds more imagery than I do in the tale because she defines the category much more broadly to include more than formal metaphors and similes. The only simile in the tale that is at all colorful is sexual: "As been thise wedded men, that lye and dare / As in a fourme sit a wery hare, / Were al forstraught with houndes grete and smale" (VII.103–5).

27. Raymond Preston, Chaucer (London: Sheed and Ward, 1952), p. 206. See also T. W. Craik, The Comic Tales of Chaucer (London: Methuen, 1964), pp. 69–70; Derek Brewer, Chaucer, 3rd ed. (London: Longman, 1973), p. 175; V. J. Scattergood, "The Originality of the Shipman's Tale," Chaucer Review 11 (1977): 210.

28. For example, complaints like those of Knight, Poetry of the Canterbury Tales, p. 137, that the poetry is "not striking" and the use of speech "unsubtle" and dull, result from expecting the same style as in Chaucer's other fabliaux. The Shipman's Tale is not inferior, it is different.

29. John C. McGalliard, "Characterization in Chaucer's Shipman's Tale," Philological Quarterly 54 (1975): 14.

30. As another example, the word frankes appears ten times in the Shipman's Tale and nowhere else in Chaucer.

31. On the large amount of dialogue, see William W. Lawrence, "Chaucer's Shipman's Tale," Speculum 33 (1958): 57.

32. Both McGalliard, "Characterization in Shipman's Tale," pp. 5–8, and Scattergood, "Originality of Shipman's Tale," pp. 222–24, discuss the importance of speech in the tale

and note that each character is given a distinct voice that varies depending on who is addressing whom.

33. Craik, *Comic Tales*, pp. 56–70.

34. For the absurdity of the wife's claim to be upholding her husband's honor, see George R. Keiser, "Language and Meaning in Chaucer's *Shipman's Tale*," *Chaucer Review* 12 (1978): 149–150. Note also her similarly hypocritical appeals to honor later at lines VII.408 and 421.

35. I am adapting Keiser's comment that the tale contains a "larger pattern of imprecise use of language by means of which characters conceal from each other and apparently also from themselves the nature of their petty and calculating motives" ("Language and Meaning," p. 147).

36. Peter Nicholson, "The 'Shipman's Tale' and the Fabliaux," *ELH* 45 (1978): 588.

37. See Claude Jones, "Chaucer's *Taillynge Ynough*," *Modern Language Notes* 52 (1937): 570; Robert A. Caldwell, "Chaucer's *Taillynge Ynough, Canterbury Tales*, B² 1624," *Modern Language Notes* 55 (1940): 262–65; Albert H. Silverman, "Sex and Money in Chaucer's *Shipman's Tale*," *Philological Quarterly* 32 (1953): 329–36. Murray Copland, "The *Shipman's Tale*: Chaucer and Boccaccio," *Medium Aevum* 35 (1966): 12, n.5, suggests a triple pun: "tail," "tally," and perhaps "tale."

38. David H. Abraham, "*Cosyn* and *Cosynage*: Pun and Structure in the *Shipman's Tale*," *Chaucer Review* 11 (1977): 319–27. For the claim that there is also a pun on *chevyssaunce* in the tale, see Lorraine K. Stock, "The Meaning of *Chevyssaunce*: Complicated Word Play in Chaucer's *Shipman's Tale*," *Studies in Short Fiction* 19 (1981): 245–49. The puns of the *Shipman's Tale* are also seen as extensive and central by Cooper, *Structure of the Canterbury Tales*, pp. 164–65.

39. Charles A. Owen, Jr., *Pilgrimage and Storytelling in the Canterbury Tales* (Norman: University of Oklahoma Press, 1977), p. 116.

40. The role reversals of monk and merchant have been noted by Bernard S. Levy, "The Quaint World of *The Shipman's Tale*," *Studies in Short Fiction* 4 (1967): 112–13. The business skills of the monk have been noted by Craik, *Comic Tales*, p. 64, and of the monk and the wife by Keiser, "Language and Meaning," pp. 149–50.

41. Keiser, "Language and Meaning," p. 151.

42. Nevill Coghill, *The Poet Chaucer* (London: Oxford University Press, 1949), p. 167.

43. Copland, "*Shipman's Tale*," p. 13; Ruggiers, *Art of the Canterbury Tales*, p. 87. See also Trevor Whittock, *A Reading of the Canterbury Tales* (Cambridge: Cambridge University Press, 1968), pp. 195–201.

44. Previous Christian interpretations of the tale, some rather strained, include Richardson, "Facade of Bawdry," pp. 309–11; Levy, "Quaint World," pp. 112–18; Joseph R. Millichap, "Source and Theme in the *Shipman's Tale*," *University of Dayton Review* 10, iii (1974): 3–6; and Gail McMurray Gibson, "Resurrection as Dramatic Icon in the Shipman's Tale," in *Signs and Symbols in Chaucer's Poetry*, ed. John P. Hermann and John J. Burke, Jr. (University, Ala.: University of Alabama Press, 1981), pp. 102–12.

45. Robert E. Kaske, "The *Canticum Canticorum* in the *Miller's Tale*," *Studies in Philology* 59 (1962): 497.

46. The irony of the monk's freshly shaved tonsure has been noted by Craik, *Comic Tales*, p. 63; by Copland, "*Shipman's Tale*," p. 13; and by Scattergood, "Originality of *Shipman's Tale*," p. 215, who also calls attention to the Sabbath as the day of assignation, as does Richardson, *Blameth Nat Me*, p. 116.

47. The literature of this debate is extensive and has been briefly mentioned in my first chapter. Perhaps the most influential proponent of the comic view of the Merchant's Tale has been Bertrand H. Bronson, "Afterthoughts on the Merchant's Tale," Studies in Philology 58 (1961): 583–96, which prompted a spirited response from E. Talbot Donaldson in defense of the older, darker view, "The Effect of the Merchant's Tale," in Speaking of Chaucer (London: Athlone Press, 1970), pp. 30–45. This debate, and many others about the tale, have been chronicled in detail by Emerson Brown, Jr., "Chaucer, the Merchant, and Their Tale: Getting Beyond Old Controversies," Chaucer Review 13 (1978): 141–56, 247–62.

48. Helen S. Corsa, Chaucer: Poet of Mirth and Morality (Notre Dame: University of Notre Dame Press, 1964), p. 165.

49. Paul E. Beichner, "Chaucer's Hende Nicholas," Mediaeval Studies 14 (1952): 151–53.

50. The Merchant's Tale does not use a particularly distinct vocabulary. In contrast to the Reeve's Tale, which has the highest percentage of nonce words in the Tales, the Merchant's Tale has one of the lowest (see Scheps, "Chaucer's Use of Nonce Words"). Occasionally, however, the poet indulges in fabliaulike wordplay for his own moral purposes. For example, the two appearances of appetyt are nicely balanced. It first occurs early in the tale to describe January's lifelong sexual promiscuity (IV.1250), and it is used again only near the end when May requests a pear in the garden (IV.2336). May implies that her hunger is the innocent result of a much-desired pregnancy, but the repetition of the word alerts us that her appetite, like January's before, is really for lechery. The poet similarly plays with the word corage to reinforce a serious theme: January's self-delusion. The first four times the word appears (IV.1254, 1513, 1725, and 1759), it is used by January and others to applaud his sexual boldness in daring to marry. In its last appearance, the truth is finally revealed; far from possessing the sexual vigor to satisfy a young wife, the old knight must resort to aphrodisiacs "t'encreessen his corage" (IV.1808).

51. Coghill, Poet Chaucer, p. 170; G. G. Sedgewick, "The Structure of The Merchant's Tale," University of Toronto Quarterly 17 (1948): 344. The poet's specific mention of other authors and works covers a wide spectrum that ranges from Cato (IV.1377) to Constantine's De Coitu (IV.1811) and from Claudian (IV.2232) to the Roman de la Rose (IV.2032). The frequent allusions to biblical and classical figures are equally varied, extending from a famous group of biblical women (IV.1362–74) to Priapus (IV.2034) and from several mentions of Venus and the Virgin to single mentions of the mysterious Wade (IV.1424) and Chaucer's own Wife of Bath (IV.1685). This extraordinary learning does not mean that the poet has abandoned the fabliau; rather, he has added a wider frame of reference by which to assess it.

52. As always with this poet, the reader cannot accept at face value the allusions presented, but must remain continually alert. During the wedding feast, for instance, January looks at May and imagines that "he that nyght in armes wolde hire streyne / Harder than evere Parys dide Eleyne" (IV.1753–54). The reader may laugh at such a grandiose comparison, but January has chosen the right story and his faulty casting perfectly defines his self-delusion. Although May is definitely Helen, it is Damyan who takes the role of Paris—leaving the old knight to play the cuckold Menelaus.

53. For some interpretations of the meaning of January's garden, see D. W. Robertson, Jr., "The Doctrine of Charity in Mediaeval Literary Gardens: A Topical Approach through Symbolism and Allegory," Speculum 26 (1951): 24–49; Kenneth Kee, "Two

Chaucerian Gardens," *Mediaeval Studies* 23 (1961): 154–62; Karl P. Wentersdorf, "Theme and Structure in *The Merchant's Tale*: The Function of the Pluto Episode," *Publications of the Modern Language Association* 80 (1965): 522–27; Bruce A. Rosenberg, "The 'Cherry-Tree Carol' and the *Merchant's Tale*," *Chaucer Review* 5 (1971): 264–76; Kenneth A. Bleeth, "The Image of Paradise in the *Merchant's Tale*," in *The Learned and the Lewed: Studies in Chaucer and Medieval Literature*, ed. Larry D. Benson, Harvard English Studies 5 (Cambridge: Harvard University Press, 1974), pp. 45–60.

54. Some kinds of speech that we have learned to expect from Chaucer's other fabliaux are either missing or greatly changed in the *Merchant's Tale*. For example, unlike the voluble clerks in the first two fabliaux (even the northern students are talkative if inarticulate), Damyan is allowed only one speech throughout the entire tale: a weak two-line plea to May for mercy (IV.1942–43). He ends where Nicholas begins. In contrast to Chaucer's other fabliaux, where speech between characters is frequent and often persuasive, is the absence of anything like conversation in the *Merchant's Tale*. The few passages of dialogue (between Justinus and Placebo or Pluto and Proserpina) are formal statements of absolutely opposed positions in which any victory is usually by default, not reasoned argument.

55. Huppé, *A Reading of the Canterbury Tales*, pp. 154–55, notes that the Parson makes clear the error of January's ways.

56. Dempster, *Dramatic Irony*, p. 57, commenting on the end of the tale (IV.2357–60), asks "Who else [but Chaucer], in the course of the ribald tale, would have devoted four long lines to the psychology of the victim?" Such attention is certainly worthy of note, but it perhaps tells us more about the special poet of the *Merchant's Tale* than about Chaucer, who shows no such interest in other ribald tales.

57. Mary C. Schroeder, "Fantasy in the 'Merchant's Tale,'" *Criticism* 12 (1970): 169. Similarly, the only passage that is anything like a portrait of Damyan actually tells us more about the foolishness of January. The squire is described to May by the old knight in terms that extol him as the ideal courtly lover (for example, "discreet" as well as "manly"), thus making January at least partly the pandar of his own cuckolding (IV.1907–12).

58. Muscatine, *Chaucer and the French Tradition*, p. 232.

59. The manipulations of the narrative voice have been discussed by most critics from Kittredge to Donaldson and remain central to recent interpretations of the poem. The voice is often identified with the teller Merchant, though there is no good reason to do so. Nothing in the account of the Merchant in the *General Prologue* or the prologue to his own tale prepares us for the learning, stylistic variety, complex irony, and brilliant nastiness exhibited by the poet of the *Merchant's Tale* and his narrative voice. See the discussion of the pilgrim Merchant's relationship to his tale in chapter I, pp. 14–16.

60. A recent summary discussion of the relationship between the narrator and January in the opening encomium is by Donald R. Benson, "The Marriage 'Encomium' in the *Merchant's Tale*: A Chaucerian Crux," *Chaucer Review* 14 (1979): 48–60.

61. On the poet's skill with "softely," see Donaldson, "Effect of the Merchant's Tale," pp. 36–37.

62. J. S. P. Tatlock, "Chaucer's *Merchant's Tale*," *Modern Philology* 33 (1936): 375.

63. For the corrosive nastiness of the narrator, see esp. Tatlock, "Chaucer's *Merchant's Tale*," pp. 367–81; Norman T. Harrington, "Chaucer's Merchant's Tale: Another Swing

of the Pendulum," *Publications of the Modern Language Association* 86 (1971): 25–31; Robin Grove, "The Merchant's Tale: Seeing, Knowing and Believing," *Critical Review* 18 (1976): 23–38; Jay Schleusener, "The Conduct of the *Merchant's Tale*," *Chaucer Review* 14 (1980): 237–50.

64. In a continually stimulating and doctrinally sound article, Emerson Brown, Jr., "Biblical Women in the *Merchant's Tale*: Feminism, Antifeminism, and Beyond," *Viator* 5 (1974): 387–412, shows that, although the praise of the four biblical women at IV.1362–74 at first seems merely ironic, these women can also be presented as religious heroines, as they are in *Melibee*, and thus they offer some answer to the cynicism of the tale.

65. That the *Merchant's Tale* contains a potentially positive view of marriage has been argued by Albert C. Baugh, "The Original Teller of the Merchant's Tale," *Modern Philology* 35 (1937): 15–26, and by C. Hugh Holman, "Courtly Love in the Merchant's and the Franklin's Tales," *ELH* 18 (1951): 241–52.

VI. The Contrasting Religious Tales of the Prioress and Second Nun

1. Mary Giffin, "Hir Hous the Chirche of Seinte Cecilie Highte," in *Studies on Chaucer and His Audience* (Hull, Québec: Les Éditions 'L'Éclair,' 1956), p. 32, notes that in MS Harleian 2382, a fifteenth-century miscellany of primarily religious pieces, the only two selections from Chaucer are the *Prioress's Tale* and the *Second Nun's Tale*.

2. For comparisons between the *Second Nun's Tale* and the *Canon's Yeoman's Tale*, see esp. Joseph E. Grennen, "Saint Cecilia's 'Chemical Wedding': The Unity of the *Canterbury Tales*, Fragment VIII," *Journal of English and Germanic Philology* 65 (1966): 466–81; Bruce A. Rosenberg, "The Contrary Tales of the Second Nun and the Canon's Yeoman," *Chaucer Review* 2 (1968): 278–91. For briefer comparisons between the *Prioress's Tale* and the *Shipman's Tale*, see Sherman Hawkins, "Chaucer's Prioress and the Sacrifice of Praise," *Journal of English and Germanic Philology* 63 (1964): 621; G. H. Russell, "Chaucer: The Prioress's Tale," in *Medieval Literature and Civilization: Studies in Memory of G. N. Garmonsway*, ed. D. A. Pearsall and R. A. Waldron (London: Athlone Press, 1969), pp. 211–13.

3. Brief comparisons between the two nuns' tales are offered by Alan T. Gaylord, "The Unconquered Tale of the Prioress," *Papers of the Michigan Academy of Science, Arts, and Letters* 47 (1962): 633–34, and by Stephen Knight, *The Poetry of the Canterbury Tales* (Sydney: Angus and Robertson, 1973), pp. 143, 175, both of whom find the *Second Nun's Tale* the more serious religious work. In a note amidst a long, appreciative discussion of the *Prioress's Tale*, Robert B. Burlin, *Chaucerian Fiction* (Princeton: Princeton University Press, 1977), p. 278, n. 11, finds the *Prioress's Prologue* far superior to the Second Nun's; Yvonne Rodax, *The Real and the Ideal in the Novella* (Chapel Hill: University of North Carolina Press, 1968), pp. 9–11, considers the *Prioress's Tale* a greater poem than the *Second Nun's Tale*. See also the more evenhanded comparison of the two tales by Patricia M. Kean, *Chaucer and the Making of English Poetry*, 2 vols. (London: Routledge and Kegan Paul, 1972), 2:201–9.

4. As often, the dramatic reading of the Prioress by George Lyman Kittredge, *Chaucer and His Poetry* (1915; reprint, Cambridge: Harvard University Press, 1972), pp. 174–82, has been influential, though hardly restrictive. Summaries of critical interpretations of

the character of the Prioress and its relation to her tale are given by Florence H. Ridley, *The Prioress and the Critics*, University of California English Studies 30 (Berkeley: University of California Press, 1965), and by Gaylord, "The Unconquered Tale of the Prioress," p. 614. The more extreme dramatic interpretations of Madame Eglentyne have
been questioned: critics from Lilian Winstanley (ed., *The Prioress's Tale: The Tale of Sir
Thopas* [Cambridge: Cambridge University Press, 1922]) to Hardy Long Frank ("Chaucer's Prioress and the Blessed Virgin," *Chaucer Review* 13 [1979]: 346–62) have cast
doubt on the popular assumption that the Prioress and her tale are meant to be seen
satirically. Even Burlin, *Chaucerian Fiction*, pp. 193–94, who is usually an enthusiastic
supporter of the dramatic approach, suggests that, instead of bringing our judgments
about the Prioress to the tale, "it seems wisest to test the purely literary evidence."

5. Norman E. Eliason, "Chaucer's Second Nun?" *Modern Language Quarterly* 3 (1942):
9–16, even argues that there is a reasonable doubt about the existence of a second
nun.

6. F. N. Robinson, ed., *The Works of Geoffrey Chaucer*, 2nd ed. (Boston: Houghton Mifflin, 1957), p. 755: "The *Second Nun's Prologue and Tale* are held generally, and with the
highest probability, to be early writings of Chaucer, which he took over, but never
really adapted, for the *Canterbury Tales*." The persistence of this opinion is found in Russell A. Peck, "The Ideas of 'Entente' and Translation in Chaucer's *Second Nun's Tale*,"
Annuale Mediaevale 8 (1967): 17, and in V. A. Kolve, "Chaucer's *Second Nun's Tale* and the
Iconography of Saint Cecilia," in *New Perspectives in Chaucer Criticism*, ed. Donald M. Rose
(Norman, Okla.: Pilgrim Books, 1981), p. 138. The case against the tale as an early and
unrevised work has been argued most persuasively by Paul M. Clogan, "The Figural
Style and Meaning of *The Second Nun's Prologue and Tale*," *Medievalia et Humanistica* n.s. 3
(1972): 213–15. For other arguments that the work is late, see William B. Gardner,
"Chaucer's 'Unworthy Sone of Eve,'" *University of Texas Studies in English* 26 (1947): 77–83;
Giffin, "Hir Hous the Chirche," pp. 29–48; Trevor Whittock, *A Reading of the Canterbury
Tales* (Cambridge: Cambridge University Press, 1968), pp. 251–52; and the critics cited
in n. 2 above who argue a close connection between the tale and the following *Canon's Yeoman's Tale*.

7. The belief that Chaucer uses the *Prioress's Tale* to criticize the Prioress's anti-Semitism is widely accepted. Two of the most influential arguments for this position are by
R. J. Schoeck, "Chaucer's Prioress: Mercy and Tender Heart," *The Bridge, A Yearbook of Ju-
deo-Christian Studies* 2 (1956): 239–55, reprinted in Richard J. Schoeck and Jerome Taylor, eds., *Chaucer Criticism: The Canterbury Tales* (Notre Dame: University of Notre Dame
Press, 1960), 1:245–58, and by E. Talbot Donaldson, ed., *Chaucer's Poetry* (New York:
Ronald, 1958), pp. 933–34; but see Ridley, *The Prioress and the Critics*. The most balanced
and convincing assessment of the question is by Albert B. Friedman, "The Prioress's Tale
and Chaucer's Anti-Semitism," *Chaucer Review* 9 (1974): 118–29. Friedman notes the
naïveté of those who argue that medieval Christianity was not deeply anti-Semitic, and
suggests that the topic has been given too much attention recently because of under-
standable modern sensibilities. See also Robert Worth Frank, Jr., "Miracles of the Virgin, Medieval Anti-Semitism, and the 'Prioress's Tale,'" in *The Wisdom of Poetry: Essays in
Early English Literature in Honor of Morton W. Bloomfield*, ed. Larry D. Benson and Siegfried
Wenzel (Kalamazoo: Medieval Institute Publications, 1982), pp. 177–88.

8. Burlin, *Chaucerian Fiction*, p. 186, calls the prologue a "gem of construction"; its au-

reate diction has been discussed by John Lawlor, *Chaucer* (1968; reprint, New York: Harper and Row, 1969), pp. 129–30. The *Prioress's Prologue* has often been praised—see, for example, Donaldson, *Chaucer's Poetry*, p. 933; Kean, *Chaucer and English Poetry*, 2:188–90, 195–96; Russell, "Chaucer: The Prioress's Tale," pp. 214–16; Knight, *Poetry of the Canterbury Tales*, pp. 139–40.

9. See Robinson, *The Works of Chaucer*, pp. 734–35, n. 453ff.; Sister M. Madeleva, "Chaucer's Nuns," in *A Lost Language and Other Essays on Chaucer* (New York: Sheed and Ward, 1951), pp. 51–55. See also Marie P. Hamilton, "Echoes of Childermas in the Tale of the Prioress," *Modern Language Review* 34 (1939): 1–8; Beverly Boyd, *Chaucer and the Liturgy* (Philadelphia: Dorrance, 1967), pp. 67–69.

10. For analysis of the prologue to the *Second Nun's Tale*, see Clogan, "Figural Style and Meaning"; Kean, *Chaucer and English Poetry*, 2:190–97; Knight, *Poetry of the Canterbury Tales*, pp. 175–77.

11. Of course, nothing like this careful investigation of what can be in a name is found in the *Prioress's Prologue*. For example, when God is invoked in the first line, his name is not analyzed intellectually but repeated as in the liturgy and then reverently praised: "O Lord, oure Lord, thy name how merveillous" (VII.453). Compare the similar repetition of Mary's name at VII.467.

12. See John L. Lowes, "The Second Nun's Prologue, Alanus, and Macrobius," *Modern Philology* 15 (1917): 193–202; Carleton Brown, "The Prologue of Chaucer's 'Lyf of Seint Cecile,'" *Modern Philology* 9 (1911): 1–16; and, for a summary of liturgical echoes, Boyd, *Chaucer and the Liturgy*, pp. 29–33. The argument by Robert Pratt, "Chaucer Borrowing from Himself," *Modern Language Quarterly* 7 (1946): 259–61, that Chaucer's direct source for the *Prioress's Prologue* is not Dante but the Second Nun's *Invocacio ad Mariam* has led at least one critic to call the latter merely a "rough draft" for the former (Burlin, *Chaucerian Fiction*, p. 278, n. 11). I believe such a conclusion misjudges the integrity and achievement of each prologue and their deliberate differences.

13. Writing is emphasized throughout the *Second Nun's Prologue* (esp. VIII.25 and 113); Peck, "Ideas of 'Entente' and Translation," esp. pp. 21ff., argues that the prologue is a defense of the importance of writing.

14. Russell, "Chaucer: The Prioress's Tale," pp. 215–16; see also Kean, *Chaucer and English Poetry*, 2:195–96. A striking example of an extended argument is the stanza between lines VIII.36 and 42. The intellectual and poetic complexity of the Second Nun's praise of Mary has been noted by Kean, *Chaucer and English Poetry*, 2:197; Peck, "Ideas of 'Entente' and Translation," pp. 22–23; Clogan, "Figural Style and Meaning," pp. 221–31.

15. On the originality of this image, see Clogan, "Figural Style and Meaning," p. 227.

16. Grennen, "Saint Cecilia's 'Chemical Wedding'"; Clogan, "Figural Style and Meaning," pp. 219–20.

17. Edward H. Kelly, "By Mouth of Innocentz: The Prioress Vindicated," *Papers on Language and Literature* 5 (1969): 370, notes that the narrator of the *Prioress's Tale* "becomes a dramatic participant in his own story."

18. Walter Morris Hart, "Some Old French Miracles of Our Lady and Chaucer's Prioresses Tale," *California University Publications in Modern Philology* 11 (1922): 40ff., notes the importance of the emotions of joy and sorrow in Gautier de Coincy's miracles of the Virgin.

19. The absence of any hint of a dramatic narrator is one reason the *Second Nun's Tale* has been considered an early work, even though all of Chaucer's major pre-Canterbury poems have intrusive, ironic narrators.

20. An example of the poet's restraint can be seen in lines VIII.358–64, which is a summary ("But atte laste, to tellen short and pleyn") of a longer passage in the sources. Indeed, the phrase "short and pleyn" perfectly describes the poet's style.

21. See also lines VIII.222, 367, 391.

22. The dialogue of the tale is praised by Knight, *Poetry of the Canterbury Tales*, pp. 178–79.

23. The significance of the trial scene is noted by Paul E. Beichner, "Confrontation, Contempt of Court, and Chaucer's Cecilia," *Chaucer Review* 8 (1974): 198–204; Sherry L. Reames, "The Sources of Chaucer's 'Second Nun's Tale,'" *Modern Philology* 76 (1978): 129.

24. Cecile's command of speech is especially evident during the extended trial scene. She begins with the most technical of verbal quibbles, a quibble that both deliberately misunderstands the point of her accuser's first question (VIII.424–25) and asserts that in his second question he "axed lewedly" (VIII.430), before she goes on to make more profound criticisms of Almachius's use of language. She compares his power to that of empty speech ("a bladdre ful of wynd" [VIII.439]) and later asserts that his claim to power is nothing but a lie (VIII.484–86). Cecile also insists that the Roman accusations against the Christians are "a wood sentence" and "nat sooth" (VIII.450–51).

25. The verb *songe* appears once in the *Second Nun's Prologue* (VIII.69) and the verb *sang* once in the *Second Nun's Tale* (VIII.135).

26. Russell, "Chaucer: The Prioress's Tale," pp. 223–24, argues that the boy's final speech is authoritative and not at all childish; Phyllis C. Gage, "Syntax and Poetry in Chaucer's *Prioress's Tale*," *Neophilologus* 50 (1966): 252–61, claims that even the syntax changes. Hawkins, "Chaucer's Prioress and the Sacrifice of Praise," argues that the child grows during the story.

27. Hamilton, "Echoes of Childermas." See also J. C. Wenk, "On the Sources of *The Prioress's Tale*," *Mediaeval Studies* 17 (1955): 214–19; Boyd, *Chaucer and the Liturgy*, pp. 64–72; Audrey Davidson, "*Alma Redemptoris Mater*: The Little Clergeon's Song," *Studies in Medieval Culture* 4 (1974): 462–63; John C. Hirsh, "Reopening the *Prioress's Tale*," *Chaucer Review* 10 (1975): 30–45. For a discussion of the emotional and liturgical style of the *Prioress's Tale*, see Alfred David, "An ABC to the Style of the Prioress," in *Acts of Interpretation: . . . Essays on Medieval and Renaissance Literature in Honor of E. Talbot Donaldson*, ed. Mary J. Carruthers and Elizabeth D. Kirk (Norman, Okla.: Pilgrim Books, 1982), pp. 147–57.

28. On the lowering of the child's age from ten to seven, see Carleton Brown, *A Study of the Miracle of Our Lady Told by Chaucer's Prioress*, Chaucer Society, 2nd ser., no. 45 (London: Kegan Paul, 1910), pp. 112–13; Gaylord, "The Unconquered Tale of the Prioress," p. 635; Hawkins, "Chaucer's Prioress and the Sacrifice of Praise," pp. 607–8.

29. Of course, as befits its subject, words like *children*, *widow*, and *mooder* appear frequently, but the use of the word *sone* is more revealing. It occurs five times in the *Prioress's Tale* (VII.466, 480, 502, 509, and 605); the first two instances are in the prologue and refer to Christ, but its three appearances in the tale refer more sentimentally to the little boy. *Son* appears eight times in the *Second Nun's Prologue and Tale*; in all

but one case—the poet's famous self-description as an "unworthy sone of Eve" (VIII.62)—the reference is to Christ (VIII.36, 42, 325, 326, 330, 345, 417).

30. Gaylord, "The Unconquered Tale of the Prioress," p. 632. See also Robert O. Payne, *The Key of Remembrance* (1963; reprint, Westport, Conn.: Greenwood Press, 1973), p. 169; Hawkins, "Chaucer's Prioress and the Sacrifice of Praise," p. 600; Kelly, "By Mouth of Innocentz," p. 366.

31. See also other doublets immediately following at VII.520, 524, 534, 545, 547, 553, 597, 600. This list does not include an even larger number of repeated phrases that are not precisely identical but whose difference is minimal, such as "foule usure and lucre of vileynye" (VII.491), "to syngen and to rede" (VII.500), and "Oure blisful Lady, Cristes mooder deere" (VII.510). See also similarly repetitious phrases at VII.501, 516, 521, 528, 533, 546, 549, 552, 558, 570, 618, 619, 628, 632, 653, 656, 663, 670.

32. Friedman, "The *Prioress's Tale* and Chaucer's Anti-Semitism," p. 125.

33. For the *Prioress's Tale* as a example of affective piety, see Hirsh, "Reopening the *Prioress's Tale*," pp. 37–39. For a recent discussion of affective piety in Middle English religious poetry, see Douglas Gray, *Themes and Images in the Medieval English Religious Lyric* (London: Routledge and Kegan Paul, 1972), pp. 18–30.

34. See, for example, Rosemary Woolf, *The English Religious Lyric in the Middle Ages* (Oxford: Clarendon Press, 1968), esp. pp. 1–15.

35. See Millett Henshaw, "The Preface of St. Ambrose and Chaucer's *Second Nun's Tale*," *Modern Philology* 26 (1928): 15–16.

36. Sherry L. Reames, "The Cecilia Legend as Chaucer Inherited It and Retold It: The Disappearance of an Augustinian Ideal," *Speculum* 55 (1980): 38–57, argues that the *Second Nun's Tale* is more pessimistic than its sources about a convert's ability or need to understand what is happening to him, and she insists that the tale consistently reduces passages that explain the intellectual basis of faith. I believe that Reames misreads the tale because she fails to distinguish between the dramatic presentation of an intellectual faith, which Chaucer has done successfully, and the literal presentation of these arguments at length, which would be inappropriate in a narrative poem (Reames apparently wants the tale to be more like the *Melibee*). In contrast, Kean, *Chaucer and English Poetry*, 2:202, notes that there is as much emphasis on "conversion by doctrine" as on marvels in the tale. The genuine concern in the *Second Nun's Tale* with learned belief is clear when the tale is read along with the *Prioress's Tale*, thus proving again the value of such comparisons.

37. The mixture of violence and sentimentality in the tale has been commented upon by many critics. See, for example, Donaldson, *Chaucer's Poetry*, p. 933; Alfred David, *The Strumpet Muse: Art and Morals in Chaucer's Poetry* (Bloomington: Indiana University Press, 1976), pp. 208–14; and, less convincingly, Maurice Cohen, "Chaucer's Prioress and Her Tale: A Study of Anal Character and Anti-Semitism," *Psychoanalytic Quarterly* 31 (1962): 232–49. The execution of the Jews in particular has frequently been criticized, but Friedman, "The *Prioress's Tale* and Chaucer's Anti-Semitism," pp. 118–19, argues that the tale is less brutal than it might have been. Nevertheless, the tale is undoubtedly melodramatic. For example, the description of the privy where the boy's body is cast after his murder appears to veer from the prudish—as seen in the euphemism "wardrobe" (John W. Draper, "Chaucer's Wardrobe," *Englische Studien* 60 [1926]: 249)—to the lurid. At the conclusion of a stanza, we are told that the body has been thrown in a

pit, but the poet then offers two additional lines of description, given special emphasis because they begin a new stanza, that intensify our disgust: "I seye that in a wardrobe they hym threwe / Where as thise Jewes purgen hire entraille" (VII.572–73).

38. The theme of busyness in the tale has been noted by Giffin, "Hir Hous the Chirche," pp. 40–41; Grennen, "Saint Cecilia's 'Chemical Wedding,'" p. 475; Rosenberg, "The Contrary Tales of the Second Nun and the Canon's Yeoman," p. 282; Clogan, "Figural Style and Meaning," pp. 218–20; Knight, *Poetry of the Canterbury Tales*, pp. 175–79; Janemarie Luecke, "Three Faces of Cecilia: Chaucer's *Second Nun's Tale*," *American Benedictine Review* 33 (1982): 335–48. The words *work, working,* and *works* occur frequently in the prologue to the *Second Nun's Tale* and occasionally in the tale itself, but not once in the *Prioress's Prologue* or *Tale* (though *labour* is used at VII.463). The words *busy, busily,* and *business* are also common in the story of St. Cecile, but the only appearance of such a word in the *Prioress's Tale* describes the widow's emotion: "With face pale of drede and bisy thoght" (VII.589).

39. This position is argued by Albert B. Friedman, "The Mysterious 'Greyn' in the *Prioress's Tale*," *Chaucer Review* 11 (1977): 328–33.

40. On the imagery of the tale, see esp. Peck, "Ideas of 'Entente' and Translation"; Whittock, *A Reading of the Canterbury Tales*, pp. 251–61.

41. Whittock, *A Reading of the Canterbury Tales*, pp. 256–58.

42. Fire images are used differently in the *Second Nun's Tale* from the *Canon's Yeoman's Tale*. Fire, which is associated with Cecile in the prologue (VIII.118), represents Valerian's fear of death should he become a Christian (VIII.313–14, 318); but when fire is actually used against Cecile it proves harmless, showing her triumph over the physical constraints of this world (and perhaps also over the flames of lust and Hell). See Giffin, "Hir Hous the Chirche," p. 47; Grennen, "Saint Cecilia's 'Chemical Wedding,'" p. 476; Peck, "Ideas of 'Entente' and Translation," pp. 24–26; Rosenberg, "The Contrary Tales of the Second Nun and the Canon's Yeoman"; Kolve, "Chaucer's *Second Nun's Tale* and Iconography." Military imagery—especially the description of the martyrs as "Cristes owene knyghtes" who have won "a greet bataille" (VII.383–87; based ultimately on 2 Timothy 4:7–8; compare VIII.34 and 353)—reinforces the paradox that the great power of the Romans is no match for the apparently helpless Christians led by a woman. The more soldiers Almachius sends to destroy the Christians, the more converts are made.

43. See esp. Peck, "Ideas of 'Entente' and Translation"; Carolyn P. Collette, "A Closer Look at Seinte Cecile's Special Vision," *Chaucer Review* 10 (1976): 337–49. See also Giffin, "Hir Hous the Chirche," p. 46; Rosenberg, "The Contrary Tales of the Second Nun and the Canon's Yeoman," pp. 282–85.

44. The rhyme is noticed by Knight, *Poetry of the Canterbury Tales*, p. 179.

45. According to Giffin, "Hir Hous the Chirche," p. 39, the *Second Nun's Tale* is the only version of the legend to end with a mention of the divine service in the church of St. Cecila.

INDEX

Adversus Jovinianum (St. Jerome), 55
Aeneas, 23
Alain de Lille, 22, 54, 134
Allen, Judson Boyce, 5
Ambrose, Saint, 141, 144
Ancrene Wisse, 38
Anselm, Saint, 140
Arnold, Matthew, 24
Arthur, 32
Astrolabe, 38
Augustine, Saint, 48, 54

Bédier, Joseph, 89
Beerbohm, Max, 33
Bernard of Clairvaux, Saint, 48, 129, 133, 140, 141
Bible, 12, 22, 35–36, 40, 55, 59, 60, 61, 96, 129; *Canticum Canticorum*, 83, 114, 119, 120, 129
Blake, William, 18
Boccaccio, Giovanni, 16, 22, 24, 34, 66, 71, 73, 75, 77, 82, 83, 115
Boethius, 22–23, 38, 42, 60, 82, 83
Bowers, R. H., 17–18
Brathwait, Richard, 17
Brewer, Derek, 18, 22, 64
Bronson, Bertrand, 5, 14
Browning, Robert, 11
Burlin, Robert, 5, 11
Burrow, John A., 33

Calderwood, James L., 49
Canon, 9
Canon's Yeoman, 9, 10, 27; woodcut of, 17
Canon's Yeoman's Prologue and Tale, 9, 107, 131, 132
Canterbury Tales: as human comedy, 4; links in, 9–11; illustrations in Hengwrt manuscript, 16; illustrations in Ellesmere manuscript, 16, 55; early illustrated manuscript of Cambridge

Gg.4.27, 16, 154 (nn. 44, 45); early editions of, 16–17; early discussion of, 17–19; poetic variety in, 20, 21–22, 23–24, 38, 43, 64, 87–88, 90, 102, 115–16, 129–30, 131, 139, 146; many poets of, 20–22; medieval precedents for variety, 22–24. *See also* Dramatic theory
Cato, 40, 69, 96, 134
Caxton, William, 3; woodcuts in edition of, 17
Chanson de Roland, 21
Chaucer the pilgrim, 26–31, 35; dramatic interpretation of, 26–31; variety of narrative voice, 27, 30–31; as narrator, 29–30, 31, 36–37
Chesterton, G. K., 34
Christ, 36, 45, 48, 51, 54, 60, 62, 129, 138, 142, 143, 145, 146
Cicero, 40
Clerk, 16, 27, 28, 131; woodcut of, 17
Clerk's Tale, 10, 14, 15, 20, 116; and *Man of Law's Tale*, 148
Coghill, Nevill, 114, 119
Commedia (Dante), 27, 133
Confessio Amantis (Gower), 23
Consolation of Philosophy (Boethius), 22, 82
Cook, 16, 27
Cook's Tale, 89, 112
Cooper, Helen, 5
Copland, Murray, 114
Corsa, Helen, 33, 117
Craik, T. W., 107

Dante, 24, 27, 133, 134
David, Alfred, 5, 11
Dean, Christopher, 82
Decameron (Boccaccio), 16, 19, 22, 66, 115
De Contemptu Mundi (Innocent III), 56
Donaldson, E. Talbot, 26–29, 38, 42, 49, 54, 77
Doyle, A. Ian, 16
Dramatic theory, 3–19, 26–31, 44–47, 49,

51, 64–66, 90–91, 99, 117, 132, 140–41,
    159 (nn. 8, 9), 163 (n. 4), 164 (n. 7), 172
    (n. 59), 173–74 (n. 4). *See also* individual
    pilgrims and tales
Dryden, John, 3, 18, 22

Eliot, T. S., 119

Fables (Dryden), 18
Falstaff, 47
Frank, Robert W., 99
Franklin, 8, 11; woodcut of, 17
Franklin's Tale, 14, 17, 148
Friar, 7, 14, 21, 27, 28
Friar's Prologue and Tale, 9, 12, 21, 89, 147

Gardner, John, 37, 42, 43
Gawain-poet, 87, 149. See also *Pearl*; *Sir Ga-
    wain and the Green Knight*
Gaylord, Alan, 31, 139
Genealogy of the Gods (Boccaccio), 34
General Prologue, 9, 10, 11, 12, 14, 18, 21,
    29, 31, 44, 46, 48, 65, 78, 132, 148; dra-
    matic interpretation of, 6–8; woodcuts
    of pilgrims, 16–17; narrator in, 26–28
Genet, Jean, 11
Gilbert and Sullivan, 33
Girlhood of Shakespeare's Heroines, 6
Goodelief, 41, 42
Gower, John, 23
Guibert de Nogent, 57
Guildsmen, 27
Guillaume de Lorris, 23. See also *Roman
    de la Rose*

Hali Meidenhad, 38, 124
Halverson, John, 45, 46, 49
Harry Bailly. *See* Host
Herbert, George, 149
Homer, 19
Horace, 59
Host (Harry Bailly), 9, 10, 11, 24, 29–31,
    34–35, 41, 42–43, 45, 59, 62, 65–66
House of Fame, 23
Howard, Donald R., 5, 11, 34, 62
Humbert of Romans, 54
Huppé, Bernard F., 30

Innocent III, 56, 57

James, Henry, 21, 30
Jean de Meun, 23, 134. See also *Roman de
    la Rose*
Jerome, Saint, 55, 56
Jordan, Robert, 5, 70

Kaske, Robert, 96, 114
Ker, W. P., 38
Kittredge, George Lyman, 3–4, 5, 7, 11,
    12, 19, 20, 44, 45–46, 62
Knight, 7, 8, 12, 13, 20, 27, 45, 62, 64; dra-
    matic interpretation of, 65, 163 (n. 4)
Knight's Tale, 13, 20, 31, 33, 64–88, 89, 90,
    91, 92, 94, 97, 102, 128, 140, 147, 148,
    149, 164 (n. 11); dramatic interpreta-
    tion of, 64–66, 163 (n. 4); and *Miller's
    Tale*, 64–88 passim; and Boccaccio's
    Teseida, 66, 71, 73, 75, 76, 82, 83; open-
    ing lines of, 67, 68; style of, 67, 70;
    marriage in, 68–69; narrative voice in,
    69, 72–74, 75, 165 (nn. 20–22); *occupatio*
    in, 69, 73, 75; characterization in, 76,
    77–78, 79; speech in, 79, 80–81; imag-
    ery in, 82; allusion in, 82–83; vocabu-
    lary in, 83–84; morality in, 85–86

Langland, William, 34, 47, 56, 87, 149. See
    also *Piers Plowman*
Lawrence, D. H., 16
Leavis, F. R., 4
"Lenvoy a Bukton," 13
"Lenvoy de Chaucer," 10
Lowes, John Livingston, 4, 6
Lumiansky, Robert, 4–5, 10
Lydgate, John, 1, 17

McGalliard, John C., 106
Macrobius, 134
Malone, Kemp, 5
Manciple, 17; woodcut of, 17
Manciple's Tale, 14
Manly, John Matthews, 6–7, 10
Mann, Jill, 7, 8
Man of Law, 12, 28, 35
Man of Law's Tale, 14, 106, 132, 142, 147;

and Clerk's Tale, 148

Mary, Blessed Virgin, 133–46 passim

Melibee, Tale of, 22, 26, 29, 31, 32, 37–43, 50, 51, 61, 64, 89, 147; teller of, 30, 35; morality in, 31; and Sir Thopas, 31–32, 35, 38, 40–41, 43; and Parson's Tale, 32; style of, 35–37, 38, 39, 40; as religious prose, 38, 43; use of authority in, 39–40; Host's assessment of, 41, 43; and Pardoner's Tale, 50

Merchant, 9, 11, 17, 27; dramatic interpretation of, 7–8, 14–16, 117, 172 (n. 59); woodcut of, 17

Merchant's Prologue and Tale, 13, 14–16, 20, 21, 40, 75, 79, 83, 89, 90, 102, 108, 109, 116–30, 147; dramatic interpretation of, 14–16, 117; as fabliau, 116–17, 119; and Shipman's Tale, 117, 118, 119, 120, 122; morality in, 117, 118, 120–21, 127–30; Christian significance of, 117, 119–20, 121–22, 127–28; opening lines of, 117–18, 122–23; and Miller's Tale, 117–26; and Reeve's Tale, 117–26; narrative voice in, 118, 124–27, 129, 172 (n. 59); language in, 118–19, 171 (n. 50); allusion in, 119, 171 (nn. 51, 52); symbolism in, 119–20; speech in, 120–21, 128–29, 172 (n. 54); characterization in, 122–24

Metamorphoses (Ovid), 22, 66

Middle English Dictionary, 68

Middleton, Anne, 34

A Midsummer Night's Dream (Shakespeare), 34

Miller, 3, 8, 20, 27, 64, 66; as narrator, 65; dramatic interpretation of, 164 (n. 7)

Miller's Prologue and Tale, 9, 12, 20, 21, 31, 47, 64–88, 147, 149, 165 (n. 19); dramatic interpretation of, 64–66, 90–91; and Knight's Tale, 64–88 passim; opening lines of, 68, 91, 92; narrative voice in, 69, 73, 74–75; imagery in, 69, 77, 82, 168–69 (n. 17); marriage in, 69–70; characterization in, 76–77, 78–79, 93–94, 95; speech in, 79–80, 81–82, 100; allusion in, 82, 83, 96; vocabulary in, 83–84; morality in, 85–86; and Reeve's Tale,

90–103 passim; wooing in, 92–93; and Shipman's Tale, 104–16 passim; and Merchant's Tale, 117–26 passim

Minnis, A. J., 22

Monk, 7, 9, 14, 24, 27, 66

Monk's Tale, 12, 14, 31, 65, 66, 147

Muscatine, Charles, 51, 70, 73, 125

Nicholson, Peter, 111

Nun's Priest, 9, 10, 11, 29

Nun's Priest's Tale, 10, 31, 38, 53, 116, 147

Ogle, George, 18

Olson, Glending, 38

Ovid, 18, 22, 23, 42, 66, 119

Owen, Charles A., Jr., 5, 11, 113

Owst, G. R., 56

Palomo, Dolores, 42

Pardoner, 8, 10, 11, 12, 16, 27, 44–60 passim, 62; dramatic interpretation of, 44–47, 49, 51, 159 (nn. 8, 9); drunkeness of, 46, 49, 160 (n. 13); sexuality of, 46–47; as preacher, 47–50, 52–58

Pardoner's Prologue and Tale, 11, 44, 45–63, 147, 149; ending of, 45, 62–63; characterization in, 48–49; and Melibee, 50; and Sir Thopas, 50; morality in, 50, 51, 57–58, 61, 62; art and doctrine in, 50, 163 (n. 51); dramatic interpretation of, 51; tavern sins in, 51, 52, 54, 56, 62; sermon in, 51, 52–58, 160 (n. 17), 161 (n. 23); exemplum in, 51, 58–63, 160 (n. 17); avarice (cupiditas) in, 54, 61; and Parson's Tale, 56, 57, 63; style of, 58–59, 60, contrasted to sermon, 59–60, 61, 62; language in, 60; symbolism in, 60, 61

Parkes, Malcolm B., 16

Parliament of Foules, 23

Parson, 7, 27, 28–29, 56, 57; woodcut of, 17

Parson's Tale, 22, 38; and Melibee, 32; and Pardoner's Tale, 56, 57, 63

Patterson, Lee, 12, 22

Pearl, 27, 140

Pearsall, Derek A., 5

Peter Pan, 32
Physician, 9, 12, 16; woodcut of, 17
Physician's Tale, 14
Piers Plowman (Langland), 9, 23, 124, 133, 137
Pittock, Malcolm, 58
Planctu Naturae, De (Alain de Lille), 22
Plowman, 27, 28; woodcut of, 17
Preaching: in Pardoner's Tale, 47–58; and ars poeticae, 48; Three Temptations in, 54; Sins of the Tavern in, 51, 52, 54, 56, 61, 62. See also Guibert de Nogent; Royal manuscript 18.B.xxiii; Thomas Aquinas, Saint; Waleys, Thomas
Prioress (Madame Eglentyne), 8, 14, 27, 28; woodcut of, 17; dramatic interpretation of, 132; as narrator, 134
Prioress's Prologue and Tale, 14, 29, 30, 31, 32, 115, 116, 131–46, 148; and Shipman's Tale, 115–16; and Second Nun's Prologue and Tale, 131–46 passim, 173 (n. 3); dramatic interpretation of, 132, 140–41, 173–74 (n. 4); anti-Semitism of, 132, 174 (n. 7), 177–78 (n. 37); emotionalism of, 133, 134, 139, 140–41, 145–46; narrative voice in, 134, 135–36; speech in, 137–38; vocabulary in, 139–40; characterization in, 142; religious faith in, 142–43; imagery in, 144

Reeve, 3, 8, 11, 16, 66; dramatic interpretation of, 90–91, 99; as narrator, 95
Reeve's Tale, 11, 75, 83, 90–103, 112, 147; and Miller's Tale, 90–103 passim; dramatic interpretation of, 90–91, 99; opening lines of, 91–92; narrative voice in, 92, 94–95; and Knight's Tale, 92, 97; wooing in, 92–93; characterization in, 94, 95–96; anti-intellectualism of, 96, 97; allusion in, 96–97; proverbs in, 97; animal imagery in, 97–98; language in, 98–99; vocabulary in, 99, 101, 169 (n. 23); speech in, 99–101; as fabliau, 102–3; and Shipman's Tale, 104–16 passim; and Merchant's Tale, 117–26 passim
Retraction, 50
Retrospective Review, 19

Robert of Basevorn, 54
Robertson, Durant W., Jr., 5, 7, 24
Roman de la Rose, 9, 23, 47, 119
Romaunt of the Rose, 106
Root, Robert Kilburn, 4, 59, 102
Royal manuscript 18.B.xxiii, 54, 55–56
Ruggiers, Paul, 31, 44, 64–65, 114
Russell, G. H., 134

Sartre, Jean-Paul, 11
Schroeder, Mary, 123
Scrutiny, 4
Second Nun, 9, 21, 29; woodcut of, 17; lack of characterization, 132
Second Nun's Prologue and Tale, 14, 17, 21, 40, 131–46, 148; and Prioress's Prologue and Tale, 131–46 passim, 173 (n. 3); dramatic interpretation of, 132; intellectualism of, 133, 136, 141–42, 143, 146; narrative voice in, 136; speech in, 136–37, 176 (n. 24); vocabulary in, 139–40; religious faith in, 143, 177 (n. 36); characterization in, 143; symbolic imagery in 144–45, 178 (n. 42); and Canon's Yeoman's Tale, 173 (n. 2)
Sedgewick, G. G., 46, 119
Shakespeare, William, 10, 18, 19, 21, 34, 46, 47
Sheridan, Richard B., 35
Shipman, 9, 12, 27, 106; woodcut of, 17
Shipman's Tale, 12–13, 21, 31, 77, 79, 89, 90, 102, 104–16, 131, 147; allusion in, 104; and Miller's Tale, 104–16 passim; and Reeve's Tale, 104–16 passim; imagery in, 105, 169 (n. 26); language in, 105, 111–13, 114; characterization in, 106; vocabulary in, 106; money in, 106–7; speech in, 107, 109–11; dialogue in, 107–11; wooing in, 108–9; opening lines of, 111; narrative voice in, 111–12, 114; puns in, 113; Christian significance of, 114–15; and Prioress's Tale, 115–16; and Merchant's Tale, 117, 118, 119, 120, 122
Siege of Thebes (Lydgate), 17
Sir Gawain and the Green Knight, 21, 23
Skelton, John, 32

Spearing, A. C., 58, 60, 99
Spearing, J. E., 99
Speirs, John, 4
Squire, 9, 27
Squire's Tale, 14, 148
Statius, 83, 134
Stevens, Martin, 5
Stow, John, 17
Summoner, 16, 27; woodcut of, 17
Summoner's Prologue and Tale, 9, 12, 21, 89, 147

Tale of Beryn, 17, 147
Tatlock, J. S. P., 126
Temple (Herbert), 149
Teseida (Boccaccio), 66, 71, 73, 75, 76, 77, 82, 83
Thebaid (Statius), 83
Thomas Aquinas, Saint, 51, 52, 53
Thopas, Tale of Sir, 22, 26, 27, 29, 30, 31, 32–35, 37, 50, 51, 61, 64, 89, 147, 148, 157

(n. 14); narrator of, 29–30; and Melibee, 31, 32, 35, 37, 38, 40–41, 43; style of, 33, 35, 40; objections to, 33–34, 35; and Pardoner's Tale, 50
Thynne, William, 17
Tolkien, J. R. R., 98–99
Troilus and Criseyde, 23–24, 72, 75, 77, 79, 83, 108, 128
Tyrwhitt, Thomas, 19

Virgil, 23

Waleys, Thomas, 52–53
Warton, Thomas, 90
Waste Land (Eliot), 119
Whittock, Trevor, 37, 42, 43, 144
Wife of Bath, 12, 16, 21, 27, 40, 44, 45, 48, 106, 131; dramatic interpretation of, 4, 5, 12, 13; woodcut of, 17
Wife of Bath's Prologue and Tale, 9, 11, 12, 148
Wodehouse, P. G., 33